D0710698

Plotinus' Mystical Teaching of Henosis

Pao-Shen Ho

Plotinus' Mystical Teaching of Henosis

An Interpretation in the Light of the Metaphysics
of the One

PETER LANG
EDITION

Bibliographic Information published by the Deutsche Nationalbibliothek
The Deutsche Nationalbibliothek lists this publication in the Deutsche Nationalbibliografie; detailed bibliographic data is available in the internet at http://dnb.d-nb.de.

Library of Congress Cataloging-in-Publication Data
Ho, Pao-Shen, 1980-
 Plotinus' mystical teaching of henosis : an interpretation in the light of the metaphysics of the one / Pao-Shen Ho.
    pages cm
Includes bibliographical references.
ISBN 978-3-631-65673-0
1. Plotinus. Enneads. 2. Mysticism. 3. Metaphysics. I. Title.
B693.E53H6 2014
186'.4--dc23
                              2014044006

ISBN 978-3-631-65673-0 (Print)
E-ISBN 978-3-653-04985-5 (E-Book)
DOI 10.3726/ 978-3-653-04985-5

© Peter Lang GmbH
Internationaler Verlag der Wissenschaften
Frankfurt am Main 2015
All rights reserved.
Peter Lang Edition is an Imprint of Peter Lang GmbH.

Peter Lang – Frankfurt am Main · Bern · Bruxelles · New York · Oxford · Warszawa · Wien

This publication has been peer reviewed.

www.peterlang.com

Abstract

Plotinus is known as both a philosopher and a mystic, and it is crucial to explain his mysticism of henosis in the light of his metaphysics of the One. In this dissertation I investigate Plotinus' mysticism on this approach, while emphasizing that the *Enneads* is a text of mystical teaching which mediates the reality of henosis by giving spiritual guidance. Thus, my investigation is orientated by two questions: First, what are the methods of Plotinus' mystical teaching? Second, how do these methods relate to henosis as their desired goal? I explain these questions in the light of Plotinus' metaphysics, according to which the One is both transcendent and immanent such that man cannot and need not know It. The conclusions reached are as follows: The methods taught by Plotinus are the practices of philosophy and negative theology, which aim at knowing intelligible beings and the transcendent One. However, these practices do not help man to attain henosis, but remind him that his failure to attain henosis pertains to his natural condition in which he is united with the One. Plotinus' mystical teaching aims not at transforming man's finite nature, but at changing man's preconceptions concerning henosis.

Contents

Acknowledgment

I would like to thank my supervisor, Prof. Dr. Edmund Runggaldier, for his generosity, tolerance and inspirations. I would also like to show gratitude to Prof. Dr. Tran Van Doan of National Taiwan University, who encouraged me to pursue the doctoral study and kindly introduced me to Prof. Runggaldier. A special thank goes to Collegium Canisianum and P. Friedrich Prassl for their hospitality and accommodation. Last not least, I am also grateful to my parents and wife for their love and support. Without these people this dissertation would not be possible.

Notes on Reference and Translations

In this dissertation references of Plotinus' *Enneads* are to *Plotini Opera*, vol. 1–3, ed. Paul Henry and Hans-Rudolf Schwyzer, Clarendon Press, Oxford, 1964–1982. I.2.3 means *Ennead* I, treatise 2, chapter 3; I.2.3–4 means *Ennead* I, treatise 2, chapter 3 and 4, and I.2.3.4–5 means *Ennead* I, treatise 2, chapter 3, line 4–5. Translations are taken from *Plotinus*, vol.1–7, tr. A. H. Armstrong, Cambridge University Press, London, 1966–1988. In Armstrong's translation the One (τò ἕν) is sometimes referred to by *He* and sometimes by *it*, while the soul (ψυχή) mostly by *it*. For the sake of clarity, I shall use *It* to refer to the One, and *she* to the soul. The brackets in my quotations of Armstrong's translations are all his, while all the italics, bracketed or not, are mine.

Abbreviations

Works of Pseudo-Dionysius the Areopagite

CH   *The Celestial Hierarchy*
DN   *The Divine Names*
EH   *The Ecclesiastical Hierarchy*
MT   *The Mystical Theology*

All references are to *Corpus Dionysiacum*, ed. B. R. Suchla, G. Heil and A. M. Ritter, Walter De Gruyter, Berlin and New York, 1990–1991; translations are quoted from *Dionysius: the Complete Works*, tr. Colm Luibheid and Paul Rorem, Paulist Press, New York, 1987.

Works of Other Authors

PI   Wittgenstein, Ludwig, *Philosophical Investigations*, tr. G.E.M. Anscombe, Blackwell Publishing, Malden, 2001.
ST   Thomas Aquinas, *Summa Theologica*, tr. Fathers of the English Dominican Province, Benzinger, New York, 1947–1948.

Introduction

This dissertation sets itself the modest task of explaining Plotinus' mystical teaching of henosis as it is presented in the *Enneads*. While my aim is fairly simple and implies an equally straightforward method, the background from which this dissertation emerges does not appear to be so. Therefore, in this introductory part, I will first look into the historical reception of Plotinus' thought (Section 1) and the scholarly approaches to mysticism as a discipline (Section 2), and finally return to specify the subject, method and structure of the dissertation accordingly (Section 3).

Section 1   The Historical Reception of Plotinus' Thought

The task of discussing the historical reception of Plotinus (205–270 C.E.) needs not strike us as overly ambitious, because Plotinus' only extant work, the *Enneads*, remains more or less underappreciated due to several historical factors. For this reason, in this section I shall only attempt to identify certain factors that hinder Plotinus' work from being understood properly in its own term.

1.1   The Extent of Plotinus' Influence

The first noteworthy issue concerns the extent of Plotinus' influence. According to the entry *Plotinus* from *The Stanford Encyclopedia of Philosophy*,

> Porphyry's edition of Plotinus' *Enneads* preserved for posterity the works of the leading Platonic interpreter of antiquity. Through these works as well as through the writings of Porphyry himself (234–c. 305 C.E.) and Iamblichus (c. 245–325 C.E.), Plotinus shaped the entire subsequent history of philosophy. Until well into the 19th century, Platonism was in large part understood, appropriated or rejected based on its Platonic expression and in adumbrations of this. The theological traditions of Christianity, Islam and Judaism all, in their formative periods, looked to ancient Greek philosophy for the language and arguments with which to articulate their religious visions. For all of these, Platonism expresses the philosophy that seemed closest to their own theologies. Plotinus was the principal source for their understanding of Platonism.[1]

---

1   Gerson, Lloyd, "Plotinus", *The Stanford Encyclopedia of Philosophy* (Summer 2013 Edition), Edward N. Zalta (ed.), URL = <http://plato.stanford.edu/archives/sum2013/entries/plotinus/>.

This account overlooks one critical detail: Porphyry's edition did preserve Plotinus' works in material format, but it did not preserve them for the posterity to *understand* them. In my opinion, we can point out at least three factors behind this phenomenon.

First, the most influential Christian Platonist (and arguably also *the* most influential Christian theologian) who helped to shape the understanding of Platonism in the Middle Ages is Augustine of Hippo (354–430 C.E.). But Augustine came under the influence of Platonism not through Porphyry's complete Greek edition of the *Enneads*, but through Marius Victorinus' Latin translations of it which Augustine called "the books by the Platonists". These books have been long lost, so we have no strong evidence as to what Augustine might have read. But recent researches identify them as Porphyry's *Philosophy from Oracles*, "containing *ex hypothesi* extracts from the *Enneads* and identified with Porphyry's *Kata christianōn*."[2] Furthermore, as A. H. Armstrong observes in his English translation of the *Enneads*, Augustine might have made adoptions of a few phrases from the *Enneads*, I.6.8[3] and V.1.2[4] in *Confessions* I.18, IX 10 and VIII 8. So it seems

---

2   Cooper, Stephen A., 'Marius Victorinus', *Cambridge History of Philosophy in the Late Antiquity*, Cambridge University Press, Cambridge, 2010, 539. See also Courcelle, Pierre, *Recherches sur les Confessions de saint Augustine*, de Boccard, Paris, 1950, 7 and Beatrice, P. F., 'Quosdam Platonicorum libros. The Platonic Readings of Augustine in Milan', *Vigilae Christianae* 43, 1989, 248–281.

3   Cf. The *Ennead* I.6.8.21–24: "Our country from which we came is there, our Father is there. How shall we travel to it, where is our way of escape? *We cannot get there on foot*; for our feet only carry us everywhere in this world, from one country to another. *You must not get ready a carriage, either, or a boat.*" See also *Confessions* I.18: "That younger son of yours in the gospel *did not hire horses or carriages, nor did he board ships, nor take wing in any visible sense nor put one foot before the other* when he journeyed to that far country where he could squander at will the wealth you, his gentle father, had given him at his departure;" and *Confessions* VIII.8: "I was groaning in spirit and shaken by violent anger because I could form no resolve to enter into a covenant with you, though in my bones I knew that this was what I ought to do, and everything in me lauded such a course to the skies. *It was a journey not to be undertaken by ship or carriage or on foot*, nor need it take me even that short distance I had walked from the house to the place where we were sitting;…"

4   Cf. The *Ennead* V.1.2.10–17: "This is how soul should reason about the manner in which she grants life in the whole universe and in individual things. Let she look at the great soul, being herself another soul which is no small one, which has become worthy to look by being freed from deceit and the things that have bewitched the other souls, and is established in quietude. *Let not only her encompassing body and the body's raging sea be quiet, but all her environment: the earth quiet, and the sea and*

2

that Plotinus' thought in the *Enneads* is not handed down to Augustine through Marius' translations, and, more important, does not influence Augustine in any substantial way. This observation can be directly confirmed by Augustine's own words:

> In them [the books by the Platonists] I read [...] that *in the beginning was the Word, and the Word was with God; he was God. He* [the Word] *was with God in the beginning. Everything was made through him; nothing came to be without him. What was made is alive with his life, and that life was the light of human kind. The Light shines in the darkness, and the darkness has never been able to master it* [...][5]

What Augustine read—or rather *read into* or *proclaimed* to understand—from Marius' translations is the Christian theology of John 1, 1–12. Consequently, the Platonism the posterity learnt from him is not Plotinus', either, but Augustine's creative appropriation of Platonism in the context of Christian theology.

Second, when the Arabic-speaking world came under the influence of Plotinus' thought in the 9th century, it is once again not via Porphyry's complete Greek edition. The book that spread Plotinus' thought in the Islam is called *The Theology of Aristotle*, a work whose authorship is wrongly ascribed to Aristotle, and which comprises only a few sections of the treatises from the last three *Enneads* and a commentary by Porphyry.[6] This circumstance makes it inevitable that what Plotinus had written is read and understood in the light of a wrong context. But more important is the fact that this version already contains certain significant modifications of Plotinus' thought. As Peter Adamson points out,

> In Arabic, the One is very clearly conceived as a creating God, frequently given epithets like 'originator' and 'creator.' On the other hand, the Arabic Plotinus acknowledges no tension between this idea of God as creator and the Plotinian metaphor of 'emanation' (Arabic words that mean 'emanation' or 'flowing,' such as *fayd*, are prominent throughout the text). In general the Arabic Plotinus agrees with Plotinus himself that God makes (creates) intellect directly, and then makes all other things 'through the intermediary of intellect' [...]. On the other hand, it has been noted that the Arabic version frequently assimilates Plotinian *nous* to the One. The Arabic version embraces the idea that the

---

air quiet, and the heaven itself at peace." See also *Confessions* IX.10: "If *the tumult of the flesh fell silent for someone, and silent too were the phantasms of earth, sea and air, silent the heavens, and the very soul silent to itself,* that it might pass beyond itself by not thinking of its own being; [...] for if anyone listens, all these things will tell him, 'We did not make ourselves; he made us who abides for ever.'"

5   *Confessions,* VII.9.
6   For a detail study of this work, see Adamson, Peter, *The Arabic Plotinus: a Philosophical Study of the "Theology of Aristotle"*, Duckworth, London, 2002.

First Cause thinks or is an intellect—an idea either rejected or mentioned only with great circumspection by Plotinus. [...] Here we see the Arabic version undoing, to some extent, Plotinus' distinction between Aristotle's self-thinking intellective god and the truly first, highest principle.[7]

In particular, Plotinus' negative theological thesis that the non-personal One is absolutely simple and ineffable is transformed into the monotheistic doctrine (Tawhid) that there is only one true God, Allah. Therefore, not only does the *Enneads* remain largely unknown to the Mediaeval Arabic world, but a small part of this work is received in a misplaced context (first under the authorship of Aristotle, and then interpreted in terms of monotheism).

Thus thirdly, when Porphyry's edition is finally translated into Latin in its entirety and published by Marsilio Ficino in 1492, the consensus about what "Platonism" is supposed to mean has already been established, and indeed in the absence of Plotinus, an important Platonic philosopher. Furthermore, at that time, it did not make sense for theologians and philosophers to deny their culture background to fully embrace the thought of a relatively unknown pagan commentator of Plato. In short, when the entire *Enneads* came into wide circulation, its readers either thought they already knew, or did not care too much to find out, what Plotinus could be really saying.

1.2 The Role of Proclus in the Reception of Neoplatonism

The second issue concerns Proclus (412–485 C.E.), another pagan Neoplatonist, and indeed on two counts: (a) his greater influence than Plotinus, and (b) his philosophical difference from Plotinus. These points combine to lead to the tendency that what we usually understand by the term Neoplatonism is Proclean for the most part rather than Plotinian. Since what I am offering here is mainly a survey regarding Plotinus' own thought, I shall not go deeply into investigating Proclus' own work; it suffices to point out certain basic facts.

(a) Proclus is more influential than Plotinus mainly for two reasons. First, Proclus' writing style, as can be seen especially in his *Elements of Theology*, is clearer, more systematic, and hence more accessible than Plotinus'. Seeing that both of them are usually classified under the umbrella term "Neoplatonism", it

---

7   Adamson, Peter, "The Theology of Aristotle", *The Stanford Encyclopedia of Philosophy* (Summer 2013 Edition), Edward N. Zalta (ed.), URL = <http://plato.stanford.edu/archives/sum2013/entries/theology-aristotle/>. See also D'Ancona, C. 'Divine and Human Knowledge in the Plotiniana Arabica', *The Perennial Tradition of Neoplatonism*, ed. J.L. Cleary, Leuven University Press, Leuven, 1997, 437–442.

is tempting and indeed helpful to clarify Plotinus' less clear Neoplatonism in terms of Proclus' much clearer Neoplatonism. Although this interpretive strategy has its strength, it sometimes misleads the readers to assuming that there is no significant difference between Plotinus and Proclus, or that this difference, if any, cannot be articulated.

Second, around the 12th century a philosophical work called *Liber de Causis* is widely circulated from the Islamic countries to the Latin West, and then commented by Albert the Great and Thomas Aquinas. Although its author remains unknown to this day, Aquinas already noticed that its content is mainly derived from Proclus' *Elements of Theology*. Thus, through *Liber de Causis* Proclus' thought—more specifically, the *Proclean* brand of Neoplatonism—became indirectly disseminated throughout the Western world. Unlike *The Theology of Aristotle*, and due to its more systematic character, *Liber de Causis* has the good fortune of being extensively studied and passed down by two of the most revered Christian philosophers in the Middle Age. This also contributes to the predominance of Proclus' Neoplatonism over Plotinus'.

(b) If there is no significant difference between Plotinus' and Plotinus' Neoplatonism, we need not lamenting over the scant historical reception of *the Enneads*. But this is not the case. Although both philosophers understand the One as the metaphysical cause of multiplicity, there are important differences between Plotinus and Proclus. According to Proposition 123 in *Elements of Theology*:

> All that is divine is in itself ineffable and unknowable (ἄρρητόν ἐστι καὶ ἄγνωστον) by any secondary being because of its supra-existential unity (ἕνωσιν), but it may be apprehended and known from the existents which participate it: wherefore only the First Principle is completely unknowable, as being unparticipated (ἄτε ἀμέθεκτον ὄν).[8]

For Proclus, for man to participate in the First Principle or the One *just is* to know It; and since the One is unknowable in itself, It must also be unparticipated. But this rules out the Plotinian approach whereby man unites with the One without knowing and speaking about It.[9] As Proposition 123 indicates, it is not simply the case that Proclus pays less attention to the obscure issue of mysticism in his sober writing; the truth is rather that his conceptions of the First Principle and of participation by knowledge make mystical unification impossible. As a result, what remains possible for him is only the degreed or "hierarchical" knowledge about the First Principle, as we see from Proposition 162:

---

8   Cf. Dodds, E. R., *Proclus: The Elements of Theology, A Revised Text with Translation, Introduction and Commentary*, Clarendon Press, Oxford, 1963, 108–111.

9   Cf. V.3.14; for further explanation see Chapter 1 and 4 of this dissertation.

All those henads [metaphysical principles inferior to the One] (ἑνάδων) which illumi-
nate true Being are secret and intelligible (κρύφιον καὶ νοητόν): secret as conjoined
(συνημμένον) with the One, intelligible as participated by Being.[10]

To sum up, from a historical point of view, the factors which shape and limit in
one way or another our understanding of Plotinus are authorship misattribution,
monotheism, and the predominance of Proclus the fellow Platonist.

Section 2 The Scholarly Approaches to Mysticism

Very roughly, by "mysticism" I mean *man's intimate experience of the ultimate
reality*, and in this section I shall use *mysticism* and *mystical experience* interchangeably unless the context indicates otherwise. It should be emphasized right
away that this characterization is not so much a definition as a suggestion that
we have no ready definition at hand, because the precise meanings of all three
components in this characterization, "intimacy", "experience" and "ultimate reality", vary from case to case across different cultural traditions. For this reason,
mysticism is a subject which is far more complicated and studied in more varied
ways than Plotinus is.

Since the subject of this dissertation only touches Plotinus' mysticism, it
seems that there is no need to review the literatures *of* and *about* mysticism in
general. But the situation is not as simple as it seems. For it is natural for us to
explain an unfamiliar phenomenon in terms of what we are familiar with, and
when things do not work out as expected, we tend to regard the unfamiliar phenomenon as abnormal or not interesting and then, instead of revising our old
conceptual framework, just leave it at that. That this might be the case not only
for Plotinus' philosophical thought, but also for his mysticism, can be expected
from the explanations in Section 1.1. Therefore, in order not to read Plotinus'
teaching of henosis in the wrong way and take it out of its proper context, it is important to first consider the possibility of refining the pre-conceived conceptual
framework in the study of mysticism. To this end, in this section I will focus on
meta-theoretical or second-order reflections upon how certain presuppositions
or conceptual schemes shape the study of mysticism. The aim, to emphasize, is
not to determine *a priori* what mysticism as such or Plotinus' mysticism in specific must be, but simply to prepare for a more humble and cautious attitude
before dealing with the subject at hand.

---

10 Cf. Dodds, 1963, 140–143.

The following analysis relies, for the most part, on Bernard McGinn's account of the theoretical foundations of modern study of mysticism in the first volume of his seminal work, *The Presence of God: A History of Western Christian Mysticism*.[11] The scope of McGinn's account is unsurpassed, covering the *theological, philosophical, psychological* and *comparative* studies of mysticism in Europe and America in the past hundred years. Since my analysis aims at meta-theoretical refinement, in what follows I will first summarize McGinn's own summary, and then remark on a few methodological features therein.

2.1 The Theological Approach to Mysticism

In general, twentieth-century German Protestant theologians (Albrecht Ritschl, Adolf Harnack, Emil Brunner, Karl Barth) tend to take a negative attitude toward mysticism, regarding its tendency toward self-deification as a deviation from the Christian faith. By contrast, English authors (Evelyn Underhill and William Inge) maintain that mysticism involves an affirmative attitude toward the world, nature and one's neighbors which is in harmony with the Gospel. The Catholic theologians, on the other hand, tend to avoid the over-simplifying criticism of mysticism as self-deification, for they see the relationship between God and man more subtly than the Protestant theologians do. Their discussions revolve around two basic questions: Whether all men (or all Christians) are called to the mystical union with God, and in what stage of man's life of prayer does the union take place. Catholic theologians from different eras address these issues in different ways. The Neo-Scholastics (Augustin-Francois Poulain, August Saudreau, Albert Farges, Reginald Garrigou-Lagrange) draw on the authoritative teachings of Thomas Aquinas, John of the Cross and Theresa of Avila, while, Karl Rahner, the most important Catholic theologian after the Second Vatican Council, draws on Joseph Maréchal's transcendental Thomism.

What ties these three theological strands together, in my opinion, is the basic intuition that the Christian way of life is fundamental, or that mysticism must be based upon a Christian "life process" (Underhill's term) in order to be acknowledged at all. Christianity provides the concrete cultural, social and historical context in which the mystical writings can be understood and the true mystics can be distinguished from the false ones. In this sense, Christian

---

11 McGinn, Bernard, *The Foundations of Mysticism: Vol. 1 of The Presence of God: A History of Western Christian Mysticism*, Crossroad, New York, 1991, 265–343.

mysticism could be understood as a further development of Christian spirituality, "the lived experience of Christian faith and discipleship".[12]

But this theological approach has difficulties from both the outside and the inside. From the outside, it has the problem of coming to term with those non-Christian mystics who claim to have intimate experiences of the ultimate reality. In our ecumenical age when inter-religious dialogue becomes an urgent task, this difficulty surfaces as one of the greatest challenges this theological approach to mysticism has to deal with.[13] And from the inside, things become even more complicated when we note that not a few Christian mystics who regarded themselves as devoted believers were treated with suspicion at their time (Evagrius Ponticus, Gregory of Palamas, Meister Eckhart, Miguel de Molinos, to name a few). The theological approach does help us to judge and evaluate them, but it seems that a more sympathetic and impartial understanding is needed.

2.2 The Psychological and Comparative Approach to Mysticism

The methodological shift from the theological to the psychological-comparative approach to mysticism is related to the *semantic change* of the term *mystical*, as Michel de Certeau observes:

> In the sixteenth or seventeenth century one no longer designates as mystical the kind of "wisdom" elevated to the recognition of a mystery already lived and proclaimed in common beliefs, but an experimental knowledge which has slowly detached itself from traditional theology or Church institutions and which characterizes itself through the consciousness, acquired or received, of a gratified passivity where the self is lost in God.[14]

This change paves the way for the psychological and comparative studies of mysticism. It is due to external factors as well, including socio-political impetus (first New Imperialism, the two World Wars, and then globalization) and scientific progress (first experimental psychology, then cognitive science), that these new studies become a growing and lasting enterprise. For this reason, in this sub-section I will not aim at an orderly run-down or a detached evaluation,

---

12 Cf. Perrin, David B., 'Mysticism', *The Blackwell Companion to Christian Spirituality*, ed. Arthur Holder, Blackwell Publishing, Malden, 2005, 442–458. See also Schneiders, Sandra M., 'Approaches to the Study of Christian Spirituality', ibid., 15–33.
13 Cf. Knitter, Paul, *Introducing Theologies of Religions*, Orbis Books, Maryknoll, 2002, 112–113, 125–126.
14 de Certeau, Michel, 'Mystique', *Encyclopaedia universalis*, 11, Encyclopaedia universalis de France, Paris, 1968, 522, cited from McGinn, 1991, 311–312.

but restrict myself to what I regard as the most influential works in this field of research.

Arguably, *the* most influential work for the psychological and comparative studies of mysticism is William James' *The Varieties of Religious Experience* (1902). According to James, mysticism or mystical experiences are *mystical states of consciousness* which are ineffable, noetic, transient and passive. Although not all psychologists and comparativists of mysticism stick to this characterization *verbatim*, they all benefit greatly from the underlying approach of James' characterization, namely the methodological *reduction* to *psychological* experience. This can be explained on two counts.

First, regarding the object of study, it strips mystical experience from the mystic's entire personal history down to a depersonalized episode of psychological experience, thereby giving the researchers something definite to focus on. It does not matter *who* has this experience or *how* this experience takes place, for it suffices for the objective-minded researchers to have before them a specimen of state of consciousness that is ineffable, noetic, transient and passive.

Second, regarding the researcher himself, James' new idea reduces personal religious experience to mystical states of consciousness, thereby freeing researchers of mysticism from any pre-theoretical commitment to a given religion. With this move, the "door" (to borrow Aldous Huxley's term) to perceiving mystical states of consciousness opens up to a wider public: not only to non-religious psychologists, but more importantly also to comparativists interested in different religions.

The second point is especially noteworthy for two reasons. First, it provides the comparativists a more reliable source, material and method to work on. Compare the Traditionalist René Guenon (1886–1951) and his contemporary Aldous Huxley (1894–1963) for example. For Guenon, all religions are based on the same sacred science which can be transmitted through spiritual or mystical initiation; Huxley, on the other hand, suggests to the effect that under the influence of psychedelic drug the Beatific Vision, Sat-Chit-Ananda and the Dharma-Body of the Buddha all become "as evident as Euclid".[15] Their basic tenets are similar—all major religions have mysticism as their inner core—but their approaches are not. Guenon's prophetic tone and proof-texting method manifest his anti-modernist position, and this is in turn based on his diagnosis of *the entire human history* based on the Hindu doctrine of Manvantara.[16] Since

---

15 Huxley, Aldous, *The Door of Perception*, Chatto and Windus, London, 1954, 12–13.

16 Cf. Guenon, René, *The Crisis of Modern World* (4th, revised edition), tr. Marco Pallis, Arthur Osborne, Richard C. Nicholson, Sophia Perennis, Hillsdale, 2001, 7: "The Hindu doctrine teaches that a human cycle, to which it gives the name *Manvantara*,

anti-modernism underlies not only Guenon's theory but also his premise, it is impossible to understand his works without pre-theoretically committing oneself to his interpretation of certain Hindu doctrines. By contrast, Huxley cites his experiment with psychedelic drugs as evidence that all mystical experiences are essentially the same because they have the same psychological features. Everyone is welcomed to take drugs so as to examine whether Huxley' claim is true; and indeed his fiercest detractor, R. C. Zaehner, experimented with mescaline and came to the opposing conclusion that such experience is "hilariously funny" and "anti-religious".[17] Leaving aside the issue whether hallucinatory experience counts as mystical experience, we still have to applaud Huxley and Zaehner for their joint attempt to secure an objective evidence for mystical experience. The study of comparative mysticism cannot make progress without first standing on a firm ground on which the basic data of mysticism can be objectively examined.

The Jamesean approach not only provides the comparativists a more reliable source, material and method to work on, but also enables them to investigate the nature of mysticism from an inter-religious point of view. In comparison with the theological approach, this new way shows a greater sensitivity and tolerance of the diversity of mystical experiences. Aldous Huxley and W. T. Stace count as two of the earliest proponents of the idea that all mystical experiences, no matter to what tradition they belong and how they are attained, have a "common core" and hence are essentially the same.[18] The most important work to criticize this view is R. C. Zaehner's *Mysticism Sacred and Profane* (1957), in which the author seeks to refute Huxley's essentialism by distinguishing three different types of mysticism (nature mysticism, monistic mysticism and theistic mysticism). Zaehner's contribution is especially noteworthy, for he is the first to

---

is divided into four periods marking so many stages during which the primordial spirituality becomes gradually more and more obscured [...] We are now in the fourth age, the *Kali-Yuga* or 'dark age', and have been so already, it is said, for more than six thousand years." Ibid., 107: "Our chief purpose in this work has been to show how it is possible, by the application of traditional data, to find the most direct solution to the questions that are being asked nowadays, to explain the present state of mankind, and at the same time to judge everything that constitutes modern civilization in accordance with truth, instead of by conventional rules or sentimental preferences."

17 Zaehner, R. C., *Mysticism Sacred and Profane: An Inquiry into some Varieties of Praeternatural Experience*, Oxford University Press, Oxford, 1960, 212–226. Clarendon University Press, Oxford, 1957, 212–226.

18 Cf. Huxley, 1954 and Stace, W. T., *Mysticism and Philosophy*, Macmillan, London, 1960.

attempt to draw a typology of mysticism based on the Jamesean, reduced conception. Later on the debate between Huxley and Zaehner will be picked up by the Anglo-American philosophers, and this also testifies to the lasting influence of James and Zaehner on the study of mysticism.

Unsurprisingly, scholars working with the theological approach will find this approach unacceptable, because their thick conception of mystical experience as a *way of life* is far richer than the thin psychological conception of mystical experience as *states of consciousness*. In their eyes, the problem of the Jamesean model is not just that it overemphasizes the mystic's transient and ineffable experience to the indifference of its historical, social and reflective dimensions. More pointedly, in focusing on the mystic's states of consciousness, the turn to psychological experience in fact misses the important *psychological* facts that the consciousness is intentional and open to the transcendent world.

This point also leads us to wonder whether the Jamesean methodological reduction to state of consciousness is too radical to accommodate the intrinsic relation among the *reality*, the *thought* and the *language* constitutive of mystical experience.[19] This problem can be seen in James' following remark:

> One may say truly, I think, that personal religious experience has its root in mystical states of consciousness; so for us, who in these lectures are treating personal experience as the exclusive subject of our study, such states of consciousness ought to form the vital chapter from which other chapters get their light. *Whether my treatment of mystical states will shed more light or darkness, I do not know, for my own constitution shuts me out from their enjoyment almost entirely, and I can speak of them only at second hand.* But though forced to look upon the subject so externally, I will be as *objective and receptive* as I can...[20]

As James admits, his own constitution shuts him out from the enjoyment of mystical experience almost entirely, and all he can do is to resort to second hand interpretations. In spite of this essential limitation (if not obstruction), he also claims that it is still possible to study mystical states of consciousness both objectively and receptively. The basic reason for James' methodological shortcut, I suppose, is this: since mystics are allegedly gifted human beings, and since the reality of mysticism is assumed to be otherworldly, the best a

---

19 The relation among reality, thought and language serves as an implicit framework in Bernard McGinn's analysis of the emergence of a new form of Christian mysticism around 1200 C.E.; cf. McGinn, Bernard, *The Flowering of Mysticism: Men and Women in the New Mysticism (1200–1350)*, Crossroads, New York, 1998, 12–30.

20 James, William, *The Varieties of Religious Experience*, Pennsylvania State University, 2002, 279–280.

psychologist can do is to appeal to second-hand interpretations. I am in no position to evaluate these presuppositions, but it is noteworthy and somewhat ironic that a psychologist like James should subscribe to presuppositions which *mystify* mystical experience, whereas a theologian like Karl Rahner maintains to the contrary that all human beings have an unthematic awareness of God in their daily experiences.

We have noted previously that the Jamesean approach enables the scholars to investigate the nature of mysticism from a more liberal, inter-religious point of view. But here we see that James wants to take this approach much further and to avail himself, paradoxically, to study mystical experience without really undergoing such experience. Perhaps his intuition is that, just as the psychiatrist can treat mental illness without suffering mental illness himself, so the scholar of mysticism can study mystical experience without enjoying it. But this analogy is too coarse. Even if the psychiatrist does not really have to suffer mental illness, he must have sufficient medical training and clinical practice in order to treat mental illness. A similar contact or acquaintance with the *reality* of mystical experience, however, is absent in James' account, for all he resorts to is the *interpretation* thereof. At all events, it suffices for James to lay down a *working hypothesis* of mystical experience for scientific investigations; the question is not brought up whether this working hypothesis can be true to the reality of mystical experience. As a result, there is no direct way to tell if a thesis advanced in such a psychological study of mysticism *corresponds* to the reality of mystical experience. I do not wish to suggest that such an approach is making unverifiable or meaningless claims about mystical experience, but it seems to me that it does overlook an essential dimension, namely the reality, of mystical experience.

A similar problem emerges in Zaehner's critique of Huxley. As we have explained, Huxley claims that the same mystical state of consciousness underlies different mystical experiences. The simplest way to refute Huxley is to offer counter-evidence, namely to show that under an experience similar to his drug-induced one, the Beatific Vision, Sat-Chit-Ananda and the Dharma-Body *do not* become "as evident as Euclid". In other words, we have to show that the Beatific Vision, Sat-Chit-Ananda and the Dharma-Body are different mystical realities, just as Jerusalem and India are different geographical realities. Now Zaehner seeks to refute him by showing that there is more than one kind of mysticism, and he does this not by *experiencing different kinds of mystical realities*, but by classifying a selection of mystical *writings*. Accordingly, the mystical experiences described in the Upanishads differ from those described by Meister Eckhart, because they are built into different systems of doctrinal beliefs. Zaehner's strategy rests on the presuppositions that different mystical writings express different mystical experiences, and that the two sets of descriptions refer to two different things. But this is wrong, for one and the same thing can have different names, and different names do not necessarily refer to different things.[21]

2.3 The Philosophical Approach to Mysticism

In inquiring into the *nature* of mysticism, philosophers of mysticism usually turn to either theology or psychology for the basic determination of their own object of inquiry. Thus, strictly speaking, what they study is not mysticism as such, but the mysticism as the theologians or the psychologists conceive it. In the first four decades of the last century, the majority of French and other continental

---

21 Cf. Stace, 1960, 35–36: "Professor R. C. Zaehner, in his book *Mysticism, Sacred and Profane* shows that he is in some sense conscious of there being a difference between the experience and the interpretation, but he is in my opinion gravely misled by his failure to hold the distinction clearly in mind, to grasp its implications, and to make effective use of it. For instance, in the records of introvertive mysticism one finds frequent descriptions of the experience of an absolute undifferentiated and distinctionless unity in which all multiplicity has been obliterated. This, as we shall see later, is described by Christian mystics such as Eckhart and Ruysbroeck on the one hand, and by the ancient Hindu mystics who composed the Upanishads on the other. The language of the Hindus on the one hand and the Christians on the other is so astonishingly similar that they give every appearance of describing identically the same experience. They were of course wholly unknown to, and independent of, one another. Yet Professor Zaehner, who is a Roman Catholic, insists that *their experiences must have been different because Eckhart and Ruysbroeck built their accounts of the experience into the orthodox Trinitarian theology which they accepted from the Church, whereas the Hindus understood it pantheistically* — pantheism being, according to Catholic theologians, a serious "heresy." We may leave the question open (for the present) whether Professor Zaehner is right in thinking that the Christian and the Indian experiences are quite different from one another in spite of the almost identical words in which they are often expressed. He may be right. We have admitted, or rather asserted, that there are two alternative hypotheses for explaining the facts. Professor Zaehner chooses one of them. We have not yet ourselves investigated the question of which is right. But the point is that *Professor Zaehner's conclusion simply does not follow from the mere fact that the beliefs which Christian mystics based upon their experiences are different from the beliefs which the Indians based on theirs.* And the difference of beliefs is really the only evidence which he offers for his view. A genuine grasp of the distinction between experience and interpretation, and especially of the difficulties involved in applying it, might have resulted in a fuller, fairer, and more impartial examination and treatment of the two possible hypotheses."

philosophers of mysticism (Friedrich von Hügel, Joseph Maréchal, Henri Bergson, Maurice Blondel, Jacques Maritain) draw inspirations from Christian (especially Catholic) theology, but the way they build personal insights about mysticism into their metaphysical systems makes it difficult to understand their premises and theses from a rationally neutral perspective.[22] As the direct impact of religion on the secularized academy decreases, such a way of doing philosophy of mysticism is on the wane.

The Anglo-American philosophers, on the other hand, mostly worked under the Jamesean conception of mystical experience as an ineffable and noetic state of consciousness.[23] Its most central issues concern the relation between mystical experience and the interpretation thereof, and, relatedly, the ineffability of mystical experience. Notably, it is the logical positivist A. J. Ayer's critical remark in 1936 that first sparked the debate surrounding these issues.

> If a mystic admits that the object of his vision is something which cannot be described, then he must also admit that he is bound to talk nonsense when he describes it [...] [In] describing his vision the mystic does not give us any information about the external world; he merely gives us indirect information about the condition of his own mind.[24]

In short, the ineffability of mystical experience contradicts its noetic quality. Following Ayer's critique, there have been several different attempts to salvage mystical experience from logical contradiction.[25] For W. T. Stace, mystical experience

---

22 Cf. McGinn's critical remark on Bergson: "The increasing religious dimension of [Bergson's] thought is evident in *The Two Sources* where Bergson's fundamental conviction about the centrality of *dureé* [...] was applied to religion and morality. From this perspective, Bergson came to see mysticism as the direct expression of the evolutionary force at the heart of all reality, the force that he described as the *élan vital*. [...] If mysticism is virtually the same thing as Bergsonianism, it would seem difficult to make use of his insights on the former without also signing on for the latter." (McGinn, 1991, 304)

23 A more sophisticated contemporary version can be found in the entry *mysticism* from *The Stanford Encyclopedia of Philosophy*, which defines mystical experience as "A (purportedly) super sense-perceptual or sub sense-perceptual unitive experience granting acquaintance of realities or states of affairs that are of a kind not accessible by way of sense-perception, somatosensory modalities, or standard introspection." (Gellman, Jerome, "Mysticism", *The Stanford Encyclopedia of Philosophy* (Spring 2014 Edition), Edward N. Zalta (ed.), forthcoming URL = <http://plato.stanford.edu/archives/spr2014/entries/mysticism/>.)

24 Ayer, A. J., *Language, Truth and Logic*, Dover Publications, New York, 1946, 118–119.

25 For a survey of more recent accounts see Gellman, Jerome, "Mysticism", *The Stanford Encyclopedia of Philosophy* (Summer 2011 Edition), Edward N. Zalta (ed.), URL = <http://plato.stanford. edu/archives/sum2011/entries/mysticism/>.

is essentially non-logical, and when the mystic says that it is ineffable, this account is only a remembrance of what has happened to him. For Ninian Smart, the mystic's intention to speak the ineffable is precisely to show *performatively* the limit of language and the transcendence of mystical experience. On top of this, the 60s and the 70s saw several other articles by Richard Gale, J. N. Findlay, Galen Pletcher, Bruce Garside, Terence Penulhum, John Hick and Ninian Smart debating over this issue.[26]

Instead of looking into this debate in detail, I shall point out an implicit meta-theoretical issue. As the above quotation of Ayer and the majority of the subsequent scholarly discussions indicate, what is debated is in fact the very *idea* that mystical experience is both ineffable and noetic, rather than an individual *case* of a certain mystic with his writings coming from a concrete historical background. No one is discussing, for instance, whether Thomas Aquinas is a mystic, whether he claims to the effect that mystical experience (or *henosis*, for that matter) is ineffable, and whether he is contradicting himself with these claims. Furthermore, supposed that a preliminary conclusion about Aquinas can be reached, no one bothers to ask to what extent this conclusion can be applied to other countless mystics. Therefore, the more precise formulation of their debate is not *Is mystical experience itself self-contradicting?*, but should be *Is the idea that mystical experience is ineffable and noetic self-contradicting?*

In this questioning, the more fundamental issue *Does the idea that mystical experience is ineffable and noetic correspond to the reality of mystical experience?* is passed over in silence most of the time. As McGinn points out, "the most recent contributions to the Anglo-American philosophical views of mysticism have been largely critical studies of the inner consistency of *theories of mysticism*

---

26 Cf. Gale, Richard M., 'Mysticism and Philosophy', *Journal of Philosophy* 57, 1960, 471–481; Findlay, J. N., 'The Logic of Mysticism', *Ascent to the Absolute: Metaphysical Papers and Letters*, Allen & Unwin, London, 1970, 162–183; Pletcher, Galen K., 'Mysticism, Contradiction, and Ineffability', *American Philosophical Quarterly* 10, 1973, 201–211; Garside, Bruce, 'Language and the Interpretation of Mystical Experience', *International Journal for the Philosophy of Religion* 3, 1972, 93–102; Penulhum, Terence, 'Unity and Diversity in the Interpretation of Mysticism', *Mystics and Scholars: The Calgary Conference on Mysticism 1976*, ed. Harold Coward and Terence Penulhum, *Sciences Reilgieuses: Supplements* 3, 1977, 71–81; Hick, John, 'Mystical Experience as Cognition', *Mystics and Scholars*, 41–56 and Smart, Ninian, 'Mystical Experience', *Sophia* 1, 1962, 19–26; idem. 'Interpretation and Mystical Experence', *Religious Studies* 1, 1965, 75–87; idem. 'Understanding Religious Experience', *Mysticism and Philosophical Analysis*, ed. Steven Katz, Oxford University Press, New York, 1978, 10–21.

whose treatment of mystical texts evidences a form of *'proof-texting'* that pays little attention to context, original language and other textual issues which any form of sound hermeneutics demands."[27] Steven Katz rightly criticizes the tendency to downplay the specificity, diversity and context-dependency of mystical experience, and argues that all mystical experiences are shaped by their respective religious tradition and other factors. There is no unmediated, "pure" experience; every experience is filtered through interpretation.

> […] in order to understand mysticism it is not just a question of studying the reports of the mystic after the experiential event but of acknowledging that the experience itself as well as the form in which it is reported is shaped by concepts which the mystic brings to, and which shape, his experience. To flesh this out, straightforwardly, what is being argued is that, for example, the Hindu mystic does not have an experience of *x* which he then describes in the, to him, familiar language and symbols of Hinduism, but rather he has a Hindu experience, i.e. his experience is not an unmediated experience of *x* but is itself the, at least partially, pre-formed anticipated Hindu experience of Brahman. Again, the Christian mystic does not experience some unidentified reality, which he then conveniently labels God, but rather has the at least partially prefigured Christian experiences of God, or Jesus, or the like. Moreover, as one might have anticipated, it is my view based on what evidence there is, that the Hindu experience of Brahman and the Christian experience of God are not the same.[28]

While Katz reminds us to look more closely into the concrete historical reality of the mystic, he tends to head to the other extremity in claiming to the effect that just because mystical experiences are all mediated by interpretations across different contexts, they cannot have any "common core" behind them. However, the fact that there are two names, say Morning Star and Evening Star, does not mean that they *must* refer to two different things. They can refer to two different things, say a cruise ship and a race car respectively. But they can *also* refer to one and the same thing, for instance to the planet Venus. We are unable to know what the case is, unless we are *both* within the linguistic context wherein these names are being used *and* in contact with the *things* they are supposed to refer to (star, ship, car). It is impossible to know what a thing really

---

27 McGinn, 1991, 319; as an indication of this tendency to over-theorization, McGinn mentions two monographs from the 80s: Wainwright, William J., *Mysticism: A Study of Its Nature, Cognitive Value and Moral Implications*, University of Wisconsin Press, Madison, 1981; and Almond, Philip C., *Mystical Experience and Religious Doctrine: An Investigation of the Study of Mysticism in World Religions*, Mouton, Berlin and New York, 1982.

28 Katz, Steven, 'Language, Epistemology and Mysticism', *Mysticism and Philosophical Analysis*, ed. Steven Katz, Oxford University Press, New York, 1978, 26.

is just by knowing its name. To restate this point in the context of comparative study of mysticism: In order to be able to tell whether or not the Hindu experience of Brahman and the Christian experience of God are the same, the scholar of mysticism should first become *both* a Hindu mystic and a Christian mystic. Textual study of a Hindu and a Christian mystical writing is important, but far from sufficient. That this condition should appear exceedingly demanding gives us no reason to take the easy way out; it is rather a warning sign and a helpful reminder that modesty, openness and caution are essential for the comparative study of mysticism.

2.4 Reflections on the Approaches to the Study of Mysticism

Let us first sum up the strength and weakness of the previous approaches. Mysticism is originally a religious and ethical phenomenon, and the theological approach correctly highlights this basic fact. But in the worst case, when a thick conception of religious way of life is carved out of this phenomenon and imposed upon an individual mystic, it tends to judge him from either a dogmatic perspective or a wrong context, thereby suffocating his originality and uniqueness.

It is this danger, I think, which makes the psychological approach appear attractive and refreshing. For its thin conception of experience not only allows the researchers something definite to concentrate on, but also welcomes non-theologians to approach mysticism from a more liberal perspective. But meta-theoretical parsimony has its negative side-effects too, for when reduction is pushed to extreme, it is no longer possible to speak anything sensible about mystical experience. To wit, it is one thing that certain mystical experiences are ineffable and mystical writings paradoxical, but quite another for researchers to *conceive* them as ineffable and paradoxical. Ineffable experiences and paradoxical writings, if any, might arouse scholarly interest to study them; but to posit ineffability and paradox as the measure of knowledge of mysticism is self-defeating for any serious intellectual inquiry.

Philosophers of mysticism, in reflecting upon the theoretical issues such as the ineffability of mystical experience and the distinction between mystical experience and interpretation, have the advantage of refining the conceptual framework of the articulation of mystical experiences. But this reflective power is surrendered when the theological and psychological conceptions of mystical experience are taken for granted and identified with mysticism as such.

The lessons we learn from these different approaches can be summarized as follows:

(1) In order both to treat fairly the mystic's concrete way of life and to focus on a definite object from an unprejudiced perspective, I suggest that we refrain from using sweeping generalizations such as "mysticism", "monistic mysticism" or "Christian mysticism", and to simply focus on the case studies of individual mystics.

(2) While we are primarily concerned with the mystical experience or experiential reality of mysticism in the case of a particular mystic, most of the time it is neither the reality itself nor the person in flesh and blood, but rather his or her *texts*, which we are directly investigating. From this it immediately follows that, as long as the texts are the direct objects of investigation, the researchers are in no position to decide whether or not the different texts describe the same experience. Even if a gifted scholar is, say, both a Hindu mystic and a Christian mystic, he is still unable to tell whether *moksha* is identical to *unio mystica*, because he cannot represent the deities (Brahman and God) involved in his experiences. Thus the question concerning the unity and diversity of mysticism is suspended.

(3) A further important consequence is that, when it comes to the textual study of mysticism, we should avoid any thick or thin preconception of mystical experience, and attend instead to how the specific text configures the relation between experience and interpretation, or reality and language. In other words, the proper method in the case study of mystical text lies in articulating the interdependency-relation among reality, thought and language as is arranged by a specific mystical text.

To see this point, compare *Life of Moses* of Gregory of Nyssa, John Climacus' *The Ladder of Divine Ascent*, *Revelations of Divine Love* of Julian of Norwich, *On the Vision of God* of Nicholas of Cusa, and *Dark Night of the Soul* of John of the Cross. All of them are classic mystical writings, so there is no reason why scholars of mysticism should overlook them. But these authors do not represent mystical experience in the same way. *Life of Moses* is a work of biblical commentary; *The Ladder of Divine Ascent* is an ascetical handbook; *On the Vision of God* is a theological treatise on beatific vision; *Revelations of Divine Love* accounts for Julian's visionary experiences, appended with her theological interpretations; and *Dark Night of the Soul* comprises stanzas and John's own explanations. Correspondingly, the *reality* of mystical experience is represented differently: as the content of wisdom teaching, as intellectual reflection, as private experience, as the goal of ascetic exercise, or as a work of art. The study of mystical writings does not focus solely on the linguistic factor, but rather on how it relates to the content of thought (via philosophical arguments, literary devices, spiritual counsel, etc.) on the one hand, and the reality of mystical experience (as lived tradition, personal experience, etc.), on the other hand.

Section 3 Subject, Method and Structure of the Present Study

For our present study of Plotinus, the gist of Section 1 and 2 boils down to three simple reminders. First, a careful study of Plotinus' own writings is needed to do justice to his thought. Second, so far as Plotinus' *mysticism* is concerned, we are not studying Plotinus' own mystical experience which he reportedly attained four times in his life, as Porphyry told us. For the direct object of our investigation should be Plotinus' more systematic account of henosis found in the *Enneads*, rather than Porphyry's cursory remarks. Third and more important, before looking into *what* Plotinus' account of henosis is, we have to explain *how* he accounts for it. In other words, we have first to attend to the genre and style of the *Enneads* as a work on mysticism.[29]

Regarding this point, major Plotinian scholars including A. H. Armstrong, Werner Beierwaltes, Émile Bréhier, John Bussanich, Pierre Hadot and John Rist are in agreement that mysticism is compatible with the philosophical thoughts presented in the *Enneads*.[30] However, John Deck and Lloyd Gerson maintain that we need not resort to mystical experience to understand Plotinus' philo-

---

29 I do not suggest that Plotinus intends to compose a work on mysticism. The *Enneads* is in fact a posthumous compilation of writings on various issues, including philosophy of nature, moral philosophy, and so on. My point is simply that in order to study Plotinus' mysticism, first we need to know how his thought is represented in and through his writings.

30 Cf. Armstrong, A. H., 'Tradition, Reason and Experience in the Thought of Plotinus', *Plotino e il Neoplatonismo in Oriente e in Occidente*, 171–194, reprinted in Armstrong, A. H., *Plotinian and Christian Studies*, Variorum, London, 1979, XVII; Beierwaltes, Werner, *Denken des Einen*, Vittorio Klostermann, Frankfurt am Main, 1985; idem., *Selbsterkenntnis und Erfahrung der Einheit: Plotins Ennead V 3, Text, übersetzung, Interpretation, Erläuterungen*, Vittorio Klostermann, Frankfurt am Main, 1991; idem., *Das wahre Selbst: Studien zu Plotins Begriff des Einen und des Geistes*, Vittorio Klostermann, Frankfurt am Main, 2001; Bréhier, Émile, *The Philosophy of Plotinus*, tr. Joseph Thomas, University of Chicago Press, Chicago, 1958; Bussanich, John, 'Plotinian Mysticism in Theoretical and Comparative Perspective', *American Catholic Philosophical Quarterly*, Vol. LXXI, No.3, 1997, 339–365; Hadot, Pierre, *Plotinus or the Simplicity of Vision*, tr. Michael Chase, University of Chicago Press, Chicago and London, 1993; and Rist, John, *Plotinus: The Road to Reality*, Cambridge University Press, Cambridge, 1967, 213–230.

sophical argumentations.[31] In this dissertation, I side with the majority of the Plotinian scholars and hold that for Plotinus, mystical experience is irreducible to philosophical argumentations (λογισμόι). As he emphasizes twice in the *Enneads*, "whoever has already seen (εἶδεν) [the One], will know (οἶδεν) what I'm saying."[32] The tenses of εἶδεν and οἶδεν indicate that the real experience of henosis precedes and grounds the reasoning about it, and arguments abstracted from their experiential context cannot be properly understood. What concerns Plotinus primarily, therefore, is the real experience itself, and a proper discourse (λόγος) thereof must be composed accordingly.

However, the *Enneads* is not a literary work on Plotinus' *personal* contact with the One, either. To be sure, we can find metaphorical descriptions and what looks like an autobiographical account of visionary experiences scattered here and there throughout his writings,[33] but their seriousness and aesthetic value do not measure up to, say, *Scivias* of Hildegard of Bingen and Jalal ad-Din Rumi's *Masnavi*. Rather, as A.H. Armstrong points out, "the primary object of all Plotinus' philosophical activity is to bring his own soul and *the souls of others* by way of Intellect to union with the One. His last words 'Try to bring back the god *in you* to the divine in the All' are a summing up of his whole life and work."[34] Thus, in terms of style and genre, the *Enneads* is neither a treatise nor an autobiography nor a poem, but stands more closely to the spiritual counsel or ascetic teaching such as *The Cloud of Unknowing*. The didactic element of Plotinus' mysticism is clearly seen in the majority of his most important treatises, such as *On Beauty* (the *Ennead*, I.6), *On the Three Primary Hypostases* (V.1), *On the Knowing Hypostases and That which is Beyond* (V.3), *On the Presence of Being* (VI.4–5), *How the Multitude of Forms Come into Being, and on the Good* (VI.7) and *On the Good or the One* (VI.9). As Armstrong remarks in his introductory note of V.1:

> It [treatise V.1] is a fine example of the way in which metaphysical reflection and personal spiritual life are always indissolubly united in Plotinus. The treatise does indeed, as its title indicates, give an account of the "three primary hypostases" [...] But it is not a textbook exposition of an abstract metaphysical system which does not involve or commit

---

31 Cf. Deck, John, *Nature, Contemplation and the One: A Study in the Philosophy of Plotinus* (2nd edition), Larson Publications, Burdett, 1991, 23–26ff. and Gerson, Lloyd, *Plotinus*, Routledge, London and New York, 1994, 218–224.
32 VI.9.9.47–48; see also I.6.7.2–3.
33 See e.g. I.6.9, IV.8.1, V.5.12, VI.7.36.10–27, VI.9.8–9 and VI.9.11.
34 Armstrong, 1966, ix–xxvi.

writer or reader, but an "ascent of the mind to God" which recalls man to an understanding of his true nature and dignity and guides him on his way to his ultimate goal.[35]

Seeing that spiritual guidance is the leitmotif behind Plotinus' writings, when he claims that "whoever has already seen [the One], will know what I'm saying," the real experience in question bears not upon *what Plotinus has already seen* in the past, but upon *what the students will have seen* when they carry out his instructions. To use his own term, Plotinus' aim is to let the students themselves "go up" (ἀναβαίνειν)[36] or "ascend" (ἀνάγειν)[37] to the One by following the methods given in his mystical teaching; and what the students will have seen is to be found in the experiential learning of the "ascent". (In this dissertation I use the technical terms "ascent to the One" and "to ascend to the One" to refer to the gist of Plotinus' mystical teaching; just what this means is the focus of my investigation.)

This point helps to specify the subject and method of our present study. The precise subject should be Plotinus' guidance, instruction or teaching concerning henosis as it is laid down in the *Enneads*, rather than the report of his personal experience, or the metaphorical descriptions about mystical vision, or (if any) the analyses and argumentations about henosis. And seeing that the kernel of Plotinus' writings lies in the methods whereby man "ascends" to the One, our method of inquiry is simply to examine the methods prescribed therein. In order to locate topics for more thorough investigations in the chapters below, I will present in what follows an exegetical survey on Plotinus' methodical teaching. What I aim at is not detailed expositions, but only a concise overview of how Plotinus guides the students along their ascent to the One. The *locus* for our exegesis is *On Dialectic* (I.3).

(i) What art is there, what method or practice, which will take us up there where we must go? Where that is, that it is to the Good, the First Principle, we can take as agreed and established by many demonstrations; and the demonstrations themselves were a kind of leading up on our way.

Τίς τέχνη ἢ μέθοδος ἢ ἐπιτήδευσις ἡμᾶς οἳ δεῖ πορευθῆναι ἀνάγει; Ὅπου μὲν οὖν δεῖ ἐλθεῖν, ὡς ἐπὶ τἀγαθὸν καὶ τὴν ἀρχὴν τὴν πρώτην, κείσθω διωμολογημένον καὶ διὰ πολλῶν δεδειγμένον· καὶ δὴ καὶ δι' ὧν τοῦτο ἐδείκνυτο, ἀναγωγή τις ἦν.[38]

---

35 Armstrong, 1984, 8.
36 Cf. I.3.1.13 and V.1.3.1–3.
37 Cf. I.3.1.2 and V.1.1.24.
38 I.3.1.1–5.

The goal is to ascend to the Good, and what the Good is and how man ascends to It are shown (δεδειγμένον) in many ways. Armstrong translates διὰ πολλῶν δεδειγμένον into *established by many demonstration*, which suggests that the Good or the One is to be shown or derived *from something else*, such as arguments (λογισμοί). This reading is incorrect because the One, qua first principle and ultimate reality, cannot be derived from anything else. In fact, δεδειγμένον is a cognate of δείκνυσθαι, which means *to show* or *to present itself*. The first principle is said to "show itself" in the sense that it is immanent in all beings which are its diverse manifestations. So when Plotinus says that the first principle is shown in many ways, he does not mean that we have many arguments for the existence of the One; the point is rather that Its manifestations or traces can be found in all beings. And since these manifestations are not man-made distortions of the One, but rather that in which the One shows *Itself*, so the ways how they are shown already lead back to the One. This is why Plotinus says that "how it is shown is a kind of ascent to the Good." For the ultimate reality to show itself and for man to "ascend" to it, consequently, boil down to one and the same thing. Such is the basic principle behind the methods laid down in Plotinus' mystical teaching, which rests upon the intuition that the ultimate reality is ultimate for everything including man, and everything is ultimately real according to its own mode of being. Plotinus' metaphysics of the One which grounds his teaching of henosis will be examined in greater detail in the opening chapter.

Within a didactic context, the most crucial implication of the One's immanence is that the One is accessible to the *students themselves*, such that they can "ascend" to It by following the "art, method or practice" (τέχνη ἢ μέθοδος ἢ ἐπιτήδευσις) given in Plotinus' mystical teaching. Thus Plotinus goes on to characterize his target students and then introduces the practices that befit them:

(ii)   But what sort of person should the man be who is to be led on this upward path? Surely one who has seen all or, as Plato says, "who has seen most things, and in the first birth enters into a human child who is going to be a philosopher, a musician or a lover."

Τίνα δὲ δεῖ εἶναι τὸν ἀναχθησόμενον; Ἀρά γε τὸν πάντα ἢ τὸν πλεῖστά φησιν ἰδόντα, ὃς ἐν τῇ πρώτῃ γενέσει εἰς γονὴν ἀνδρὸς ἐσομένου φιλοσόφου μουσικοῦ τινος ἢ ἐρωτικοῦ;[39]

The One manifests Itself in different *lovers*: lover of sensual pleasure, lover of fine art, and philosopher, i.e. lover of wisdom (φιλο-σόφος). So the target students

39   I.3.1.5–9.

are those who are driven by the desire for material and immaterial beauties, and gratify themselves in the attainment thereof. Stated differently, the starting point of Plotinus' teaching of henosis lies in man's *ordinary experience of desire* through which the One is accessible to him. How man should ascend from his experience of desire to the One, is explained in Plotinus' description of the philosopher, the noblest of all the lovers:

(iii)   But the philosopher—he is the one who is by nature ready to respond and "winged", we may say, and in no need of separation like the others. He has begun to move to the higher world, and is only at a loss for someone to show him the way.

Ὁ δὲ φιλόσοφος τὴν φύσιν ἕτοιμος οὗτος καὶ οἷον ἐπτερωμένος καὶ οὐ δεόμενος χωρίσεως, ὥσπερ οἱ ἄλλοι οὗτοι, κεκινημένος τὸ ἄνω, ἀπορῶν δὲ τοῦ δεικνύντος δεῖται μόνον.[40]

Propelled by the desire for knowledge, the philosopher inquires with his intellect into the intelligible beings, and aims ultimately at knowing just what it *is* that he really desires. Accordingly, one of the basic ideas behind Plotinus' mystical teaching is that man should know about his own desire and what he desires, and indeed by means of the practice of philosophy, namely *the intellectual inquiry into intelligible beings*.[41]

But as Plotinus immediately warns us in the same passage, philosophy is only an underdeveloped stage in the mystical ascent to the One, for the philosopher would be "at a loss for someone to show him the way". Why is the philosopher at a loss, and who would show him the way? These questions are explained as follows:

(iv)   So he must be shown and set free, with his own good will, he who has long been free by nature. He must be given mathematical studies to train him in philosophical thought and accustom him to firm confidence in the existence of the immaterial—he will take to them easily, being naturally disposed to learning; he is by nature virtuous, and must be brought to perfect

---

40 I.3.3.1–4.

41 For brevity's sake, in this dissertation "philosophy" and "Plotinus' philosophy" refer specifically to the *method* or *practice* of philosophical activity instructed in his mystical teaching. The same applies to the technical terms "negative theology" and "Plotinus' negative theology". All these terms should not be confused with the *content* of Plotinus' own thought, the bulk of which I shall discuss under the heading "Plotinus' metaphysics of the One".

his virtues, and after his mathematical studies instructed in *dialectic*, and made a complete dialectician.

Δεικτέον οὖν καὶ λυτέον βουλόμενον καὶ αὐτὸν τῇ φύσει καὶ πάλαι λελυμένον. Τὰ μὲν δὴ μαθήματα δοτέον πρὸς συνεθισμὸν κατανοήσεως καὶ πίστεως ἀσωμάτου—καὶ γὰρ ῥάδιον δέξεται φιλομαθὴς ὤν—καὶ φύσει ἐνάρετον πρὸς τελείωσιν ἀρετῶν ἀκτέον καὶ μετὰ τὰ μαθήματα λόγους διαλεκτικῆς δοτέον καὶ ὅλως διαλεκτικὸν ποιητέον.⁴²

Λυτέον βουλόμενον καὶ αὐτὸν τῇ φύσει καὶ πάλαι λελυμένον literally means "one must set him free who is willing and has long been free by nature". That is to say, the philosopher is by nature free from the "will", namely desire for knowledge, in which he appears to be occupied. To be freed from the loss or confusion (ἀπορίας), therefore, is just to be freed from this illusory desire. To this end, Plotinus tells us, the philosopher should learn the art of *dialectic*. But what is the art of dialectic, and why is the philosopher by nature always free from the desire for knowledge? As Plotinus goes on to clarify:

(v) It *[dialectic]* stops wandering about the world of sense and settles down in the world of intellect, and there it occupies itself, casting off falsehood and feeding the soul in what Plato calls "the plain of truth," using his method of division to distinguish the Forms, and to determine the essential nature of each thing, and to find the primary kinds, and weaving together by the intellect all that issues from these primary kinds, till it has traversed the whole intelligible world; then it resolves again the structure of that world into its parts, and comes back to its starting-point; …

Παύσασα δὲ τῆς περὶ τὸ αἰσθητὸν πλάνης ἐνιδρύει τῷ νοητῷ κἀκεῖ τὴν πραγματείαν ἔχει τὸ ψεῦδος ἀφεῖσα ἐν τῷ λεγομένῳ ἀληθείας πεδίῳ τὴν ψυχὴν τρέφουσα, τῇ διαιρέσει τῇ Πλάτωνος χρωμένη μὲν καὶ εἰς διάκρισιν τῶν εἰδῶν, χρωμένη δὲ καὶ ἐπὶ τὰ πρῶτα γένη, καὶ τὰ ἐκ τούτων νοερῶς πλέκουσα, ἕως ἂν διέλθῃ πᾶν τὸ νοητόν, καὶ ἀνάπαλιν ἀναλύουσα, εἰς ὃ ἂν ἐπ᾽ ἀρχὴν ἔλθῃ, …⁴³

Plotinus' so-called "dialectic" is not the same as the original Platonic one. The Platonic dialectic is concerned with investigating the world of intelligible beings, which is tantamount to Plotinus' practice of philosophy explained in passage (iii). But as is emphasized repeatedly in the *Enneads*, the world of intelligible

---

42 I.3.3.5–10.
43 I.3.4.9–16.

beings is not the "starting-point" or the first principle (ἀρχὴ) mentioned in (v).[44] For this reason, in striving to truly know the object of his desire, the philosopher must go *beyond* the intelligible beings to find out the ultimate reality. Plotinus' dialectics, entitled "the second stage of the ascent to the One"[45] and "the nobler part of philosophy",[46] is designed precisely for this task. It proceeds by "resolving" or reducing the world of intelligible beings so radically that the ultimate reality resulting from this operation turns out to be beyond all of them. In this sense, what Plotinus means by "dialectic" is actually a version of *negative theology* which inquires into the ultimate reality which is beyond all beings by removing all beings from It.

Now, considering that the ultimate reality of the intelligible beings is beyond all of them, the philosopher must be said to be "by nature always free from the desire for knowledge" (cf. (iv)) for two reasons. First, the desire for knowledge is an inferior one and therefore should be overcome, insofar as it is directed not toward the ultimate reality but toward the *intelligible beings*. Second, the desire for knowledge is illusory and must be overcome just as well, insofar as it is directed toward *the ultimate reality* which is in fact beyond intelligible beings. In the last analysis, then, the basic idea behind Plotinus' mystical teaching is not simply that man should know what his desire and his desired object really are (cf. (iii)). What man should know, rather, is that his desire is an illusion because the things he desires do not measure up to the ultimate reality. In view of this, the second basic idea behind Plotinus' mystical teaching is to work against this desire for knowledge, and to have man *put to rest his desire for knowledge* altogether. As Plotinus goes on to explain:

(vi) [...] and then, keeping quiet (for it is quiet in so far as it is present There) it busies itself no more, but contemplates, having arrived at unity.

[...] τότε δὲ ἡσυχίαν ἄγουσα, ὡς μέχρι γε τοῦ ἐκεῖ εἶναι ἐν ἡσυχίᾳ οὐδὲν ἔτι πολυπραγμονοῦσα εἰς ἓν γενομένη βλέπει, ...[47]

---

44 For Plotinus *principle* (ἀρχή) refers primarily to the first metaphysical cause of reality. In this sense, the term *ultimate reality* would be more appropriate than *first principle*, which might suggest that that of which it is a principle of bears upon man's explanations of certain phenomena and problems, or that the principle serves explanatory function. Cf. Gerson, Lloyd, *Plotinus*, Routledge, London and New York, 1994, 3–4.

45 I.3.1.14–18.

46 I.3.5.9.

47 I.3.4.16–18.

Since the practice of "dialectics" or negative theology leads to the cessation of all inquiries into henosis, beyond which there is nothing else for the students to do, it is properly speaking the last stage of Plotinus' teaching of henosis.

On the whole, then, Plotinus' mystical teaching is made up of two practices only, namely philosophy and negative theology, and leads to the cessation of any active doing on the students' part. The majority of the most important treatises in the *Enneads* can be understood as exercises or demonstrations of these two methods. Consider for example the so-called *Großschrift*, consisting of *On Nature, and Contemplation and the One, On the Intelligible Beauty, That the Intelligibles are not Outside the Intellect and on the Good*, and *Against the Gnostics* (the *Enneads* III.8, V.8, V.5 and II.9; No. 30, 31, 32, 33 in chronological order). In treatises III.8 and V.8, the subject of which is the contemplation of the sensible world and the intelligible beauty, we see Plotinus' philosophical inquiry into intelligible beings. Starting with V.5.3, Plotinus shifts the focus to the One. The arguments that the intelligible beings depend on the One (V.5.3–5) and that the One is beyond the intelligible beings (V.5.6) belong to the stage of negative theology, in which rational inquiry is applied to that which is beyond all beings. In V.5.7–8 Plotinus takes another turn and concludes that the intellect will be at a loss (ἀπελθόντος) when it tries to know and speak about the One. The One, for example, "was within, and was not within (ἔνδον ἄρα ἦν καὶ οὐκ ἔνδον αὖ);"[48] and "came as one who did not come (ἦλθεν ὡς οὐκ ἐλθών)."[49] These startling theses bring the inquiry of negative theology to an abrupt end, only to see Plotinus claim that "one must not chase after It [the One], but wait quietly till It appears [...] as the eye awaits the rising sun,"[50] that "men have forgotten that which from the beginning until now they want and long for",[51] and that "We [...] must not add any of the things which are later and lesser."[52]

Similarly, in the treatise *On the Knowing Hypostasis and That Which is Beyond* (the *Enneads* V.3) Plotinus starts by explaining the nature of intellect and its proper activity, namely apprehending the intelligible objects, which is ultimately actualized in the intellect's self-thinking (V.3.1–9). This part can be understood as Plotinus' further explanation of his practice of philosophy introduced in I.3.3. The resolution or reduction of philosophy to negative theology is the subject of V.3.10–13, in which Plotinus demonstrates that the One must be beyond

---

48 V.5.7.36.
49 V.5.8.15.
50 V.5.8.3–6.
51 V.5.12.6–7.
52 V.5.13.17–18.

intelligible beings and truly ineffable. Then in V.3.14, the total silence to which negative theology is further reduced is highlighted by the claim that "we are not prevented from having It [the One] even if we do not speak."[53] The treatise ends with Plotinus' famous dictum in which he appeals for the suspension of all intellectual inquiry, whether into intelligible beings or that which is beyond them: "Take away everything (ἄφελε πάντα)!"[54]

Plotinus' teaching of henosis, so far as we have seen, can be characterized as follows: First, its spiritual message is open to all human beings and addresses their everyday concerns and pursuits, for it takes their experiences of desire as the starting point of the ascent to the One. Second, its method of ascent is rational and accommodates ordinary intuition, for all it demands is that man should know what he really desires. Third, it owes its spiritual profundity not to any mythical fabrication of the ultimate reality, but to man's radicalization of reason which resolves the knowledge about his desire into that which is beyond it and which, in the last analysis, nullifies his own inquiries into henosis.

As investigators of Plotinus' mystical writing, we have to remind ourselves at this point that the texts under examination, such as those surveyed above, are the specific configurations of the relation between what henosis is and how Plotinus the author represents them. Now it is our main methodological premise (cf. p.20–21 ff.) that Plotinus neither intends to describe his personal experience nor submits a certain instance of mystical experience under discursive analyses and argumentations, but seeks to offer his students the *methods* by which they can "ascend to the One" on their own. Thus, in addition to examining the methods themselves, we also have to examine the specific way in which these methods relate to the desired goal, i.e. the reality of henosis. To wit, not all methods relate to their respective desired goal in the same way. In some cases such as cookery, the method is *constitutive* of the goal: whether frozen food is deep-fried, baked or heated by microwave makes a difference to its taste and color. But in some other, the method is *abolished* when the goal is reached: for instance, a vehicle is no longer needed when the destination is reached. Seeing that Plotinus' teaching ends up with the cessation of all inquiries, we should try to explain, in the light of Plotinus' metaphysics of the One, whether and in what sense this seemingly undesirable result has anything to do with henosis.

Accordingly, in the following chapters I shall first investigate the methods or practices given in Plotinus' teaching of henosis, as well as their methodological

---

53 V.3.14.8.
54 V.3.17.38.

presuppositions. Chapter 1 deals with Plotinus' metaphysics of the One, in which I attend specifically to Its simplicity, transcendence and ineffability. The subject of Chapter 2 is the practice of philosophy or intellectual inquiry into intelligible beings, and my focus will be on the *constitutive* role of desire for knowledge therein. In Chapter 3 I investigate the practice of negative theology, namely the intellectual inquiry into that which is beyond all beings, and especially the *dissolution* of the intellect resulting from it. Finally, in Chapter 4 I attempt to explain how Plotinus understands the relation between his teaching of henosis and henosis itself, and the focus is on how the practice of negative theology relates to its desired goal.

Chapter 1 Plotinus' Metaphysics of the One

To understand Plotinus' teaching of henosis, first we have to explain how our subject, namely the One, is accessible at all. The condition of possibility of our study therefore depends on two critical issues: first, how the One "*exists*", and second, what the One "*is*." Now it is clear that for Plotinus both the "existence" and the "essence" of the One are not to be taken in the ordinary sense (hence the scare quotes) because the One, as the first principle that grounds and explains all beings, is itself irreducible to any being (τὸ ὄν, οὐσία). What is not, but should have been made clear, however, is Plotinus' subtle approach to these formal requirements. For this reason, this chapter will not directly explain these questions, but proceeds through critical discussions of scholarly interpretations of the *Enneads*. In Section 1 I present the standard account which is upheld by several Plotinian commentators and bears an interesting similarity to Thomas Aquinas' doctrine of God, and argue that this account does not really capture the basic intuition underlying Plotinus' reflections upon the One. Section 2 focuses on the doctrine that the One radically transcends even the apophatic claims made about It. Finally, Section 3 explains how this radical transcendence implies the radical immanence which provides access to the One in our daily experience, thereby paving the way for the first stage of Plotinus' teaching of henosis, to be discussed in the next chapter.

Section 1 The Standard Account

Does the One "exist", and what "is" It? According to John Deck,

> For Plotinus, the doctrine of the One appears to be susceptible of proof. Thus, in the treatise on contemplation, he argues [... that] any multitude is posterior to a one. But the Nous [i.e. intellect] [...] is a two, a duality of intelligence and intelligible. Therefore, the Nous is posterior to another principle, which is the One [... The] argument proceeds from the lower principle, the Nous; the nature of the Nous is seen to demand the One. The doctrine of the One appears in Plotinus' philosophy by rational exigency. Therefore, for a philosophic treatment of his doctrines, Plotinus' "mystical" or para-mystical experience of the One may safely be left to one side. [...] The One, or Good, was demonstrated by the need of the Nous for a principle and a good.[1]

---

1   Deck, John, *Nature, Contemplation and the One: A Study in the Philosophy of Plotinus* (2nd edition), Larson Publications, Burdett, 1991, 23–24. For a similar interpretation see Gerson, Lloyd, *Plotinus*, Routledge, London and New York, 1994, 12–14.

To sum up Dock's interpretation in brevity: the One "is" oneness or the cause of multitude, and must necessarily exist because its effect exists. Similar accounts can be found in the *Enneads* III.8.9, V.3.12, V.5.6, V.6.3, and so on. A stripped-down argument would look like this:

(1) The multiplicity of intellect demands explanation.
(2) Oneness or unity is the best explanation.
(3) The One "is" oneness.
(4) Therefore we must hypothesize that the One "exists"; for otherwise the multiplicity of intellect cannot be explained.

Call this the abductive argument for the existence of the One. It is neither a deduction nor an induction, but an inference to the best explanation which infers X as explanation of Y. "Must" in (4) does not imply any logical or metaphysical necessity by which the One Itself is constrained, but simply a conjecture made on the intellect's demand for explanation and made by its leap into hypothesis.[2] The best-known application of this reasoning in philosophical theology can be found in Thomas Aquinas' Five-Ways.[3] A brief look at the first Way can help us target the critical issue within the standard account of Plotinus' argument:

> It is certain, and evident to our senses, that some things in the world are in motion. Now whatever is in motion is put in motion by another, for nothing can be in motion except it is in potentiality to that towards which it is in motion; whereas a thing moves inasmuch as it is in act. [...] If that by which it is put in motion be itself put in motion, then this also must needs be put in motion by another, and that by another again. But this cannot go on to infinity, because then there will be no first mover, and, consequently, no other mover; seeing that subsequent movers move only inasmuch as they are put in motion by the first mover; [...] Therefore it is necessary to arrive at a first mover, put in motion by no other; and this everyone understands to be God.[4]

---

2   Note that the Greek term for *cause*, αἰτία, primarily means *charge* and *request*; αἰτεῖν means both *to demand* and *to postulate*.

3   It is beyond the scope of the present dissertation to consider the innumerable interpretations of Thomas' arguments. I base my interpretation on following passages: te Velde, Rudi, *Aquinas on God: the "Divine Science" of the Summa Theologiae*, Ashgate Publishing, Farnham, 2006, 47–48; Velecky, Lubor, *Aquinas' Five Arguments in the Summa Theologiae 1a 2, 3*, Kok Pharos Publishing House, Kampen, 1994, 39–42; Shanley, Brian J., *Thomas Aquinas: The Treatise on the Divine Nature, Summa Theologiae I 1–13*, Hackett Publishing, Indianapolis, 2006, 186–191. See also Swinburne, Richard, *The Existence of God* (2nd edition), Oxford University Press, Oxford, 2004, 4–22, 26–34.

4   *ST* I, q.2, a.3, c.

In this argument Thomas presupposes two principles or premises: first, "whatever is in motion is put in motion by another"; and second, "this [the first principle] cannot go on to infinity, because then there will be no first mover, and, consequently, no other mover." In order to explain the empirical fact that something is put in motion under the constraint of these conditions, we must hypothesize a first mover. Now, in order to understand this argument appropriately, it is crucial to remember that it does not consist in deducing the conclusion from the premises, but in inferring to the best explanation under the constraint of these conditions. There are several ways to challenge this argument: either by rejecting both or either one of the two conditions, or by arguing that these two conditions run counter to other conditions of intelligibility, or by hypothesizing a better *explanans* than the first mover. If none of these ways is available, we have to accept that there must be a first mover which moves and is not moved. Such is Thomas' abductive argument in a nutshell, which is not essentially different from the abductive argument for the existence of the One according to Deck's interpretation of Plotinus.

After establishing from the above-mentioned principles and empirical facts the necessity of the first mover's existence, Aquinas goes on to claim that "this [the first mover] everyone understands to be God". This claim is not a part of the abductive argument, but a theological interpretation of the concept of the first mover. Its point is neither to conjure the objectivity of God from subjective opinions nor to identify His essence with the first mover, but to show that what everyone (or at least most people) understands to be God rests on empirical evidence and can be rationally justified. Furthermore, it does not assert that everyone subscribes to a full body of Christian beliefs, but that everyone has a *vague idea* about what it is to be God. The more indefinite the intuition is, the more people it is able to accommodate; and the more people agree that the first mover is God, the more persuasive the argument becomes.

Now let us return to the abductive argument for the existence of the One, and consider thesis (3) that the One "is" oneness. In order to establish the highly generally or even universally valid claim that what must "exist" is not simply oneness but rather the One, we must first reach an agreement that the One is oneness. Accordingly, (3) should mean that *everyone understands oneness to be the One*. But is this the case? The above comparison with *Doctor communis* indicates that this question must be answered in the negative for several reasons.

First, we can follow Aquinas and modify (3) to the effect that everyone understands oneness to be God (θεός). There are two *prima facie* reasons why this assumption is no more implausible than Aquinas' claim that everyone understands the first mover to be God. First, both oneness and the first mover are hypothesized as the best explanation of certain empirical facts. Second, both claims make appeal only to a very indefinite intuition about what it is to be God; they make no impossible demand to turn everyone into a Christian. Accordingly, (3) would be true *if God and the One are one and the same thing*. However, in the *Enneads* the term *God* is ambiguous, referring sometimes to the intellect, and sometimes to the One.[5] Therefore what everyone understands to be God does not refer to the same thing referred to by Plotinus. Consequently, not everyone understands oneness to be the One.

Second, in those cases where Plotinus uses "the One" and "God" as two interchangeable terms, it seems that they refer to one and the same thing. For example, *the One* means the life and source of all beings, the principle of beauty, of well-being and of goodness, and the most lovable "object", which all agree with our intuition about God.[6] But even so, nowhere does Plotinus confirm that these terms are interchangeable because they have the same extension or that *the One* refers to a deity worshipped by a certain religious community. The case is rather the other way round: these terms are interchangeable simply because they have the same intension, namely *perfections*. Therefore, even if everyone understands oneness to be God, it does not follow from this that this God is the One.

Third and more important, as Porphyry's biography informs us, Plotinus belongs to no specific religion extant at his time.[7] Therefore, his conception and talk of perfections cannot be constrained by any extant religion. In this respect, one of the most distinctive and difficult features of his philosophical theology is that he places the One unrelated to and even *beyond* all deities. Therefore, when he talks about θεός and invokes Plato's dictum "to be made like God" (θεῷ ὁμοιωθῆναι) as man's final destination,[8] it must have been the case that none of his students really knew what he was talking about:

> When Amelius grew ritualistic and took to going round visiting the temples at the New Moon and the feasts of the gods and once asked if he could take Plotinus along, Plotinus

---

5   For "God" as the intellect, see V.1.4, V.1.5, V.1.7, V.8.3, V.8.9, V.8.12, V.9.7, VI.4.14, VI.5.7, VI.5.12, VI.7.1, and VI.7.9; for "God" as the One, see I.1.8, I.8.2, II.9.6, II.9.8, V.5.9, V.5.11, VI.7.19, VI.9.5, VI.9.6, VI.9.9 and VI.9.11.

6   Cf. VI.5.12, VI.7.35, I.4.8, V.5.13, VI.7.35, VI.9.9.

7   For Plotinus' attitude and relation to religions in the third century Rome see Miles, Margaret R., *Plotinus on Body and Beauty: Society, Philosophy and Religion in the Third-century Rome*, Blackwell Publishing, Oxford, 1999,10–16.

8   Cf. I.2.1.3; quoted from Plato, *Theaetetus*, 176A-B.

said, 'They [the gods] ought to come to me, not I to them.' *What he meant by this exalted utterance we could not understand and did not dare to ask.*[9]

Since Plotinus seeks to elaborate his theology of the One outside of any given religious context, and since "the One" is not a conventional name such as *Apollo* in the first place, it seems that hardly anyone but Plotinus himself knows what "the One" means. Therefore the abductive argument for the "existence" of the One outlined above, in the strict sense, is acceptable only to very few people and hence not entirely persuasive. At any event, it is not as persuasive as Thomas' version, in which the incomprehensive and imprecise meaning of "God" is immediately agreed upon.

But the above consideration does not simply show that Plotinus' unconventional approach makes his philosophical theology of the One untenable from the very beginning. The point, in my opinion, is rather that Plotinus is raising certain fundamental questions concerning the very possibility of theology as such: Are theological reflections upon God or (to use a neutral term) "the ultimate reality" possible only within the context of a given religion? If yes, how should we explain the fact that religions as well as non-religious thinkers like Plotinus make different claims about God? If not, how should a trans-contextual reflection upon God proceed? As his argument for the existence of oneness suggests, Plotinus would maintain that the *diversity* of God-talks must be explained by a *unified* conception of God across different religions. However, he does not approach it in light of inter-religious dialogue or comparative religion; as we shall see below, his ambition is to reflect upon the ultimate reality *as such*, transcending all religious contexts and their references.

Section 2   The Radical Transcendence of the One

Plotinus' reflections upon the One or the ultimate reality appears unnecessarily convoluted, because the technical term he uses, "the One", connotes several meanings which are often confused in our ordinary language. Usually we mean by "one" following things: an ordinal number (εἷς); a cardinal number or the first; an individual thing; a single thing, solitary in type; *the* unique thing without equals or parallels, either relatively (as in "this is the one") or absolutely (as in "God is *the* one"); a unity considered with respect to its composition (e.g. an army is a unity of soldiers); a simple thing considered in itself; and so on. Plotinus does

---

9   Porphyry, *The Life of Plotinus*, 10, cited from *Plotinus*, vol.1, tr. A. H. Armstrong, Harvard University Press, Cambridge, 1966, my italics.

not take all these meanings into consideration, because he is not a philosopher of language, but above all a philosophical theologian of the ultimate reality. For him, the three most important meanings of the term "the One" are: (1) *oneness*, or the attribute of providing unified explanation of beings; (2) *simplicity*, or the identity between the ultimate reality and its oneness; (3) the pragmatic marker of *illocutionary self-denial*, whereby the speaker denies that he is claiming the ultimate reality to be absolutely simple and ineffable. In the following three sub-sections I shall explain these three meanings or functions of the One in order.

2.1 "The One" as Oneness

To start with, the most basic meaning of "the One" is *oneness*, in the sense of metaphysical principle of beings (τὰ ὄντα). The reason Plotinus adduces is that to be is to be one, or that being (τὸ εἶναι) is identical to oneness:

(i)   It is *by the one* that all beings are beings, both those which are primarily beings and those which are in any sense said to be among beings. For what could anything be if it was not one? For if things are deprived of the one which is *predicated* of them, they are not those things.

Πάντα τὰ ὄντα τῷ ἑνί ἐστιν ὄντα, ὅσα τε πρώτως ἐστὶν ὄντα, καὶ ὅσα ὁπωσοῦν λέγεται ἐν τοῖς οὖσιν εἶναι. τί γὰρ ἂν καὶ εἴη, εἰ μὴ ἓν εἴη; ἐπείπερ ἀφαιρεθέντα τοῦ ἓν ὃ λέγεται οὐκ ἔστιν ἐκεῖνα.[10]

As long as Plotinus understands oneness to be the ultimate reality, the preceding argument for its existence can be established. We could therefore conclude that the existence of the One or ultimate reality can be proved, and that its essence is oneness. But this is not entirely the case. Note that in (i) Plotinus does not talk about *oneness as such* (τὸ ἕν), but rather "*by the one*" (τῷ ἑνί) and "the one which is *predicated* (λέγεται) of [things]". These qualifications mark the *reflexive* character of Plotinus' approach to the ultimate reality.[11] On the one hand, he is

---

10 VI.9.1-2. By *oneness* is meant the state of unity, individuality or singularity *simpliciter*, rather than composition, which is oneness considered in terms of its composites. *Unity* is also to be distinguished from *henosis* or unification with the One.

11 Cf. V.1.1.31-35: "For that which investigates is the soul, and she should know what she is as an investigating soul, so that she may learn first about herself, whether she has the power to investigate things of this kind, and if she has an eye of the right kind to see them, and if the investigation is suitable for her. For if the objects are alien, what is the point? But if they are akin, the investigation is suitable and discovery is possible." V.1.10.1-6: "It has been shown that we ought to think that this is how things are,

not *skeptical* about the "existence" of the ultimate reality and our access to it; but on the other hand, he does not embrace the *naivety* that reality remains what it is irrespective to our mode of experience. He neither rejects nor accepts our everyday experience as it appears, but rather takes a step back to consider what its appearance is. "One must perceive each thing by the appropriate organ (Χρὴ δὲ βλέπειν ᾧ ἕκαστα δεῖ αἰσθάνεσθαι);"[12] in other words, there are degrees of beings as well as degrees of knowledge because—from an epistemological perspective—there are degrees of perceiving things.

From this reflexive point of view, oneness is always ascribed to the ultimate reality as an *explanans* which necessarily presupposes and depends on an *explainer* and an *explanandum*.[13] As in an abduction argument, oneness is invoked as the best explanation of certain facts under certain theoretical constraint and hence remains essentially hypothetical and open to correction. Consequently, oneness is not self-explanatory, self-evident or self-sufficient (αὐτάρκης)—it is at most *the ultimate explanation*, but should not thereby be confused with the *ultimate reality* as such.[14]

2.2 "The One" as Simplicity

In order to signify the self-sufficiency of the ultimate reality, Plotinus gives "the One" a more radical meaning, namely *simplicity* (ἁπλότης, τὸ ἁπλούστατον). To wit, if the ultimate reality is a composite, it would be *dependent* on its components; but this is absurd, for if a metaphysical principle is ultimate, it cannot be dependent:

(ii)   For there must be something simple before all things, and this must be other than all the things which come after it, existing by itself, not mixed

---

that there is the One beyond being, of such a kind as our argument wanted to show, so far as demonstration was possible in these matters, and next in order there is Being and Intellect, and the nature of Soul in the third place. And just as in nature there are these three of which we have spoken, so we ought to think that they are present also in ourselves."

12 V.5.12.1.

13 Cf. VI.9.1–2.

14 Cf. VI.9.6.34–38: "But a principle is not in need of the things which come after it, and the principle of all things needs none of them. For whatever is in need is in need as striving towards its principle; but if the One is in need of anything, It is obviously seeking not to be one; so It will be in need of Its destroyer;…" That is to say, if the One is in need of anything, It will not be the One, which is absurd; therefore the One must not be in need of anything.

with the things which derive from it, and all the same able to be present in a different way to these other things, being really one, and not a different being and then one; it is false even to say of it that it is one, and there is "no concept or knowledge" of it; it is indeed also said to be "beyond being". For if it is not to be simple, outside all coincidence and composition, it could not be a [sic] first principle;...

δεῖ μὲν γάρ τι πρὸ πάντων εἶναι ἁπλοῦν, τοῦτο καὶ πάντων ἕτερον τῶν μετ᾽ αὐτό, ἐφ᾽ ἑαυτοῦ ὄν, οὐ μεμιγμένον τοῖς ἀπ᾽ αὐτοῦ, καὶ πάλιν ἕτερον τρόπον τοῖς ἄλλοις παρεῖναι δυνάμενον, ὂν ὄντως ἕν, οὐχ ἕτερον ὄν, εἶτα ἕν, καθ᾽ οὗ ψεῦδος καὶ τὸ ἓν εἶναι, οὗ μὴ λόγος μηδὲ ἐπιστήμη, ὃ δὴ καὶ ἐπέκεινα λέγεται εἶναι οὐσίας—εἰ γὰρ μὴ ἁπλοῦν ἔσται συμβάσεως ἔξω πάσης καὶ συνθέσεως καὶ ὄντως ἕν, οὐκ ἂν ἀρχὴ εἴη—...[15]

From a reflexive point of view, a being (τὸ ὄν) is always accessible to us as an instance of explanation, namely as an explanandum explained by us in terms of the explanans. There is an essential conceptual distinction among the act of explanation, the explanandum and the explanans, such that all beings are necessarily composite. But the ultimate reality is simple. Therefore the ultimate reality must be transcendent or beyond all beings.

(iii) But if all things are in that which is generated [from the One], which of the things in It are you going to say that the One is? Since It is none of them, It can only be said to be beyond them. But these things are beings, and being: so It is "beyond being". This phrase "beyond being" does not mean that It is a particular thing—for it makes no positive statement about It—and it does not say Its name, but all it implies is that It is "not this". But if this is what the phrase does, it in no way comprehends the One...

εἰ οὖν τὰ πάντα ἐν τῷ γενομένῳ, τί τῶν ἐν τούτῳ ἐκεῖνο ἐρεῖς; οὐδὲν δὲ τούτων ὂν μόνον ἂν λέγοιτο ἐπέκεινα τούτων. ταῦτα δὲ τὰ ὄντα καὶ τὸ ὄν· ἐπέκεινα ἄρα ὄντος. τὸ γὰρ ἐπέκεινα ὄντος οὐ τόδε λέγει—οὐ γὰρ τίθησιν—οὐδὲ ὄνομα αὐτοῦ λέγει, ἀλλὰ φέρει μόνον τὸ οὐ τοῦτο. τοῦτο δὲ ποιοῦν οὐδαμοῦ αὐτὸ περιλαμβάνει·[16]

---

15 V.4.1.5–13. See also Gerson 1994,4–6and Bussanich, John, 'Plotinus' Metaphysics of the One', *The Cambridge Companion to Plotinus*, ed. Lloyd Gerson, Cambridge University Press, Cambridge, 1996, 42–43.
16 V.5.6.8–15.

Since the notion of simplicity is introduced mainly in order to save the ultimate realty from falling into pure self-reflexivity and to prevent us from reducing it to an *ad hoc* hypothesis (albeit a very powerful one), it bears first and foremost upon overcoming the distinction among explainer, *explanandum* and *explanans*, and consequently upon our inability of explaining and saying anything about it. Therefore the ultimate reality is not only simple, but also *ineffable*.

(iv) It *[the One]* is, therefore, truly ineffable: for whatever you say about It, you will always be speaking of a "something". But "beyond all things and beyond the supreme majesty of Intellect" is the only one of all the ways of speaking of It which is true; it is not Its name, but says that It is not one of all things and "has no name", because we can say nothing of It: we only try, as far as possible, to make signs to ourselves about It.

Διὸ καὶ ἄρρητον τῇ ἀληθείᾳ· ὅ τι γὰρ ἂν εἴπῃς, τὶ ἐρεῖς. ἀλλὰ τὸ "ἐπέκεινα πάντων καὶ ἐπέκεινα τοῦ σεμνοτάτου νοῦ" ἐν τοῖς πᾶσι μόνον ἀληθὲς οὐκ ὄνομα ὂν αὐτοῦ, ἀλλ᾽ ὅτι οὔτε τι τῶν πάντων οὔτε ὄνομα αὐτοῦ, ὅτι μηδὲν κατ᾽ αὐτοῦ· ἀλλ᾽ ὡς ἐνδέχεται, ἡμῖν αὐτοῖς σημαίνειν ἐπιχειροῦμεν περὶ αὐτοῦ.[17]

Simplicity and ineffability characterize the absoluteness of the ultimate reality in two complementary ways. Simplicity, as well as the names *self-sufficiency* (αὐτάρχεια: V.3.17.12–14), *causa sui* (αἴτιον ἑαυτοῦ: VI.8.14.41), *the Good* (τὸ ἀγαθόν: I.3.1.3, V.4.1.32–34, VI.9.3.16) and *the first* (τὸ πρῶτον: V.4.1.3, VI.9.3.16), highlight the absoluteness as such. On the other hand, ineffability, as well as negative terms like *beyond* (ἐπέκεινα: V.3.17.13–14, V.4.1.10, .5.6.10–11, VI.8.16.34, VI.8.19.13), *formless* (ἄμορφον: VI.7.17.17 and VI.7.33.4) and *infinite* (ἀπείρον: V.5.10.19–21), emphasize its difference from the beings dependent on it.[18] Unlike perfection-terms, these two classes of names make no direct reference to other beings.

Introducing the notion of ineffability has serious consequences. For one, to ascribe oneness to the ultimate reality already makes a claim about it which fails to measure up its self-sufficiency. As a result, thesis (3) in the abductive argument for the existence of the One should be rejected, for it is impossible to predicate anything to the One. Plotinus' radical position can be clarified in light of a brief contrast with Aquinas' doctrine of divine simplicity. In *Summa Theologiae* I, q.3, a.1-a.6, Aquinas first considers several types of metaphysical composition between, say, matter and

---

17 V.3.13.1–6.
18 Cf. Gerson, 1994,15–22 and Bussanich, 1996, 42–45.

form, essence and existence, subject and predicate, and so on. He then proceeds to demonstrate that all the composites in question remain dependent upon their respective components and hence give rise to untenable results when applied to God, for He is form itself (ipsa forma) or being itself (ipsum esse).[19]

Two things are to be noted from this line of thought. First, what Aquinas does is to *deny* of God several types of metaphysical composition, rather than to *affirm* what some contemporary philosophers of religion presume to be the logical consequence of his argument, such as the identity between God's existence and essence, and the identity among all of His attributes.[20] In particular, since Aquinas explicitly denies that negating P of God amounts to ascribing non-P to God,[21] the aforementioned interpretation is inaccurate: that God is not composed does not imply that God just is identical to His attributes.

Second, one way to challenge Aquinas' argument is to bring up counter-examples, namely types of metaphysical composition in which the composite itself is *not* dependent on its components. Such a mode, I think, can be found in Plotinus' doctrine that the self-thinking intellect is at once one and two, simple and not simple:

(v)   There is a difference between one thing thinking another and something thinking itself; the latter goes further towards escaping two. The former wants to escape being two and think itself, but is less capable of it; for it has what it sees with itself, but none the less it is different from it. But the latter is not substantially distinct [from its object], but keeps company with itself and so sees itself. It becomes a pair, therefore, while remaining one. It thinks more genuinely, therefore, and thinks primarily, because *the thinking principle must be one and two*. For if it is not one, that which thinks and that which is thought will be different—it would not therefore be the primary thinker, [...] but if it is, on the other hand, one and not two, it will have nothing to think: so that it will not even be a thinking principle. It must, then, be simple and not simple.

Τὸ μέν ἐστι νοεῖν ἄλλο ἄλλο, τὸ δὲ αὐτὸ αὐτό, ὃ ἤδη φεύγει μᾶλλον τὰ δύο εἶναι. τὸ δὲ πρότερον λεχθὲν βούλεται καὶ αὐτό, ἀλλ᾽ ἧττον δύναται· παρ᾽

---

19 Cf. ST I, q.3, a.7, c.

20 See e.g. Plantinga, Alvin, *Does God Have a Nature?*, Marquette University Press, Milwaukee, 1980, 47; Stump, Eleonore, and Kretzmann, Norman, 'Absolute Simplicity', *Faith and Philosophy*, Vol.2, Issue 4, 1985, 338–353; Leftow, Brian, 'Divine Simplicity', *Faith and Philosophy*, Vol.23, Issue 4, 2006, 365–380.

21 *ST* I, q.3, prol.: "[...] we cannot know what God is, but rather what He is not;" that is to say, *not knowing what God is* is not equivalent with *knowing what God is not*.

αὐτῷ μὲν γὰρ ἔχει ὃ ὁρᾷ, ἕτερόν γε μὴν ὂν ἐκείνου. τὸ δὲ οὐ κεχώρισται τῇ οὐσίᾳ, ἀλλὰ συνὸν αὐτῷ ὁρᾷ ἑαυτό. ἄμφω οὖν γίνεται ἓν ὄν. μᾶλλον οὖν νοεῖ, ὅτι ἔχει, καὶ πρώτως νοεῖ, ὅτι τὸ νοοῦν δεῖ ἓν καὶ δύο εἶναι. εἴτε γὰρ μὴ ἕν, ἄλλο τὸ νοοῦν, ἄλλο τὸ νοούμενον ἔσται—οὐκ ἂν οὖν πρώτως νοοῦν εἴη […] εἴτε ἓν μέν, μὴ δύο δὲ αὖ ἔσται, ὅ τι νοήσει οὐχ ἕξει· ὥστε οὐδὲ νοοῦν ἔσται. ἁπλοῦν ἄρα καὶ οὐχ ἁπλοῦν δεῖ εἶναι.[22]

In this instance the composite itself, namely the intellect which thinks itself, is not dependent on its components, namely the act of intellection and the intelligible object. The case is rather that the composite and the components depend on each other and constitute a "self-organizing" or self-*sufficing* system that depends on nothing but *itself*.

Whether a self-sufficing composite is possible, and whether Aquinas would reject or rather welcome such a possibility, cannot be discussed in any detail here. My point is simply that Aquinas' argument only proves that the types of metaphysical composition he takes into consideration cannot be predicated of God. And since he does not consider *all* possible types, the kind of divine simplicity thus demonstrated remains a relatively weak one. Plotinus' approach, on the other hand, can be understood as a radical correction of Aquinas'. Unlike Aquinas, he does not pay too much attention to analyzing types of metaphysical composition; his strategy is to deny in a sweeping fashion the very possibility of *predicating* (τὸ λέγειν) anything of the ultimate reality. The focus is not on whatever types of metaphysical composition, but rather on the possibility of saying anything about the ultimate reality, as we saw in quotations (i) and (ii) of this chapter. Whereas Aquinas articulates the doctrine of divine simplicity by negating certain types of metaphysical compositions, Plotinus approaches it via the correlated doctrine of ineffability. His argument could be simplified like this: Since the ultimate reality is ineffable, it is *a priori* impossible to ascribe any types of composition to the ultimate reality.

However, the apophatic claim that the ultimate reality is ineffable already makes a claim about it, and what exactly it means does not seem very clear. To introduce Plotinus' own explanation in greater detail in the next sub-section, let us first consider two possible approaches.

The first approach takes the apophatic claim out of its proper context and treats the ultimate reality like any object of other discourses. This leads to the rejection of the apophatic claim on the ground that it contradicts the "grammar" or "logic" of those discourses. For example, we can formalize the apophatic claim

---

22 V.6.1.1–14; see also V.3, V.5, V.810, V.9, VI.7.

into a self-defeating statement with which the speaker affirms what he negates.[23] But since serious negative theologians such as Plotinus, Pseudo-Dionysius the Areopagite (henceforth Dionysius) and Aquinas are not concerned with formal language, but rather with the ultimate reality which is "beyond beings", this approach is irrelevant to their concern.

The second approach privileges a special discourse which does not directly speak of the ultimate reality, but merely insinuates its transcendence. In this way, it manages to find a balance between the ultimate reality and language. Metaphoric and expressive discourses, for instance, describe not what the ultimate reality essentially is, but only what it is like and how we feel about it. But the most famous example is arguably Aquinas' doctrine of analogy found in *Summa Theologiae* I, q.13. a.5.[24]

> Now names are thus used [i.e. in an analogous sense, or according to proportion] in two ways: either according as many things are proportionate to one, thus for example "healthy" predicated of medicine and urine in relation and in proportion to health of a body, of which the former is the sign and latter the cause: or according as one thing is proportionate to another, thus "healthy" is said of medicine and animal, since medicine is the cause of health in the animal body. And in this way some things are said of God and creatures analogically, and not in a purely equivocal nor in a purely univocal sense. For we can name God only from creatures. Thus whatever is said of God and creatures, is said according to the relation of a creature to God as its principle and cause, wherein all perfections of things pre-exist excellently. Now this mode of community of idea is a mean between pure equivocation and simple univocation. For in analogies the idea is not, as it is in univocals, one and the same, yet it is not totally diverse as in equivocals; but a term which is thus used in a multiple sense signifies various proportions to some one thing…[25]

2.3 "The One" as the Illocutionary Self-Denial

Plotinus' own approach is similar to Aquinas' above-mentioned doctrine of analogy in that both seek to save the ultimate reality from reduction. But unlike Aquinas' approach, it rejects the apophatic claim on the ground that not even

---

23 Cf. Alston, William, 'Ineffability', *The Philosophical Review*, Vol.65, No.4, 1956, 506–522.

24 Cf. te Velde, 2006, 97: "Analogy is the key term in Thomas' solution to the problem of how the infinite and transcendent God can be named by names which are originally at home in the finite and immanent sphere of the human world. It is by means of analogy that Thomas wants to explain how human discourse on God can be in truth a discourse on God, without thereby treating God as a particular object among others." (te Velde's italics)

25 *ST* I, q.13, a.5, c.

a privileged discourse about the ultimate reality can adequately measure up to it—after all, is it not much loftier for the ultimate reality to transcend even any apophatic claim than to be accessible by it? Therefore, while the basic motive of Plotinus' approach is similar to Aquinas' doctrine of analogy, its result is closer to the approach which rejects the apophatic claim, although for obviously different reasons: the former for the sake of transcendence of the ultimate reality, the latter for the sake of a standardized discourse. This extreme measure is taken up by Plotinus and marks his *most* radical position regarding the transcendence of the ultimate reality:

(vi) But perhaps this name "One" contains [only] a negation of multiplicity. [...] But if the One—name and reality expressed—was to be taken positively it would be less clear than if we did not give It a name at all: for perhaps *this name [One] was given It in order that the seeker*, beginning from this which is completely indicative of simplicity, *may finally negate this as well*, because, though it was given as well as possible by its giver, not even this [name] is worthy to manifest that nature;…

τάχα δὲ καὶ τὸ "ἕν" ὄνομα τοῦτο ἄρσιν ἔχει πρὸς τὰ πολλά. [...] εἰ δὲ θέσις τις τὸ ἕν, τό τε ὄνομα τό τε δηλούμενον, ἀσαφέστερον ἂν γίνοιτο τοῦ εἰ μή τις ὄνομα ἔλεγεν αὐτοῦ· τάχα γὰρ τοῦτο ἐλέγετο, ἵνα ὁ ζητήσας, ἀρξάμενος ἀπ᾽ αὐτοῦ, ὃ πάντως ἁπλότητός ἐστι σημαντικόν, ἀποφήσῃ τελευτῶν καὶ τοῦτο, ὡς τεθὲν μὲν ὅσαν οἷόν τε καλῶς τῷ θεμένῳ οὐκ ἄξιον μὴν οὐδὲ τοῦτο εἰς δήλωσιν τῆς φύσεως ἐκείνης,…[26]

The suggestion that simplicity and ineffability properly characterize the ultimate reality, once maintained in (ii), (iii) and (iv), is now turned down by Plotinus. These names are indeed more appropriate than, say, "oneness", but in the last analysis they remain names all the same, and should be negated for just this reason. Especially noteworthy is Plotinus' claim that the name "One" is not *predicated* to the One (ἔλεγεν αὐτοῦ), but rather *uttered* in a speech act to be performed for a certain purpose (τοῦτο ἐλέγετο, ἵνα…). The negativity implied by this term does not pertain to the negative proposition about the ultimate reality, but rather marks the illocutionary self-denial whereby the speaker denies that *he* is making any apophatic claim. Thus understood, Plotinus' discourse of "the One" functions as a linguistic performance which refrains from making any claim about what the ultimate reality is.

---

26 V.5.6.26–34.

Later on, Anselm took up a similar approach to God in the *Proslogion*. In Chapter 2, Anselm says that God is "that than which nothing greater can be conceived (cogitari)". That is to say, God is the greatest thing conceivable, or the most perfect reality represented by the concept of the highest perfection. This formulation corresponds to Plotinus' conception of the ultimate reality as simplicity and ineffability, for both of them are used to designate the self-sufficiency and absoluteness as such. After enumerating various perfections of God, however, Anselm's experience of prayer drives him into despair:

> But, if thou [my soul] hast found (invenisti) Him, why is it that thou dost not feel (sentis) thou hast found Him? Why, O Lord, our God, does not my soul feel thee, if it hath found thee?[27]

Thus Anselm claims in *Proslogion*, Chapter 15 as follows:

> Therefore, Lord, Thou art not only that than which a greater cannot be conceived, *but thou art something greater than can be* conceived (quiddam maius quam cogitari posit). For, since it can be conceived that there is such a being (esse aliquid huiusmodi), then, if Thou art not this very being (hoc ipsum), a greater than Thou can be conceived. But this is impossible.[28]

That is, God is not simply the greatest thing conceivable, but beyond all conceivable greatness; He is the perfect reality to which no concept of perfection can correspond. The context shows that Anselm's insight is not an inference to God's perfection, but rather a confession of thought's inability to conceive it. From a comparative perspective, although their respective meanings bear remarkable differences, Anselm's *perfection* and Plotinus' *simplicity* are meant to be adequate characterizations of God and the ultimate reality. Both thinkers, furthermore, not only take seriously the abysmal gap between characterization as such and the reality which transcends it, but also seek to go beyond mere characterization to come nearer to the transcendent reality. But their approaches are different: what Plotinus emphasizes by pragmatic marker is set forth by Anselm in a devotional context ("Therefore, Lord, not only are You…").[29]

---

27 *Proslogion* Chapter 14, from *St. Anselm: Proslogium; Monologium; an Appendix in Behalf of the Fool by Gaunilon; and cur Deus Homo*, tr. Sidney Norton Deane, Open Court, La Salle, 1903.

28 Ibid. Chapter 15.

29 Cf. Fulmer, J. Burton, 'Anselm and the Apophatic: "Something Greater than Can Be Thought"', *New Black Friars*, Vol.89, Issue 1020, 2008,177–193and Marion, Jean-Luc, 'Is the Ontological Argument Ontological? The Argument According to Anselm and Its Metaphysical Interpretation According to Kant', *Journal of the History of Philosophy*, Vol.30, No.2, 1992, 201–218.

The extremity of passage (vi) in its difference to the *Proslogion*, Chapter 15 becomes more palpable if we recall that this passage comes from a *non-theistic* thinker for whom the experience and doctrines of faith have little relevance. Not only does "The One" designate no deity like Yahweh or the Triune God, but it is not a vocative like "O Lord" addressed in prayer, either. Its linguistic function is not to open and hand oneself over to a transcendent deity, but to deny one's own claim on the absolute reality and thereby to remove any definite approach to it. It seems more likely that Plotinus comes up with this strategy of self-denial out of the concern, shared with Plato, that the transmission of teaching is liable to misinterpretation and abuse by the students. According to *The Seventh Letter*:

> So much at least I can confirm with confidence about any who have written or propose to write on these questions, pretending to a knowledge of the problems with which I am concerned, whether they claim to have learned from me or from others or to have made their discoveries from themselves: it is impossible, in my opinion, that they can have learned anything at all about the subject. *There is no writing of mine about these matters, nor will there ever be one. For this knowledge is not something that can be put into words like other sciences*; but after long-continued intercourse between teacher and pupil, in joint pursuit of the subject, suddenly, like light flashing forth when a fire is kindled, it is born in the soul and straightway nourishes itself.[30]

Similarly, according to *Phaedrus*:

> SOCRATES: Would a sensible farmer, who cared about his seeds and wanted them to yield fruits, plant them in all seriousness in the garden of Adonis in the middle of the summer and enjoy watching them bear fruit within seven days? Or would he do this as an amusement and in honor of the holiday, if he did it at all? Wouldn't he use his knowledge of farming to plant the seeds he cared for when it was appropriate and be content if they bore fruit seven months later?

> PHAEDRUS: That's how he would handle those he was serious about, Socrates, quite differently from the others, as you says.

> SOCRATES: Now what about the man who knows what is just, noble and good? Shall we say that he is less sensible with his seeds than the farmer is with his?

> PHAEDRUS: Certainly not.

> SOCRATES: Therefore, he won't be serious about writing them in ink, sowing them, through a pen, with *words that are as incapable of speaking in their own defense as they are of teaching the truth adequately.*

> PHAEDRUS: That wouldn't be likely.[31]

---

30 *The Seventh Letter* 341b-d; cf. Cooper, John (ed.), *Plato: Complete Works*, Hackett, Indianapolis, 1997.

31 *Phaedrus* 276b-d; cf. Cooper, John (ed.), *Plato: Complete Works*, Hackett, Indianapolis, 1997.

Thus, drawing on Plotinus' claim in passage (vi) that naming the One would be less clear than *not* naming It, we can imagine Plotinus respond to Anselm as follows:[32]

"It is not really the case that the ultimate reality or God is beyond all conceivable greatness. For with this claim you are already picking out God as the subject of discourse, and this God-talk is true only within the context of a certain religion. But this implies that its truth-condition lies in said religion and the orthodoxy of its believers, rather than in the ultimate reality itself, which is absurd. Like I said, 'we must perceive each thing with the appropriate organ.' So, instead of saying that the ultimate reality or God is beyond all conceivable greatness, it is more accurate to say that what is beyond all conceivable greatness lies beyond the ultimate reality we are talking about. But still more appropriate would it be for us to deny having made all these God-talks, for nothing you say about the ultimate reality has anything to do with the transcendent and ineffable ultimate reality itself."

Section 3 The Radical Immanence of the One

For Plotinus, the ultimate reality is not simply transcendent in the sense that it is ineffable; it is rather *radically* transcendent, so much so that we cannot talk about it in any way. This uncompromising attitude seems to lead to insoluble difficulties. The first one is that to say the ultimate reality is radically transcendent *still* says something about it. As we saw, Plotinus resorts to illocutionary self-denial to solve this problem: he denies that he has said anything about the ultimate reality, or that what he has "said" amounts to having made a positive claim about it. We can criticize his self-denial for being insincere, but Plotinus might counter that his intention is sincere even if his speech-act does not seem so, and that if

---

32 This imaginary reply is a paraphrase of VI.7.38.1–10, replacing "the Good" with "God": "But It *[the One]* is not even the "is" (Εστι δὲ αὐδὲ τὸ "ἔστιν"); for It has no need whatever even of this; for "It is good" is not applicable to It either, but to that to which the "is" applies; but the "is" [, when said of It,] is not said as one thing of another, but as indicating what It is. But we say "the Good" about It, not speaking of It Itself or predicating of It that good belongs to It, but saying it is Itself; so then, since we do not think it proper to say "is good" or to put the article before It, but are unable to make ourselves clear, if one takes it away altogether, we say "the good" so as not to still need the "is", that we may not make one thing and then another." Note that the One is called "the Good" not because this name properly designate Its simplicity and ineffability, but is only for the sake of clarifying our thoughts and words, which remain inaccessible to the One itself.

his interlocutors are more sympathetic they could appreciate his intention.[33] But at any rate, we might as well set aside this problem because it does not receive much discussion in the *Enneads*. More noteworthy and serious is the second issue, which can also be understood as the leitmotif of Plotinus' teaching of henosis: If the ultimate reality is so transcendent and ineffable that we cannot talk about it in any way, is not his teaching henosis just an empty talk? What should we *do* if we do not *talk* about the ultimate reality at all?

This difficulty is discussed in a highly compressed passage from the *Ennead* V.3.14. Plotinus' explanation, stated with maximum brevity, is that the ultimate reality is transcendent in such a way that we "have" it already without having to speak about it. Thus the ultimate reality is not simply immanent or "within us", but above all radically immanent because we have it within us *unaware*. This explanation is not so much a compromise with his radical position regarding the transcendence of the One as a *further radicalization* of it, although this somehow makes his stance intuitively acceptable, to the point of sheer platitude. According to V.3.14.1–8:

(vii) How then do we ourselves speak about It *[the One]*? We do indeed say something about It, but we certainly do not speak It, and we have neither knowledge or [sic] thought of It. But if we do not have It in knowledge, do we not have It at all? But we have It in such a way that we speak about It, but do not speak It. For we say what It is not and not what It is, so that we speak about It from what comes after It. *But we are not prevented from having It, even if we do not speak It.*

Πῶς οὖν ἡμεῖς λέγομεν περὶ αὐτοῦ; ἢ λέγομεν μέν τι περὶ αὐτοῦ, οὐ μὴν αὐτὸ λέγομεν οὐδὲ γνῶσιν οὐδὲ νόησιν ἔχομεν αὐτοῦ. πῶς οὖν λέγομεν περὶ αὐτοῦ, εἰ μὴ αὐτὸ ἔχομεν; ἢ εἰ μὴ ἔχομεν τῇ γνώσει, καὶ παντελῶς οὐκ ἔχομεν; ἀλλ᾽ οὕτως ἔχομεν, ὥστε περὶ αὐτοῦ μὲν λέγειν, αὐτὸ δὲ μὴ λέγειν. καὶ γὰρ λέγομεν ὃ μὴ ἔστιν· ὃ δέ ἐστιν, οὐ λέγομεν· ὥστε ἐκ τῶν ὕστερον περὶ αὐτοῦ λέγομεν. ἔχειν δὲ οὐ κωλυόμεθα, κἂν μὴ λέγομεν.[34]

We cannot "speak the One", namely· designate Its "essence" and "have It in knowledge". So the question that (vii) poses is this: Do we still have the One in any other way? This question is explained in the last three sentences of (vii). Note

33 Plotinus is concerned with persuasion (πειθώ) where arguments fail. (cf. V.3.6.9–10; VI.4.4.5; VI.5.11.7; VI.7.40.4; VI.8.13.4) This indicates that he is willing to cope with incomprehension and misunderstandings of his intention and message.

34 V.3.14.1–8.

that, when translating the last phrase κἂν μὴ λέγομεν, Armstrong puts an extra neutral pronoun "It", although a more literal translation should simply be *"even if we do not speak"*. So the key sentences which explain the present question run as follows:

(1) But we have It in such a way that we speak about It, but do not speak It.

(2) For we say what It is not and not what It is, so that we speak about It from what comes after It.

(3) But we are not prevented from having It, *even if we do not speak*.

Let us first consider two interpretations. According to Lloyd Gerson:

> The contrast between "speaking it" and "speaking about it" is [...] primarily the contrast between positive and negative predication. The former is proscribed just in so far as it implies compositeness. The latter approach accordingly would seem to be limited merely to saying that the One is incomposite. Does not that say it all? No, for "what comes after it" is not merely the class of composites different from their incomposite ἀρχή, but also the effects of the causal activity of that ἀρχή. *We can know of the One both whatever follows from incompositeness and whatever follows from its being a cause of its effects.*[35]

That is, we "have" the One in the sense of speaking about the One analogically "from what comes after It", rather than designating Its "essence". Accordingly, (3) becomes a restatement of (1), and the claim that we "do not speak" (μὴ λέγωμεν) is modified to "do not speak *It*". This interpretation therefore recommends an *analogical* discourse in talking about the ultimate reality. The second interpretation is provided by Werner Beierwaltes:

> Basically, all talks "about" the One are metaphors, whether with explicit qualification or not. Such a metaphor is an absolute one, which cannot and should not be reduced to an identificatory, definite and unambiguous concept. This provisional and relativistic character of the talk about the One results, however, in its interminability, which amounts to an infinite process of approximation. This process does not enable the speaker to say *what* the One in and of Itself is. Rather, conscious of this limitation, the thought nonetheless knows that the limitation, in pointing beyond its limit (im ausgrenzenden Umschreiben), points towards something which is greater than what is said or hinted and which, as such, transcends what is directly expressible. In this respect, the thinker and the speaker about the One are like those who are "divinely possessed," [...] for they also have within themselves something "greater," without "knowing" exactly what it is.[36]

---

35 Gerson, 1994, 16, my italics.

36 Beierwaltes, Werner, *Selbsterkenntnis und Erfahrung der Einheit: Plotins Ennead V 3, Text, übersetzung, Interpretation, Erlaüterungen*, Vittorio Klostermann, Frankfurt am Main, 1991, 151–152, my translation.

For Beierwaltes, we do not use essentialist language to "speak the One", but we can use the metaphor to "speak *about* It". Just as the metaphor points beyond its surface meaning to insinuate an implicit one in an imprecise, non-literal way, so too the intellect possesses an implicit and imprecise "hunch" about the transcendent One. As such, we "have" the One in the qualified sense that we have a "hunch" of It. But Beierwaltes seems to overlook the notion of analogy implied in (2) which has been correctly noted by Gerson. On the other hand, like Gerson, Beierwaltes also treats (3) as a restatement of (1) and modifies "do not speak" into "do not speak *It*". Both Gerson and Beierwaltes, then, maintain that we "have" the One in the sense of speaking about It *indirectly*. Their interpretations diverge as to what this indirect mode of speech should be—for Gerson it is analogy, for Beierwaltes metaphor. However, at any rate, they do not see how it is possible to have the One in *utter silence*.

From an exegetical perspective, there are several difficulties in the previous two readings, for they overlook the context in which Plotinus' explanation is presented. To wit, passage (vii) begins with a question, "How do we ourselves speak about the One?" From this follows a dialectics between contrasting claims: First, "we do indeed say something about It, but certainly do not speak It." Then second, "*but* (ἤ) if we do not have It in knowledge, do we not have It at all?" Then third, "*but* (ἀλλ᾽) we have It in such a way that we speak about It but do not speak It." Now it is plausible to suppose that, within this context, (3) is not a mere repetition of (1), but also a contrasting claim against (1). Its conjunction *but* (δὲ), which like ἤ and ἀλλά signifies contrast or opposition, lends support to this speculation.

Another difficulty is that it does not make much sense to use "have" (ἔχειν), which connotes a *strong* and tight connection between its subject and its accusative object, to describe the *weak*, analogical or metaphorical discourse which only speaks about the One indirectly. Therefore the question which (3) raises against (1) could be this: Why bother saying that we have the One, if all we have is an inexact knowledge of the One based on things derived from It? It is like saying: "Alice is thirty years old—I mean she is in her thirties." Is not such a manner of speech utterly misleading?

The third problem is that these interpretations distort the original text in (3) by putting an extra αὐτὸ behind κἄν μή λέγωμεν. There is no reason for doing this if κἄν μή λέγωμεν can be given a coherent and meaningful explanation.

In light of these problems, we can re-interpret the message behind (3) as follows: According to (1) and (2), we have the One in the *weak* sense of speaking about It; *however*, we are not prevented from having It even if we do not speak *at all.* In V.3.14.8–11, Plotinus explains what this stronger mode of having the One is:

(viii) But just as those who have a god within them and are in the grip of divine possession may know this much, *that* they have something greater within them, even if they do not know *what*…

> […] οἱ ἐνθουσιῶντες καὶ κάτοχοι γενόμενοι ἐπὶ τοσοῦτον κἂν εἰδεῖν, ὅτι ἔχουσι μεῖζον ἐν αὐτοῖς, κἂν μὴ εἰδῶσιν ὅ τι…[37]

The One is immanent in man; on the other hand, man can be vaguely aware only so far *that* (ὅτι) the One is immanent in him, but just *what* It is (ὅ τι) is beyond his knowledge. His awareness, we could say, is about the "thatness" or "existence", rather than the "whatness" or "essence" of the One. However, since man's vague awareness depends on the *fact* that the One is immanent in him, whereas this fact is *independent* from it, he is rightly said to "have" the One even when he is not aware of or speaking about It.

Plotinus' point, I think, can be clarified in light of our ordinary intuition about the relation between reality and language. For example, the desk before our eyes will not disappear and appear again as we blink, but remains there independently from our perception. A true claim about the desk, we also believe, neither creates the desk out of nothing nor makes it "true"; and a false claim about the desk does not annihilate or makes the desk "false", either. So the desk does not depend on our linguistic representation, but our linguistic representation must depend on the desk.

However, since "desk" is itself a name given to that real thing which is called "desk", it would be more accurate to add that that real thing which we call "desk" is itself ineffable. But more importantly, although that real thing is ineffable, its reality does not consist in being ineffable, because ineffability is only a property that describes the irreversible relation of language to reality. Therefore, in order to prevent our mistaking ineffability for reality, it would be more advisable to revoke this inadequate negative expression.

Now, when we stop talking about that thing called "desk", are we cut off from it altogether? No. Whether something is real or not has nothing to do with our linguistic representation, but with our interaction with it which can be either linguistic or non-linguistic, consciously or unaware.[38] For example, that thing

---

37 V.3.14.8–11.
38 Cf. V.1.12.1–10: "Why then, when we have such great possessions, do we not consciously grasp them, but are mostly inactive in these ways, and some of us are never

which is called "desk" is already actually and effectively real, as long as we are reading and writing on it, and it does not matter whether we use it consciously or not. Moreover, there is no strong reason against believing this thing would become unreal when we are not interacting with it. It is true that such a belief is falsified when someone else destroys that thing behind our back; however, that thing would not become unreal *just because* there is no interaction from our part. What is primary for us in our daily experience is not our thought or language, but our openness to and dependence on what is real.

The basic idea of (viii) is this everyday intuition writ large, for the One is none other than the ultimate reality of all beings, including that thing called "desk". Thus in the last analysis, it is our thought and language that depend on the ultimate reality, and not the other way round. Even if we do not form any belief about the ultimate reality, the ultimate reality itself is not thereby negated, for what is lacking is only the belief thereof. Similarly, what can be proved and refuted is our claim about the ultimate reality, not the ultimate reality itself. The fact that we have no belief and make no claim about it whatsoever, as well as the fact that our beliefs and claims about it are inadequate, does not sever the tie by which we depend on it.

The upshot of the above analysis, then, is that the One or the ultimate reality is at once radically transcendent and radically immanent *insofar as it underlies our daily experience*. We cannot and need not prove Its "existence" and "essence", not because It is entirely disconnected from us, but rather because It is always already there by or within us. Conversely, no extraordinary power is required to establish our contact with the One, for our daily experience itself already provides an access to It and hence constitutes the formal condition of Plotinus' teaching of henosis. But exactly what is this access? Plotinus' explanations are scattered throughout the *Enneads*; let us start from V.3.14–19, which immediately follows passage (viii):

(ix) […] and from the ways in which they are moved and the things they say *[they]* get a certain awareness of the god who moves them, though these

---

active at all? They are always occupied in their own activities: Intellect, and that which is before Intellect, always in itself, and soul, which is in this sense "ever moving". For not everything which is in the soul is immediately perceptible, but it reaches us when it enters into perception; but when a particular active power does not give a share in its activity to the perceiving power, that activity has not yet pervaded the whole soul. We do not therefore yet know it, since we are accompanied by the perceptive power and are not a part of soul but the whole soul."

are not the same as the mover; so we seem to be disposed towards the One, divining, when we have our intellect pure, that this is [...] more and greater than anything said about It, because It is higher than speech and thought and awareness; It gives us these, but It is not these Itself.

[...] ἐξ ὧν δὲ κεκίνηται καὶ λέγουσιν, ἐκ τούτων αἴσθησίν τινα τοῦ κινήσαντος, λαμβάνουσιν ἑτέρων ὄντων τοῦ κινήσαντος, οὕτω καὶ ἡμεῖς κινδυνεύομεν ἔχειν πρὸς ἐκεῖνο, ὅταν νοῦν καθαρὸν ἔχωμεν, χρώμενοι, ὡς οὗτός ἐστιν [...] καὶ πλέον καὶ μεῖζον ἢ λεγόμενον, ὅτι καὶ αὐτὸς κρείττων λόγου καὶ νοῦ καὶ αἰσθήσεως, παρασχὼν ταῦτα, οὐκ αὐτὸς ὢν ταῦτα.[39]

"They" refers to "those who have a god within them and are in the grip of divine possession" in passage (viii), or the men in whom the One is immanent. Plotinus highlights man's endeavor to use the intellect to articulate the awareness of the One. This endeavor is described as a *risk, hazard* or *venture* (κίνδυνος, a cognate of κινδυνεύειν), because he does not really know *what* the One is, but have at most a certain vague awareness (αἴσθησίν τινα) about Its immanence in himself. This intellectual venture provides man the access to the One which is always already immanent.

But this seems problematic: if man cannot and does not need to speak about the One because It is always already there in him, why is he even motivated to do so? Beierwaltes explains as follows:

> [...] if we "had" the One in a direct or dominating (verfügende) way, then we would also know and speak It as It is, and meanwhile destroy Its absolute simplicity, uniqueness and original self-sufficiency. But if we did not have the One in or by ourselves in another (indirect, non-dominating) way, then surely no impulse would arise in us to want to think and speak about the One. So, above all else, we must "have" the One in us in an implicit yet effective way which we are initially unaware of, and which can and does make us aware of It, and indeed as something "greater" to be realized. It is therefore crucial for us to make "use" of that which is within us but is not yet brought into full presence or essential moment of our self-consciousness. [...] To "have" the One in this unconscious or pre-conscious way while being "moved" by It at the same time—just like those "divinely possessed" do—is the ontological and life-historical precondition for being bit by bit "snatched away" (Hingerissensein, ἁρπασθείς) by the One as the true origin of movement that transcends all things moved.[40]

On Beierwaltes' interpretation, man is said to "have" the One not in the sense that the One is immanent in him without him being aware of It, but in the sense

39 V.3.14.11–19.
40 Beierwaltes, 1991, 152–153, my italics and translation.

that the One somehow arouses in him a vague awareness thereof, such that the articulation of this awareness will lead to henosis. Accordingly, man is motivated to speak about the One, because the One is both the efficient cause and the final cause of his intellectual venture.

I disagree with this interpretation. To see why, let us observe more closely what Plotinus says in (viii) and (ix):

> But just as those who have a god within them and are in the grip of divine possession may know this much, that they have something greater within them, even if they do not know what, and *from the ways in which they are moved and the things they say* get a certain awareness of the god who moves them, *though these are not the same as the mover,* so we seem to be disposed towards the One…

Note that man is said to "get a certain awareness of the god [namely the One]" *not* from the One Itself, but "from the ways in which [he is] moved and the things [he says]". These ways, however, "are *not the same as the mover*". In other words, the immanence of the One in man is one thing, and his vague awareness thereof quite another. There are two reasons to account for this difference. First, the immanent One is ineffable, whereas man's vague awareness is derived from the impulse to speak *per impossibile* about It. Second, according to our explanation of (viii), the fact that the One is immanent is *independent* from man's awareness, while his vague awareness thereof *depends* on this fact. It is precisely due to this difference that the One is at once radically transcendent and radically immanent in man. In order to emphasize that the immanent One remains transcendent at the same time, in V.3.14.13 Plotinus describes man's intellectual effort to articulate the One specifically with the term κινδυνεύομεν, which means literally *take risk*, or *act under uncertainty*. For him, such an effort is not courageous (ἀνδρεῖος) so much as audacious (τολμηρός), for it makes man oblivious of the transcendence of the One. Plotinus elaborates this point as follows:

(x)   What is it, then, which has made the souls forget their father, God, and be ignorant of themselves and It, even though they are parts which come from Its higher world and altogether belong to It? The beginning of evil for them was audacity and coming to birth and the first otherness and the wishing to belong to themselves. Since they were clearly delighted with their own independence, and made great use of self-movement, running the opposite course and getting as far away as possible, they were ignorant even that they themselves came from that world;…

Τί ποτε ἄρα ἐστὶ τὸ πεποιηκὸς τὰς ψυχὰς πατρὸς θεοῦ ἐπιλαθέσθαι, καὶ μοίρας ἐκεῖθεν οὔσας καὶ ὅλως ἐκείνου ἀγνοῆσαι καὶ ἑαυτὰς καὶ ἐκεῖνον;

ἀρχὴ μὲν οὖν αὐταῖς τοῦ κακοῦ ἡ τόλμα καὶ ἡ γένεσις καὶ ἡ πρώτη ἑτερότης καὶ τὸ βουληθῆναι δὲ ἑαυτῶν εἶναι. τῷ δὴ αὐτεξουσίῳ ἐπειδήπερ ἐφάνησαν ἡσθεῖσαι, πολλῷ τῷ κινεῖσθαι παρ᾽ αὐτῶν κεχρημέναι, τὴν ἐναντίαν δραμοῦσαι καὶ πλείστην ἀπόστασιν πεποιημέναι, ἠγνόησαν καὶ ἑαυτὰς ἐκεῖθεν εἶναι·[41]

In other words, from a human perspective, it is *not* enough for man just to have the One immanent in him, for he also *desires to know* just what It is. The ultimate reality which underlies man's daily life, he suddenly realizes, no longer makes sense for him and calls for an explanation. How does this desire to know the One come about? This question is explained in Plotinus' account of the generation of intellect, quoted from V.6.5 in its entirety:

(xi)   And again, the multiple might seek itself and wish to converge on and be conscious of itself. But by what way will that which is altogether one go to itself? At what point will it need self-consciousness? But it is one and the same thing which is better than self-consciousness and better than all thinking. For thinking does not come first either in reality or in value, but is second and is what has come into being when the Good [already] existed and *moved what had come into being* to Itself, and it was moved and saw. And this is what thinking is, *a movement towards the Good in its desire of that Good; for the desire generates thought* and establishes it in being along with itself: for desire of *sight* is seeing. The Good itself, then, must not think anything: for the Good is not other than Itself. For when what is other than the Good thinks It, it does so by being "like the Good" and having a *resemblance* to the Good, and it thinks It as Good and as desired by itself, and as if it had a *mental image* of the Good. And if it is like this for ever, it thinks the Good for ever. And again, in thinking the Good it thinks itself accidentally, for it is in looking to the Good that it thinks itself; for it thinks itself in actual activity; and the actual activity of all things is directed to the Good.

Ἔτι τὸ πολὺ ζητοῖ ἂν ἑαυτὸ καὶ ἐθέλοι ἂν συννεύειν καὶ συναισθάνεσθαι αὑτοῦ. ὃ δ᾽ ἐστι πάντη ἕν, ποῦ χωρήσεται πρὸς αὐτό; ποῦ δ᾽ ἂν δέοιτο συναισθήσεως; ἀλλ᾽ ἔστι τὸ αὐτὸ καὶ συναισθήσεως καὶ πάσης κρεῖττον νοήσεως. τὸ γὰρ νοεῖν οὐ πρῶτον οὔτε τῷ εἶναι οὔτε τῷ τίμιον εἶναι, ἀλλὰ δεύτερον καὶ γενόμενον, ἐπειδὴ ὑπέστη τὸ ἀγαθὸν καὶ τὸ γενόμενον ἐκίνησε πρὸς αὐτό, τὸ δ᾽ ἐκινήθη τε καὶ εἶδε. καὶ τοῦτό ἐστι νοεῖν, κίνησις

41 V.1.1.1–9.

πρὸς ἀγαθὸν ἐφιέμενον ἐκείνου· ἡ γὰρ ἔφεσις τὴν νόησιν ἐγέννησε καὶ συνυπέστησεν αὐτῇ· ἔφεσις γὰρ ὄψεως ὅρασις. οὐδὲν οὖν δεῖ αὐτὸ τὸ ἀγαθὸν νοεῖν· οὐ γάρ ἐστιν ἄλλο αὐτοῦ τὸ ἀγαθόν. ἐπεὶ καὶ ὅταν τὸ ἕτερον παρὰ τὸ ἀγαθὸν αὐτὸ νοῇ, τῷ ἀγαθοειδὲς εἶναι νοεῖ καὶ ὁμοίωμα ἔχειν πρὸς τὸ ἀγαθὸν καὶ ὡς ἀγαθὸν καὶ ἐφετὸν αὐτῷ γενόμενον νοεῖ καὶ οἷον φαντασίαν τοῦ ἀγαθοῦ λαμβάνον. εἰ δ᾽ ἀεὶ οὕτως, ἀεὶ τοῦτο. καὶ γὰρ αὖ ἐν τῇ νοήσει αὐτοῦ κατὰ συμβεβηκὸς αὐτὸ νοεῖ· πρὸς γὰρ τὸ ἀγαθὸν βλέπων αὐτὸν νοεῖ. ἐνεργοῦντα γὰρ αὖ ἑαυτὸν νοεῖ· ἡ δ᾽ ἐνέργεια ἁπάντων πρὸς τὸ ἀγαθόν.[42]

Plotinus makes an implicit but crucial distinction between the generation or coming-into-being (τὸ γεννᾶν) of the intellect on the one hand, and the putting-in-motion (τὸ κινεεῖν, κίνησις) whereby the intellect becomes active on the other hand. The intellect is "secondary and generated" (δεύτερον καὶ γενόμενον); and after it has been generated and come into being, it is described as a "movement towards the Good" (κίνησις πρὸς ἀγαθὸν), and a movement which "the Good moves to Itself" (ἐκίνησε πρὸς αὐτό) and which "is moved and sees" (ἐκινήθη τε καὶ εἶδε).[43] That is to say, the One does not generate the intellect or its activity of thinking, but is only said to "move" the intellect when it has *already* come into being through its own desire (ἔφεσις) for the One. Put more pointedly, the intellect is at first a desire which *generates itself before* the One "moves" it.[44]

But this account raises two problems. First, if the One is the cause of all beings, how could It not also generate the intellect's desire for It? Second, in what sense is the One said to "move" the intellect? Let us attempt an explanation in order. The reason why the cause of all beings is not the cause of the intellect's desire for the One, I suppose, is that this desire is not a being but rather non-existent, insubstantial and illusive. It is, so to speak, a lack or nothingness which cannot

---

42 V.6.5.1–10.

43 Armstrong translates the Greek aorist tense into the English past tense; but a more appropriate translation would be in the present tense, highlighting the perfective aspect of the action.

44 Cf. V.1.7: "How does It [i.e. the One] generate (γεννᾷ) the intellect? Because by its return to It it sees, and this seeing is intellect." It seems that Plotinus means by γεννᾷ what he means by ἐκίνησε in (xi), namely the final cause represented by the intellect. See also V.3.11.12–13: "So this intellect had an immediate apprehension of the One (ἐπεβάλε μὲν ἐκείνῳ); but by grasping it *became* intellect (λαβὼν δὲ ἐγένετο νοῦς), perpetually in need [of the One] and having become at once Intellect and substance and intellection when it thought; for before this it was not intellection since it did not possess the intelligible object, nor Intellect since it had not yet thought."

be said to "be" in the proper sense. For the intellect purports to desire the One, but only turns out to "seek itself" and "wish to converge on and be conscious of itself", because its desire for the One is in truth the desire to know the One. But since the One is unknowable and ineffable, this desire ends up in vain: either it fails to know the unknowable One as such, or it confuses its failure with the true knowledge of the One. In any event, what is accessible to the intellect's desire is not the One as such, but the "vision" (ὄψις), "resemblance" (ὁμοίωμα) or "mental image" (φαντάσια) of the One insofar as it is desired (καὶ ὡς ἀγαθὸν καὶ ἐφετὸν) as an intelligible being.

In this light, we can explain how the One "moves the intellect when it has already come into being" and why the intellect is a "movement towards the Good in its desire of that Good". Without any doubt, the "motion" at issue cannot be the One's metaphysical causation, for it follows and depends upon the intellect's generation. It is not the efficient cause of the intellect, either, for the intellect generates itself. Perhaps we can say that the One is the *intentional object* of the intellect, "for it [the intellect] is in *looking to the Good* that it thinks itself". But as the preceding analysis indicates, the intellect's desire is directed not to the One as such, but to the image of the One as an intelligible being. This is why Plotinus immediately adds that "for it [the intellect] thinks itself in actual activity, and the actual activity of all things is directed to the Good;" that is to say, for the intellect, the activity of thinking is primary, and its direction to the Good only accidental. Therefore, strictly speaking, what "moves the intellect when it has already come into being" is not the One as such, but the image of the One; and this image is not produced by the One Itself, but derived from the intellect's desire to know the One as an intelligible being.

According to our analysis of (xi), Plotinus is advancing two points the significance of which cannot be overstated. First, the intellect's desire to know the One does not come from the One, but is self-generating. Second, this desire is not real but illusive. This tension is expressed more sharply in the claim that the intellect "*desired one thing*, having vaguely in itself a kind of image (φάντασμά) of it, but *came out having grasped something else* which it made many in itself."[45] Thus, accurately speaking, it is not the case that the intellect desires the One or desires to know the One. What it really desires and is able to attain with its desire, as Plotinus explains below, is the pretension to the One, namely *beauty*:

(xii) But the more ancient, unperceived desire of the Good proclaims that the Good itself is more ancient and prior to beauty. All men think that when

---

45   V.3.11.6–8.

they have attained the Good it is sufficient for them: for they have reached their end. But not all see beauty, and when it has come into existence they think it is beautiful for itself and not for them; this applies also to beauty here: it belongs to the one who has it. And it is enough for people to seem to be beautiful, even if they are not really, but they do not want to have the Good in seeming only.

ἡ δὲ ἀρχαιοτέρα τούτου καὶ ἀναίσθητος ἔφησις ἀρχαιότερον φησι καὶ τἀγαθὸν εἶναι καὶ πρότερον τούτου. καὶ οἴονται δὲ τἀγαθὸν λαβόντες ἀρκεῖν αὑτοῖς ἅπαντες· εἰς γὰρ τὸ τέλος ἀφῖχθαι· τὸ δὲ καλὸν οὔτε πάντες εἶδον γενόμενον τό τε καλὸν αὐτῷ οἴονται εἶναι, ἀλλ᾽ οὐκ αὐτοῖς, οἷα καὶ τὸ τῇδε κάλλος· τοῦ γὰρ ἔχοντος τὸ κάλλος εἶναι. καὶ καλοῖς εἶναι δοκεῖν ἀρκεῖ, κἂν μὴ ὦσι· τὸ δ᾽ ἀγαθὸν οὐ δόξῃ ἐθέλουσιν ἔχειν.[46]

Plotinus' understanding of beauty in this passage is surprisingly modern on several points. First, the enjoyment of beautiful things is not separate from aesthetic judgment, but always involves the operation of the *intellect* leading to an aesthetic criticism. Hence second, beauty "belongs to the one who has it" and "has come into being like themselves [those who have beauty]". In other words, aesthetic judgment is based on *subjective* taste; beauty is relative to the eyes of the beholder. Third, beauty "is beautiful for itself, rather than for them [men themselves]". That is to say, beauty is *free from ulterior concern* because it is for its own sake.

These three points combine to draw a highly paradoxical consequence: as soon as we claim that a thing is beautiful only for us and not for other people, this thing becomes irrelevant to us. This is why Plotinus says that "it is enough for people to seem to be beautiful, even if they are not really," for beauty can be enjoyed only in a *deceptive* image. The Good or the One, on the other hand, is contrasted against beauty on all of these counts. First, it is "unperceived" and pre-intellective, such that we cannot make any judgment about the One which implies a subject-object distinction between the One Itself and us. Hence second, the Good is not a subjective possession for each individual person, but belongs impartially to all those who "have" It.[47] Third, the One is free from ulterior concern, not because It is for its own sake, but because It is of universal value.

---

46   V.5.12.17–24.
47   Cf. V.5.13.

Chapter Summary

The basic intuition of Plotinus' metaphysics is that the One is at once radically transcendent and radically immanent. From the perspective of man, this point can be restated to the effect that man's daily experience consists of two conflicting aspects. On the one hand, the One is already immanent in him; but on the other hand, man also desires to *know* the One, which in effect wrongly reduces the One to an intelligible being. Man is naturally united with the One, but he somehow alienates himself from It through his inquiry into this natural condition; he is at once at home with his true origin and estranged from it. Plotinus' conception of man's daily experience is outlandish to say the least, but it helps to put into perspective the basic structure of his teaching of henosis, for its task is neither to unite with a deity of a certain religion nor to attain an extraordinary experience, but to dissolve the apparent tension intrinsic in one's own existence. Furthermore, it takes as its starting point the source of this tension, namely the inquiry into henosis. Finally, the method is to explain how the inquiry into henosis clashes with henosis on the one hand, but can be brought into coherence with it on the other hand.

Chapter 2 The Practice of Philosophy

According to the *Ennead* I.3, the first stage of Plotinus' mystical teaching is the practice of philosophy, namely the intellectual inquiry into intelligible beings.[1] Since further methodological details about this practice are not explicitly set forth in I.3, in this chapter I will refer to other passages from the *Enneads* and attempt a more systematic explanation thereof from a specific perspective, namely *the desire for knowledge*. The curious place of the desire for knowledge in Plotinus' conception of man's ordinary experience is already suggested in Chapter 1: on the one hand, man is originally united with the One but his desire to know the One breaks off this union; on the other hand, man can somehow return to the original union by striving to know the One. Since both the leitmotif and the dramatic tension of Plotinus' mystical teaching reside in this desire for knowledge, it provides us a vantage point to develop a more systematic account of Plotinus' practice of philosophy.

Section 1 Different Desires and the Desire for Knowledge

In this section I address a preparatory issue: the relation between *different modes of desire* and *the desire for knowledge* according to Plotinus. As far as exegesis is concerned, it is intended to order the different terms used in the *Enneads* which refer to the phenomenon of desire. From a more systematic perspective, this also deepens our understanding of Plotinus' desire for knowledge and facilitates our explanation of the methodological details of Plotinus' practice of philosophy in the next section.

In Section 1.1 I suggest an interpretation of Plotinus' discussions of different modes of desire. To explain the relation among them, I reject the hierarchy account on the ground that it fails to take into consideration each desire's relation to the One (Section 1.2). On the reflexive account, by contrast, each desiring agent relates to the One indirectly via his self-relation which lies in *contentment* (Section 1.3). Plotinus' thesis that contentment consists in contemplation is explained in the light of his doctrine of intellect (Section 1.4), according to which the desire for *contemplation* (his technical term for knowledge) is not an attitude directed toward desired *objects* distinct from the desiring agent, but is the agent's reflexive attitude toward *his own* desire.

---

1   Cf. Introduction, Section 3.

1.1 Toward an Interpretation of the Diversity of Desire

In the *Enneads* we can find different terms which denote what is ordinarily and variously understood as the phenomena of striving, will, desire and love (for brevity's sake, henceforth I shall use the term *desire*). According to *Lexicon Plotinianum*, the terms for these phenomena include βούλεσθαι (to will, to wish), ἐπιβάλλειν (to turn one's attention to, to apprehend), ἐπιθυμεῖν (to desire), ἐρᾶν (to love), ἐφιέσθαι (to desire), ζητεῖν (to seek, to search for), ὀρέγεσθαι (to desire), ὁρμᾶν (to have an impulse, to strive), ποθεῖν (to long for, to yearn), σπεύδειν (to hasten, to seek eagerly) and their cognates.[2] Plotinus seldom defines or clarifies his terminology, and it seems that most of the time he does not even have in mind a technical term for his discussion in the first place.[3] To complicate the matter, it seems that sometimes these terms are used liberally by a stretch of anthropomorphism. For instance, the heaven (οὐρανός), the earth, plants, and even parts of the animal, such as its hoofs and claws, are all said to "strive" in one way or another to attain perfection. Different beings, so to speak, "desire" different things in different ways.

It would do us a disservice, I think, if we take this claim about desire in nature as a central doctrine of Plotinus' philosophy. Instead, in order to accommodate the didactic approach in Plotinus' teaching of henosis, I suggest that we opt for a more modest, qualified interpretation that different *people* desire different things in their own ways, or simply that there are different modes or "ways of life" of desire. This interpretation of desire as an *existential phenomenon* turns our focus from the pantheistic-sounding treatises such as II.1–3, III.5 and III.8 to the methodological discussion in I.3. Accordingly, the basic insight behind Plotinus' discussion of desire is not a fanciful anthropomorphism, but rather a *robust realism concerning men's diverse ways of life.* Contrary to the widespread prejudice that Neoplatonism is misanthropic, Plotinus affirms the richness and plurality of human desires, and his mystical teaching is intended for all kinds of "lovers" or desiring agents. To see in what sense Plotinus' message is universal, we

---

2   Sleeman, J. H. and Pollet, Gilbert, *Lexicon Plotinianum*, Brill, Leiden, 1980. For a brief explanation of the meaning of these terms see Arnou, René, *Le Désir de Dieu dans la Philosophie de Plotin* (3rd edition), Presses de L'Université Grégorienne, Rome, 1967, 59–64. Arnou does not include in his analysis ἐπιβάλλειν, ζητεῖν and σπεύδειν.

3   As is noted in Arnou 1967, 59, most of these terms are conventional jargons already circulating in previous Greek writings. Therefore, lacking a set of clear terminology, it is natural for Plotinus to use them in a less than consistent way.

still have to explain the relation among different desires. In the next two sections I shall address this issue.

1.2 The Hierarchy Account of the Relation among Desires

On the standard account of the Plotinian scholarship, the relation among different modes of desire resides in the *hierarchy*, or grade of desirability, regarding the *object* of desire. Of all modes of desire, it is the *desire for knowledge* which ranks at the top. As Werner Beierwaltes remarks:

> [...] Plotinus sets out a concept of beauty that is characterized primarily by intelligibility or "intellect, spirit" [...] Beautiful is what participates in form or logos [i.e. its intelligible foundation] and is shaped by form and logos into a single ordered whole, whether by nature or by art. [...] Plotinus' reflections on the concept of the beautiful, particularly as he develops them in Enneads I 6 and V 8, are, briefly stated, determined by the view that the ground of visible beauty is beautiful in the true sense. The joy, fear, delight, wonder, desire, and eros experienced already at the sight of sensible beauty become all the more intense in the face of the rediscovered or recollected intelligible [beauty], since this is the "true" itself. [...] Thus, in Plotinus' view the extended answer to the question of what beauty is would have to be as follows: It is what really or actually exists, which is intellect or absolute thought (nous) and being itself; as such it gives rise to sensible beauty by means of logos or reflective thinking about the ideas.[4]

The basic theses of the hierarchical account can be analyzed as follows. First, it considers a mode of desire in light of the relation between the *lover* (ὁ ἐραστής) or the desiring agent and his *beloved* or desired *object* (τὸ ἐραστόν). Second, it defines the desiring agent and the mode of desire from the perspective of the desired object. For example, a philosopher is defined as someone who loves wisdom, and a hedonist is one who pursues pleasure (ἡδονή). Third, it posits a measure or *paradigm* against which these modes of desire can be compared with one another. Last not least, the paradigm is the *intelligibility* of the desired object.

The relation among modes of desire can be derived by comparing their respective objects against the yardstick of intelligibility. The more intelligible an object is, the higher ranks the corresponding mode of desire and the desiring agent. Since knowledge presupposes intelligibility, the desire for knowledge must rank at the top of the hierarchy. As René Arnou observes, ἔφεσις, ὄρεξις, and πόθος usually designate the *nobler* kind of desire for knowledge, whereas ἐπιθυμία stands for the *lower* kind of sensible desire susceptible to suffering and

---

4   Beierwaltes, Werner, 'The Love of Beauty and the Love of God', *Classical Mediterranean Spirituality: Egyptian, Greek, Roman*, ed. A. H. Armstrong, Routledge, London, 1986, 299–300, my italics.

excitement.[5] But this hierarchy account has the not-so-appealing implication that, except for the philosopher, no other desiring agent can readily receive Plotinus' mystical teaching.

Although Plotinus does not deny that one way of life could be nobler or more beautiful than another,[6] the hierarchy interpretation misses an important aspect in Plotinus' thought on this issue. This account recognizes no higher principle than the paradigm of intelligibility; and as a matter of fact, the very idea of hierarchy is that there should be a definite measure by which things are graded. However, the highest principle in Plotinus' philosophy is neither intelligibility nor the intellect, but the One. Ontologically, the One is radically beyond the intellect, because the former is infinite, whereas the latter is limited by its being necessarily related to the intelligible object. For the same reason, the One is not a paradigm, because the latter is a definite form by which something is measured, whereas the former cannot be limited by any definite form. Consequently, there is no place for the One in any hierarchy; and there can be no hierarchy in the realm of the One, either: "For of the things which are said to be one each is one in the way in which it also has what it is".[7] In this sense, Plotinus' mystical teaching does not privilege a certain class of students, namely the philosophers, but is universal and open to all human beings as long as they desire anything at all.

Of course, as Plotinus points out, this does not mean that the One is ignoble or devoid of beauty. Rather, it means that the One is infinitely beautiful and hence not just beautiful in this or that particular way,[8] such that its beauty cannot be fully appreciated from any derived and restricted perspective. This last point also helps explain why Plotinus can consistently maintain that, on the one hand, one mode of desire is *indeed* nobler than another, and on the other hand, the comparison in question does *not* appeal to a specific paradigm. The reason is that "the things which are less beings have the One less, and those which are

---

5   Cf. Arnou, 1967, 59–64. See also I.4.6.17: ἔφεσις πρὸς τὸ κρεῖττον; III.5.1.64: ἔφεσις ἀγαθοῦ; III.5.6.29: τοῦ ἀγαθοῦ καὶ καλοῦ; VI.9.11.24: ἔφεσις πρὸς ἀφὴν; I.1.5.25: ὄρεξις... ἐπὶ ἀφροδισίων; I.2.1.14: ὄρεξις... τῶν νοητῶν; IV.8.4.1: ὄρεξις νοερά; VI.5.1.16: ἡ ὄρεξις τοῦ ἀγαθοῦ; I.6.7.12: ποίους ἂν ἴσχοι ἔρωτας, ποίους δὲ πόθους; II.8.15.14: Ἐπεὶ οὐδ' ἐπιθυμίαι οὐδ' αὖ λῦπαι, οὐ θυμοί, οὐ φόβοι. However, Arnou reminds us that this is only a rather general and exegetical summary which still requires further systematic precision.

6   Cf. I.4.9; I.4.14; I.6.5; I.6.9; VI.7.22.

7   VI.9.1.26–27; for Plotinus' critique of this hierarchical account see VI.4.7.

8   Cf. I.8.2.8; V.8.8.21; VI.7.33.29.

more beings, more."[9] That is to say, a certain way of life is nobler than another simply by its "having the One more" and "nearer still (ἐγγυτέρῳ) [to the One]".[10]

So the real issue is to understand the peculiar relation among different modes of desire, including the desire for knowledge, *from the perspective of the One.* To modify the hierarchical account, Beierwaltes suggests that the experience of desire actually has *two* points of reference: one is the intellect or intelligibility, and the other is the One which, due to Its transcendence, is to be understood as the ground or principle of the intellect.[11] But this is question-begging, for we still need to explain the relation between desire and the One. More accurately, it is not the case that *there are two* points of reference, the one being the paradigm and the other being the One which is beyond paradigm, but rather that these points do not obtain in a univocal sense, for the former is *derived* from the latter. Consequently, the hierarchy account is at best partially true, but at worst misleading. For clarity's sake, I suggest we drop the imprecise expression "two points of reference" and stick to what is clear and simple: there is only one ultimate, basic point of reference, which is none other than the One.

Three points are to be noted from the above argument against the hierarchy account. First, the relation among different modes of desire cannot be hierarchical, and therefore the desire for knowledge cannot be the noblest of them. Second, the relation among different modes of desire should be derived from the One which is beyond any possible paradigm, and we have to specify the place of the desire for knowledge anew accordingly. Thus third, from the non-paradigmatic perspective of the One, we cannot directly compare the desires against one another; rather, the relation among them is to be derived indirectly from their respective relation to the One. These last two issues will be explained in the next sub-section.

1.3 The Reflexive Account of the Relation among Desires

The desire's primary relation to the One is overlooked in the hierarchy account. In the *Enneads*, by contrast, this relation is explained from a *reflexive* point of view by taking into consideration the desiring agent's relation to himself.

(i)   [...] the desire of the good, that is of itself, leads to what is really one, and every nature presses on to this, to itself. For this is the good to this one nature, belonging to itself and being itself: but this is being one. It is in this

---

9   VI.9.1.27–28.
10   VI.9.1. 34.
11   Beierwaltes, 1986, 304.

sense that the good is rightly said to be our own; therefore one must not seek it outside.

[...] ἡ ὄρεξις τοῦ ἀγαθοῦ, ὅπερ ἐστὶν αὐτοῦ, εἰς ἓν ὄντως ἄγει, καὶ ἐπὶ τοῦτο σπεύδει πᾶσα φύσις, ἐφ᾽ ἑαυτήν. τοῦτο γάρ ἐστι τὸ ἀγαθὸν τῇ μιᾷ ταύτῃ φύσει τὸ εἶναι αὐτῆς καὶ εἶναι αὐτήν· τοῦτο δ᾽ ἐστὶ τὸ εἶναι μίαν. οὕτω δὲ καὶ τὸ ἀγαθὸν ὀρθῶς εἶναι λέγεται οἰκεῖον· διὸ οὐδὲ ἔξω ζητεῖν αὐτὸ δεῖ.[12]

It might be more appropriate to translate φύσις into *being* in the context of (i), for the One is not only the cause of beings in the natural world of becoming, but also the cause of the world of intelligible beings. The Good or the One is said to be "of Itself" (ἐστὶν αὐτοῦ) in the sense that It is absolute and self-sufficient. But since the One is absolute, It must not be separate from any being, but must also be immanent in all beings as their cause.[13] So when Plotinus says that every being desires the One, this is because every being desires the One, *insofar as the One is immanent in each and every being itself*. This is also why in this passage Plotinus uses the neutral pronoun τοῦτο which refers to τὸ ἕν, and the feminine pronoun ἑαυτήν which refers to φύσις, *interchangeably*: "and every nature presses on to this, to itself (καὶ ἐπὶ τοῦτο σπεύδει πᾶσα φύσις, ἐφ᾽ ἑαυτήν)."

From a metaphysical point of view, each being desires the One insofar as the One is immanent in it. By extension, from a more specific anthropological and psychological point of view, every man desires to be self-sufficient, insofar as self-sufficiency pertains to the *subjective* condition of desire, namely *contentment*:

(ii)   If then its life is satisfactory to it, it is clear that it seeks nothing.

εἰ οὖν ἀγαπητὸν τούτῳ τὸ ζῆν, δῆλον ὅτι οὐδὲν ζητεῖ.[14]

That is to say, if man's life is satisfactory to him, then he will no longer seek anything. As this passage indicates, Plotinus understands desire first and foremost as a human attitude rather than a natural phenomenon, and it is especially the desiring agent's *reflexivity* or relation toward himself that counts the most in his analysis of desire. From this point of view, the attainment of the desired object might *gratify* (ἥδεθαι) the desiring agent; but since in this case it is still possible

---

12   VI.5.1.16–21.
13   The *Enneads* VI.5 treats of this issue in detail. See also Chapter 1 of this dissertation.
14   V.3.16.26. Plotinus uses different terms to refer to contentment, including ἡσυχία, τὸ ἀγαπᾶν, τὸ ἀρκεῖν, τὸ ἀρέσκειν, τὸ πληροῦν. Cf. V.3.8.30, V.3.6.13, V.3.13.17, V.3.16.24–27, V.5.5.6, V.8.4.30, V.9.1.5, V.9.5.23, VI.7.26.15, VI.7.28.18, VI.7.38.23, VI.7.39.27, VI.8.7.40, VI.8.13.42, VI.8.15.27, VI.8.16.25, VI.9.6.16.

for the desiring agent to desire other things, his desire is not yet *fulfilled* (πλήρης, πληρούμενος). For Plotinus, desire is fulfilled only when the desiring agent himself is content and desires nothing more.

(iii) But the attainment is confirmed when a thing becomes better and has no regrets [sic], and fulfillment comes to it and it remains with the Good and does not seek something else. This is why pleasure is not self-sufficient; for one is not satisfied with the same thing; for what pleasure is satisfied with again is not the same; for that which gives one pleasure is always something else.

ὅτι δ᾽ ἔτυχε, πιστοῦται, ὅταν βέλτιόν τι γίνηται καὶ ἀμετανόητον ᾖ καὶ πεπληρῶσθαι αὐτῷ γίγνηται καὶ ἐπ᾽ ἐκείνου μένῃ καὶ μὴ ἄλλο ζητῇ. διὸ καὶ ἡ ἡδονὴ οὐκ αὔταρκες· οὐ γὰρ ἀγαπᾷ ταὐτόν· οὐ γάρ, ὅ τι ἡδονὴ πάλιν, ταὐτόν· ἄλλο γὰρ ἀεὶ τὸ ἐφ᾽ ᾧ ἥδεται.[15]

According to Plotinus' reflexive account of desire, there is no given object-related paradigm against which different modes of desire can be compared with one another. But on the other hand, we can still compare them by considering each desiring agent's relation to himself. As Plotinus says:

(iv) For everything seeks not another, but itself, and the journey to the exterior is foolish or compulsory. A thing exists more, not when it comes to be many or large, but when it belongs to itself: and it belongs to itself in tending to itself. But the desire to be great in this way is the property of something which does not know what true greatness is and is hastening not where it should but to the exterior; but the direction towards itself was inward.

---

15 VI.7.26.12–15. See also I.8.8.35–37: "When we are full (Πλήρεις) we are different, both in our desires and our thoughts, from what we are when we are empty, and when we have eaten our fill of one kind of food we are different from what we are when we are filled (πληρωθέντες) with another." III.5.7.12–22: "So Love is not a pure rational principle, since he has in himself an indefinite, irrational, unbounded impulse; for he will never be satisfied (πληρώσεται), as long as he has in him the nature of the indefinite. [...] And Love is like a 'sting', without resources in his own nature; therefore, even when he attains his object he is without resources again; he cannot be satisfied (πληροῦσθαι) because the mixed thing cannot be; only that is truly satisfied which has already attained full satisfaction in its own nature (πεπλήρωται τῇ ἑαυτοῦ φύσει);..."

ἕκαστον γὰρ οὐκ ἄλλο, ἀλλ᾽ αὐτὸ ζητεῖ, ἡ δ᾽ ἔξω πορεία μάταιος ἢ
ἀναγκαία. μᾶλλον δέ ἐστιν ἕκαστον, οὐχ ὅταν γένηται πολὺ ἢ μέγα, ἀλλ᾽
ὅταν ἑαυτοῦ ᾖ· ἑαυτοῦ δ᾽ ἐστὶ πρὸς αὐτὸ νενευκός. ἡ δὲ ἔφεσις ἡ πρὸς τὸ
οὕτως μέγα ἀγνοοῦντός ἐστι τὸ ὄντως μέγα καὶ σπεύδοντος οὐχ οὗ δεῖ,
ἀλλὰ πρὸς τὸ ἔξω.[16]

Overall, there are three aspects to see how the reflexive approach frees the desiring agent from the rigid relation to a given desired object. First, a mode of desire
can be nobler than another one even if its *object* is inferior (and vice versa). Second, it is possible for the same agent to desire different objects and for the same
object to be desired by different agents. Or better: the same agent can desire ever
new things, and the same object can be desired in different ways by different
agents. For instance, it is not the case that the philosopher desires no other object
called "wisdom as such"; the case is rather that he can find wisdom in different
things. Likewise, the same thing, for example carnal love, can be desired by both a
philosopher and a hedonist in different ways, for the former finds wisdom therein, but the latter seeks gratification from it. Third and most important, desire is
actualized not when the desired object is attained, but when the desiring agent is
content. Contentment pertains to the subjective condition of the actualization of
desire; for man to desire, in the last analysis, is to be content. In the next section
I shall turn to Plotinus' further explanation of contentment.

1.4 Contentment and Contemplation

For Plotinus, desire is essentially a reflexive attitude which is ultimately fulfilled
in contentment. As he goes on to explain, contentment is not simply an emotional state, but involves a certain noetic element called *contemplation* (θεορία,
τὸ θεορεῖν). This point is set forth in the highly convoluted passage below:

(v)   For, again, when they reach what they want […] so that they should know
       it and *see it present in their soul*, it is, obviously, an object set for contempla-
       tion. This is so, too, because they act for the sake of a good; but this means,
       not that the good arising from their action should be outside them, or that
       they should not have it, but that they should have it. But where do they have
       it? In their soul. So action bends back again to contemplation, for *what
       someone receives in his soul, which is rational form—what can it be other
       than silent rational form?* And more so, the more it is within the soul. For
       the soul keeps quiet then, and seeks nothing because she is filled, and the

---

16   VI.6.1.10–16; see also I.6.5, II.2.1, III.2.9, VI.5.1, VI.5.9, VI.6.1, VI.7.30, VI.9.9.

contemplation which is there in a state like this rests within because it is confident of possession. And, in proportion as the confidence is clearer, the contemplation is quieter, in that it unifies more, and what knows, insofar as it knows, [...] comes into unity with what is known. [...] For this reason, the rational principle must not be outside but must be united with the soul of the learner, until she finds that it is her own.

Καὶ γὰρ οὗ ὅταν τύχωσιν οὗ βούλονται [...] ἵνα γνῶσι καὶ παρὸν ἴδωσιν ἐν ψυχῇ, δῆλον ὅτι κείμενον θεατόν. Ἐπεὶ καὶ ἀγαθοῦ χάριν πράττουσι· τοῦτο δὲ οὐχ ἵνα ἔξω αὐτῶν, οὐδ᾽ ἵνα μὴ ἔχωσιν, ἀλλ᾽ ἵνα ἔχωσι τὸ ἐκ τῆς πράξεως ἀγαθόν. Τοῦτο δὲ ποῦ; Ἐν ψυχῇ. Ἀνέκαμψεν οὖν πάλιν ἡ πρᾶξις εἰς θεωρίαν· ὃ γὰρ ἐν ψυχῇ λαμβάνει λόγῳ οὔσῃ, τί ἂν ἄλλο ἢ λόγος σιωπῶν εἴη; Καὶ μᾶλλον, ὅσῳ μᾶλλον. Τότε γὰρ καὶ ἡσυχίαν ἄγει καὶ οὐδὲν ζητεῖ ὡς πληρωθεῖσα, καὶ ἡ θεωρία ἡ ἐν τῷ τοιούτῳ τῷ πιστεύειν ἔχειν εἴσω κεῖται. Καὶ ὅσῳ ἐναργεστέρα ἡ πίστις, ἡσυχαιτέρα καὶ ἡ θεωρία, ᾗ μᾶλλον εἰς ἓν ἄγει, καὶ τὸ γινῶσκον ὅσῳ γινώσκει [...] εἰς ἓν τῷ γνωσθέντι ἔρχεται. [...] Διὸ δεῖ μὴ ἔξωθεν τὸν λόγον εἶναι, ἀλλ᾽ ἑνωθῆναι τῇ ψυχῇ τοῦ μανθάνοντος, ἕως ἂν οἰκεῖον εὕρῃ.[17]

Plotinus' somewhat chaotic explanation can be summed up as follows. First, the desiring agent "keeps quiet and seeks nothing because he is content." Second, contentment is to be found in *contemplation* (θεωρία) and attained in the act of contemplating (τὸ θεωρεῖν) the "silent rational principle" which is "united with" the agent *himself*. Thus third, all modes of desire "bend back" or is reflexively grounded in contemplation. In addition to restating the reflexive account of desire from Section 1.3, this passage also introduces a new thesis: the agent's contentment is linked to *contemplation*.

To clarify Plotinus' new thesis, first we have to note that, as is explained previously, it is through contentment that the desiring agent is related indirectly to the One. Because of this peculiar "connection" between contentment and the One, contentment is *irreducible* to contemplation or any other intellectual activity. Thus, when it is said in (v) that contentment consists in contemplating the rational principle, this claim is in fact a qualified explanation of contentment in terms of intellectual contemplation, rather than an *identification* of contentment with contemplation, much less a *reduction* of contentment into contemplation.

Now the basic reason why Plotinus explains contentment in terms of contemplation is simply that the intellect is held to be man's most important faculty.

---

17   III.8.6.4–22.

This privileged faculty serves as a better explanans than any other inferior faculty such as sensation and imagination. Thus it is said in (v) that when the agent has what he wants, he "sees it present," "has it," and "receives it in his soul", rather than has it "outside".

Another more complicated reason has to do with Plotinus' notoriously difficult doctrine that the intellect is identical to the intelligible objects when the act of intellection is actualized (henceforth abbreviated as *the identity thesis*). As is also explained in III.8.6:

(vi) For if they *[the knower and the known objects]* are two, the knower will be one thing and the known another, so that there is a sort of juxtaposition, and contemplation has not yet made this pair akin to each other, as when rational principles present in the soul do nothing.

Εἰ γὰρ δύο, τὸ μὲν ἄλλο, τὸ δὲ ἄλλο ἔσται· ὥστε οἷον παράκειται, καὶ τὸ διπλοῦν τοῦτο οὔπω ᾠκείωσεν, οἷον ὅταν ἐνόντες λόγοι ἐν ψυχῇ μηδὲν ποιῶσι.[18]

In V.5.1 Plotinus makes a similar argument:

(vii) Now when Intellect knows, and knows the intelligibles [sic], if it knows them as being other than itself, how could it make contact with them? For it is possible that it might not, so that it is possible that it might not know them, or know them only when it made contact with them, and it will not always possess its knowledge. But if they are going to say that the intelligibles and Intellect are linked, what does this "linked" mean? Then the acts of intelligence will be impressions; but if this is what they are, they come to it from outside and are impacts.

ὁ δὴ νοῦς γινώσκων καὶ τὰ νοητὰ γινώσκων, εἰ μὲν ἕτερα ὄντα γινώσκει, πῶς μὲν ἂν συντύχοι αὐτοῖς; ἐνδέχεται γὰρ μή, ὥστε ἐνδέχεται μὴ γινώσκειν ἢ τότε ὅτε συνέτυχε, καὶ οὐκ ἀεὶ ἕξει τὴν γνῶσιν. εἰ δὲ συνεζεῦχθαι φήσουσι, τί τὸ συνεζεῦχθαι τοῦτο; ἔπειτα καὶ αἱ νοήσεις τύποι ἔσονται· εἰ δὲ τοῦτο, καὶ ἐπακτοὶ καὶ πληγαί.[19]

For Plotinus, whether the knower relates to the known objects via the weak "juxtaposition" or via the stronger "link", the result is equally undesirable: there remains a *gap* between the knower and the known objects which hinders the

---

18   III.8.6.17–19.
19   V.5.1.20–25.

former from infallibly knowing the latter as it truly is.[20] There is only one way for the knower to truly know the objects to be known:

(viii) [...] the contemplation must be *the same as* the contemplated [sic], and Intellect the same as the intelligible; for, if not the same, there will not be truth, for the one who is trying to possess realities will possess an impression different from the realities, and this is not truth. For truth ought not to be the truth of something else, but to be what it says.

[...] δεῖ τὴν θεωρίαν ταὐτὸν εἶναι τῷ θεωρητῷ, καὶ τὸν νοῦν ταὐτὸν εἶναι τῷ νοητῷ· καὶ γάρ, εἰ μὴ ταὐτόν, οὐκ ἀλήθεια ἔσται. τύπον γὰρ ἕξει ὁ ἔχων τὰ ὄντα ἕτερον τῶν ὄντων, ὅπερ οὐκ ἔστιν ἀλήθεια. τὴν ἄρα ἀλήθειαν οὐχ ἑτέρου εἶναι δεῖ, ἀλλ᾿ ὃ λέγει, τοῦτο καὶ εἶναι.[21]

But if the intellect is identical to the intelligible object, then the act of intellection must be an act of self-thinking.

(ix) All together are one, Intellect, intellection, the intelligible. If therefore Intellect's intellection is the intelligible, and the intelligible is itself, it will itself think itself: for it will think with the intellection which it is itself and will think the intelligible, which it is itself. In both ways, then, it will think itself, in that intellection is itself and in that the intelligible is itself which it thinks in its intellection and which is itself.

ἓν ἅμα πάντα ἔσται, νοῦς, νόησις, τὸ νοητόν. εἰ οὖν ἡ νόησις αὐτοῦ τὸ νοητόν, τὸ δὲ νοητὸν αὐτός, αὐτὸς ἄρα ἑαυτὸν νοήσει· νοήσει γὰρ τῇ νοήσει, ὅπερ ἦν αὐτός, καὶ νοήσει τὸ νοητόν, ὅπερ ἦν αὐτός. καθ᾿ ἑκάστερον ἄρα ἑαυτὸν νοήσει, καθότι καὶ ἡ νόησις αὐτὸς ἦν, καὶ καθότι τὸ νοητὸν αὐτός, ὅπερ ἐνόει τῇ νοήσει, ὃ ἦν αὐτός.[22]

---

20 Plotinus speaks of the identity in question in terms of *internality* in V.9.5–8, and Eyjólfur Kjalar Emilsson bases his interpretation of Plotinus' identity thesis on these passages (cf. Emilsson, Eyjólfur Kjalar, *Plotinus on Intellect*, Oxford University Press, Oxford, 2007,141–152). However, the internality thesis cannot meet Plotinus' exceedingly high demand of true knowledge as much as the identity thesis advanced in V.3.5 and V.5.1 does. Furthermore it should also be noted that in V.9 Plotinus pays very little attention to the One and the intellect's relation to It in his discussion of the nature of intellect, which is not the case in the discussions in V.3 and V.5. These are the two reasons why, to my mind, the internality thesis in V.9.5–8 does not fully represent Plotinus' doctrine of intellect.

21 V.3.5.21–26.

22 V.3.5.44–49.

Plotinus' notion of self-thinking, to emphasize, is not the same as the act of thinking oneself as an object; nor is the Plotinian self-knowledge engendered by self-thinking the same as knowledge of oneself. An example of the latter case is when John thinks about who he was ten years ago. His self-thinking amounts to an act of remembering, and his self-knowledge a memory. Although it is John himself who is being thought and becomes the content of knowledge, this John is in fact a historical John distinct from the present John who is thinking. What we have in this case is merely one and the same name "John" used to describe two distinct entities, "thinking" and "being thought". What Plotinus emphasizes in (ix), however, is precisely that the entities themselves, namely the intellect and the intelligible object, must be one and the same, and that the act of self-thinking is simply the intellect itself which is identical to the intelligible object.

So far as our present discussion is concerned, it is not necessary to draw from this thesis all the implications for Plotinus' epistemology,[23] although one might already expect that in his mystical teaching, the insistence on the absolute simplicity and ineffability of the One often *overrides* other epistemological issues. For now, I shall only emphasize that Plotinus' peculiar notion of "knowledge" or contemplation of the identity thesis should not be confused with our commonsensical understanding of knowledge and cognition. Ordinarily, the mind is held to be object-related or *intentional*: "Intentionality is the power of minds to be about, to represent, or to stand for, things, properties and states of affairs."[24] By contrast, Plotinus' intellect is unintentional in the weak sense that it is self-thinking and hence unrelated to things, properties and states of affairs. More important, it is also unintentional in the stronger sense that it seeks not to know a certain object, but precisely to suspend intentional knowing and ordinary knowledge, for if the objects to be known are already identical to the knower, then the intention to know them would not arise and the act of knowing (in the ordinary sense) would not take place at all. The same point is demonstrated more concisely in terms of Plotinus' metaphysics as follows:

(x)   A trace of the Good is seen in it *[the intellect]*, and it is in the likeness of this that one should conceive its true archetype, forming an idea of it in oneself

---

23   Plotinus will have more to say about this thesis in his teaching of negative theology (cf. Chapter 4 of this dissertation). For a more detailed philosophical study of Plotinus' doctrine of intellect and epistemology see Emilsson, 2007, 124–175.

24   Jacob, Pierre, "Intentionality", *The Stanford Encyclopedia of Philosophy* (Fall 2010 Edition), Edward N. Zalta (ed.), URL = <http://plato.stanford.edu/archives/fall2010/entries/intentionality/>.

from the trace of it which plays upon Intellect. The Good, therefore has given the trace of itself on Intellect to Intellect to have by seeing, so that in Intellect there is desire, and it is always desiring and always attaining, but the Good is not desiring—for what could it desire?—and attaining, for it did [sic] not desire [to attain anything].

Οἷον δὲ ἐνορᾶται ἐπ᾽ αὐτῷ ἴχνος τοῦ ἀγαθοῦ, τοιοῦτον τὸ ἀρχέτυπον ἐννοεῖν προσήκει τὸ ἀληθινὸν ἐκείνου ἐνθυμηθέντα ἐκ τοῦ ἐπὶ τῷ νῷ ἐπιθέοντος ἴχνους. Τὸ μὲν οὖν ἐπ᾽ αὐτοῦ ἴχνους αὐτοῦ τῷ νῷ ὁρῶντι ἔδωκεν ἔχειν· ὥστε ἐν μὲν τῷ νῷ ἡ ἔφεσις καὶ ἐφιέμενος ἀεὶ καὶ ἀεὶ τυγχάνων, ἐκεῖνος δὲ οὔτε ἐφιέμενος—τίνος γάρ;—οὔτε τυγχάνων· οὐδὲ γὰρ ἐφιέτο.[25]

Since the intellect aims at the transcendent One which neither desires nor attains nor thinks, its act of self-thinking is in fact aiming at something which is beyond knowledge.

Plotinus' bizarre conception of knowledge or contemplation might appear less counter-intuitive if we put it in the context of his mystical teaching and compare it with the various techniques of *meditation* aiming not at a body of scientific knowledge, but at mental absorption and stillness, such as *dhyana* in Hinduism and Buddhism, or *hesychasm* and contemplative prayer in Christianity. The following passage is a good example of how Plotinus incorporates his identity thesis about knowledge and mind into such a practice:

(xi)   But why should not intellect itself be active [without perception], and also its attendant soul, which comes before sense perception and any sort of awareness? There must be an activity prior to awareness if "thinking and being are the same". It seems as if awareness exists and is produced when intellectual activity is reflexive and when that in the life of the soul which is active in thinking is in a way projected back, as happens with a mirror-reflection when there is a smooth, bright, untroubled surface. In these circumstances when the mirror is there the mirror-image is produced, but when it is not there or is not in the right state the object of which the image would have been is [all the same] actually there. In the same way as regards the soul, when that kind of thing in us which mirrors the images of thought and intellect is undisturbed, we see them and know them in a way parallel to sense perception, along with the prior knowledge that it is intellect and thought that are active. But when this is broken when the harmony

25   III.8.11.19–26.

of the body is upset, thought and intellect operate without an image, and then intellectual activity takes place without a mind-picture. So one might come to this sort of conclusion, that intellectual activity is [normally] accompanied by a mind-picture, but is not a mind-picture. One can find a great many valuable activities, theoretical and practical, which we carry on both in our contemplative and active life even when we are fully conscious, which do not make us aware of them. The reader is not necessarily aware that he is reading, least of all when he is really concentrating [...] Conscious awareness, in fact, is likely to enfeeble the very activities of which there is consciousness; only when they are alone are they pure and more genuinely active and living; and *when good men are in this state their life is increased, when it is not spilt out into perception, but gathered together in one in itself.*

Αὐτὸς δὲ ὁ νοῦς διὰ τί οὐκ ἐνεργήσει καὶ ἡ ψυχὴ περὶ αὐτὸν ἡ πρὸ αἰσθήσεως καὶ ὅλως ἀντιλήψεως; Δεῖ γὰρ τὸ πρὸ ἀντιλήψεως ἐνέργημα εἶναι, εἴπερ τὸ αὐτὸ τὸ νοεῖν καὶ εἶναι. Καὶ ἔοικεν ἡ ἀντίληψις εἶναι καὶ γίνεσθαι ἀνακάμπτοντος τοῦ νοήματος καὶ τοῦ ἐνεργοῦντος τοῦ κατὰ τὸ ζῆν τῆς ψυχῆς οἷον ἀπωσθέντος πάλιν, ὥσπερ ἐν κατόπτρῳ περὶ τὸ λεῖον καὶ λαμπρὸν ἡσυκάζον. Ὡς οὖν ἐν τοῖς τοιούτοις παρόντος μὲν τοῦ κατόπτρου ἐγένετο τὸ εἴδωλον, μὴ παρόντος δὲ ἢ μὴ οὕτως ἔχοντος ἐνεργείᾳ πάρεστιν οὗ τὸ εἴδωλον ἦν ἄν, οὕτω καὶ περὶ ψυχὴν ἡσυχίαν μὲν ἄγοντος τοῦ ἐν ἡμῖν τοιούτου, ᾧ ἐμφαίνεται τὰ τῆς διανοίας καὶ τοῦ νοῦ εἰκονίσματα, ἐνορᾶται ταῦτα καὶ οἷον αἰσθητῶς γινώσκεται μετὰ τῆς προτέρας γνώσεως, ὅτι ὁ νοῦς καὶ ἡ διάνοια ἐνεργεῖ. Συγκλασθέντος δὲ τούτου διὰ τὴν τοῦ σώματος ταραττομένην ἁρμονίαν ἄνευ εἰδώλου ἡ διάνοια καὶ ὁ νοῦς νοεῖ καὶ ἄνευ φαντασίας ἡ νόησις τότε· ὥστε καὶ τοιοῦντον ἄν τι νοοῖτο μετὰ φαντασίας τὴν νόησιν γίνεσθαι οὐκ οὔσης τῆς νοήσεως φαντασίας. Πολλὰς δ' ἄν τις εὕροι καὶ ἐγρηγορότων καλὰς ἐνεργείας καὶ θεωρίας καὶ πράξεις, ὅτε θεωροῦμεν καὶ ὅτε πράττομεν, τὸ παρακολουθεῖν ἡμᾶς αὐταῖς οὐκ ἐχούσας. Οὐ γὰρ τὸν ἀναγινώσκοντα ἀνάγκη παρακολουθεῖν ὅτι ἀναγινώσκει καὶ τότε μάλιστα, ὅτε μετὰ τοῦ συντόνου ἀναγινώσκοι· [...] ὥστε τὰς παρακολουθήσεις κινδυνεύειν ἀμυδροτέρας αὐτὰς τὰς ἐνεργείας αἷς παρακολουθοῦσι ποιεῖν, μόνας δὲ αὐτὰς οὔσας καθαρὰς τότε εἶναι καὶ μᾶλλον ἐνεργεῖν καὶ μᾶλλον ζῆν καὶ δὴ καὶ ἐν τῷ τοιούτῳ πάθει τῶν σπουδαίων γενομένων μᾶλλον τὸ ζῆν εἶναι, οὐ κεχυμένον εἰς αἴσθησιν, ἀλλ' ἐν τῷ αὐτῷ ἐν ἑαυτῷ συνηγμένον.[26]

---

26   I.4.10.3–33.

In short, when man's mind is still, there is no reflective consciousness or awareness (ἀντίληψις) of what he is doing. And when the mind becomes active and
the body stays in harmony, the mind is perfectly aware of its object, just as a
smooth mirror reflecting its image. But when the harmony of the body is broken, the mind will also be disturbed and lose the perfect awareness of its object.
Like many practitioners of meditation in the Christian and Buddhist traditions,
Plotinus links the harmony of body with mental awareness, but does not reduce
the psycho-somatic equilibrium to perfect mental stillness, which is a state more
closely related to mystical experience. Thus understood, it might be no exaggera-
tion to say that Plotinus' identity thesis of contemplation is intended not so much
to establish a robust theory of knowledge for its own sake, as to incorporate it
into his mystical teaching.

The preceding clarifications help us to put in perspective Plotinus' thesis that
contentment is linked to contemplation. When Plotinus seeks to explain contentment in terms of contemplation, the explanandum is not how contentment can
be (*per impossibile*) gratified, nor is the explanans a certain body of knowledge
which induces gratification. Rather, the explanandum is how the actualization
of desire can be independent from such gratification, and the explanans is the
unintentional act of contemplating oneself. Plotinus' explanation, then, is to this
effect: *as long as the agent contemplates, he is freed from the gratification of desired
object and always already content.*

1.5 Section Summary

With the above explanations we are finally in the position to answer the guiding
question of Section 1, namely the relation between different modes of desire and
desire for knowledge. Plotinus does not understand knowledge in the ordinary
sense, but rather as *contemplation*. For instance, it is claimed in III.8.1 that "all
things desire contemplation" (πάντα θεωρίας ἐφίεσθαι), and in III.8.7 it is said
that "actions have their goal in knowledge, and their driving force is desire for
knowledge (ἔφεσις γνώσεως)." Desire for contemplation, however, is not one
of the various modes of desire, such as *curiosity* or the desire to know something. Since all modes of desire have their common intrinsic structure in the
agent's self-relation, such that they are actualized only when the agent is content,
and since contemplation leads to contentment, it follows that desire for contemplation is a reflexive attitude in which contentment can be attained and desire
fulfilled.

Section 2 The Constitutive Role of Desire for Knowledge in the Practice of Philosophy

The task of Section 2, as is planned in the beginning of this chapter, is to articulate the methodological details in Plotinus' practice of philosophy in the light of the desire for knowledge. In the *Enneads*, however, Plotinus rarely explains his teaching explicitly in terms of this concept. But since desire for knowledge is the desiring agent's attitude toward himself (cf. Section 1), we can still approach our task in the light of the philosopher's attitude toward himself. Philosopher (φιλο-σόφος), on Plotinus' act-theoretical characterization, is someone who desires knowledge of intelligible beings.[27] Accordingly, how the philosopher relates to himself amounts to *how he treats his own desire*. Thus, in what follows I shall distinguish the various senses of the term *desire* in III.8.1 and other related passages which describe the activity of philosophical inquiry, thereby showing that the philosopher is said to consider his own desire to be related to his philosophical inquiry in certain ways. Specifically speaking, it will be demonstrated that the philosopher regards his desire as constitutive of the origin, object, method and goal of his philosophical inquiry. The upshot is that, just as desire for knowledge is not the curiosity to know something but the desiring agent's attitude toward himself, so too philosophy is not a set of philosophical questions and arguments compiled in a textbook, but properly speaking an attitude toward one's own desire. Assuming such a philosophical attitude, therefore, practically amounts to conducting philosophical inquiry.

2.1 The Origin of Philosophical Inquiry

An example of how philosophical inquiry proceeds according to Plotinus is given in the opening chapter of III.8, *On Nature, Contemplation and the One*. What follows is the first half of this crucial chapter, quoted in its entirety:

(xii) Suppose we said, playing at first before we set out to be serious, that all things aspire to contemplation, and direct their gaze to this end—not only rational but irrational living things, and the power of growth in plants, and the earth which brings them forth—and that all attain to it as far as possible for them in their natural state, but different things contemplate and attain their end in different ways, some truly, and some only having an imitation and image of this true end—could anyone endure the oddity of this line of thought? Well, as this discussion has arisen among ourselves, there will be

---

27   Cf. I.3.1–3.

no risk in playing with our own ideas. Then are we now contemplating as we play? Yes, we and all who play are doing this, or at any rate this is what they aspire to as they play. And it is likely that, whether a child or a man is playing or being serious, one plays and the other is serious for the sake of contemplation, and every action is a serious effort towards contemplation; compulsory action drags contemplation more towards the outer world, and what we call voluntary, less, but, all the same, voluntary action, too, springs from the desire of contemplation.

Παίζοντες δὴ τὴν πρώτην πρὶν ἐπιχειρεῖν σπουδάζειν εἰ λέγοιμεν πάντα θεωρίας ἐφιέσθαι καὶ εἰς τέλος τοῦτο βλέπειν, οὐ μόνον ἔλλογα ἀλλὰ καὶ ἄλογα ζῷα καὶ τὴν ἐν φυτοῖς φύσιν καὶ τὴν ταῦτα γεννῶσαν γῆν, καὶ πάντα τυγχάνειν καθ᾽ ὅσαν οἷόν τε αὐτοῖς κατὰ φύσιν ἔχοντα, ἄλλα δὲ ἄλλως καὶ θεωρεῖν καὶ τυγχάνειν καὶ τὰ μὲν ἀληθῶς, τὰ δὲ μίμησιν καὶ εἰκόνα τούτου λαβάνοντα—ἆρ᾽ ἄν τις ἀνάσχοιτο τὸ παράδοξον τοῦ λόγου; Ἡ πρὸς ἡμᾶς αὐτοῦ γινομένου κίνδυνος οὐδεὶς ἐν τῷ παίζειν τὰ αὐτῶν γενήσεται. Ἆρ᾽ οὖν καὶ ἡμεῖς παίζοντες ἐν τῷ παρόντι θεωροῦμεν; Ἡ καὶ ἡμεῖς καὶ πάντες ὅσοι παίζουσι τοῦτο ποιοῦσιν ἢ τούτου γε παίζουσιν ἐφιέμενοι. Καὶ κινδυνεύει, εἴτε τις παῖς εἴτε ἀνὴρ παίζει ἢ σπουδάζει, θεωρίας ἕνεκεν ὁ μὲν παίζειν, ὁ δὲ σπουδάζειν, καὶ πρᾶξις πᾶσα εἰς θεωρίαν τὴν σπουδὴν ἔχειν, ἡ μὲν ἀναγκαία καὶ ἐπιπλέον τὴν θεωρίαν ἕλκουσα πρὸς τὸ ἔξω, ἡ δὲ ἑκούσιος λεγομένη ἐπ᾽ ἔλαττον μέν, ὅμως δὲ καὶ αὕτη ἐφέσει θεωρίας γινομένη.[28]

Let us set aside the content of discussion, namely the thesis that all things desire contemplation, and focus instead on its *formal* elements. The first one concerns the *origin* or starting point of philosophical inquiry. As *"playing at first before* we set out to be serious" indicates, philosophy does not boil down to a set of philosophical problems and the attempted solutions thereof, but should be exercised as an intellectual inquiry which originates from a "play".

On Kevin Corrigan's interpretation, "play" refers to *dialogues*, which is the medium where philosophical ideas are communicated among friends, or teacher and students: "the free play necessary for the birth of new thought requires in such dialogue the sympathy of friends and an affinity with the subject."[29] That is to say, it is the dialogical character of play which engenders new thought. But this

---

28   III.8.1.1–18.

29   Cf. Corrigan, Kevin, *Reading Plotinus: A Practical Introduction to Neoplatonism*, Purdue University Press, West Lafayette, 2005, 102–103.

interpretation is at odds with our commonsense, for not all dialogues engender new thought, and not all new thoughts are engendered from dialogue. Indeed, a great number of philosophical thoughts and works of art are borne from seclusion and solitude in varying degrees, and there are great scientists and artists who died without being recognized by their peers.

Moreover, nowhere in III.8.1 is it said that the philosopher *talks* with others as he plays. What Plotinus states is rather that the philosopher *contemplates* or *desires for contemplation* as he plays: "[…] are we contemplating as we play? Yes, we and all who play are doing this, or at any rate this is what they desire as they play." We have already given a brief account of Plotinus' notion of contemplation in the context of his mystical teaching. For now, let us note that dialogue, as a communication of opinions among more than two parties, is not contemplation but a kind of "compulsory action [which] drags contemplation towards the outer world". The thought compelled and constrained by such an action is weak, poor, insignificant (ἀσθενής), and far from philosophical: "Men, too, when their power of contemplation weakens, make action a shadow of contemplation and reasoning. […] since their souls are weak and they are not able to grasp the vision sufficiently, and therefore are not filled with it, but still long to see it, they are carried into action, so as to see what they cannot see with their intellect."[30]

In accordance with the didactic approach of his mystical writing, Plotinus conceives philosophy neither as social behavior such as dialogue nor as a set of questions and arguments, but primarily as what his target student, i.e. the philosopher, does, namely the action of philosophical inquiry. The focus is on the philosopher's agency as someone who desires knowledge. Crucial to this conception is that something *matters* to the philosopher, such that he is *motivated* toward his inquiry into it. This is exactly why in (xii) Plotinus prefaces his discussion first with a "play", rather than proceeds directly to "serious inquiry" (ἐπιχειρεῖν σπουδάζειν). The "play" in question refers to the desire which inspires and motivates philosophical inquiry. In this sense, desire plays a constitutive role in the origination or motivation of philosophical inquiry.

The connection between the motivating desire and the One is especially noteworthy. According to Plotinus' mystical teaching, the practice of philosophy is the first stage in man's "acent" to the One. Now since such a practice originates from desire, it follows that this motivating desire must be somehow connected to the One from the very beginning. This connection between the motivating desire

---

30   III.8.4.31–36.

and the One is the condition of possibility of philosophical inquiry. As Plotinus explains in VI.5.1:

(xiii) A general opinion affirms that what is one and the same in number is everywhere present as a whole, when all men are naturally and spontaneously moved to speak of the god who is in each one of us one and the same. And if someone did not ask them how this is and want to examine their opinion rationally, this is what they would assume, and with this active and actual in their thinking they would come to rest in this way somehow supporting themselves on what is one and the same, and they would not wish to be cut away from this unity. And this is the firmest principle of all, which our souls cry out, as it were, not summed up from individual instances, but preceding all the individuals…

Τὸ ἓν καὶ ταὐτὸν ἀριθμῷ πανταχοῦ ἅμα ὅλον εἶναι κοινή μέν τις ἔννοιά φησιν εἶναι, ὅταν πάντες κινούμενοι αὐτοφυῶς λέγωσι τὸν ἐν ἑκάστῳ ἡμῶν θεὸν ὡς ἕνα καὶ τὸν αὐτόν. καὶ εἴ τις αὐτοὺς τὸν τρόπον μὴ ἀπαιτοῖ μηδὲ λόγῳ ἐξετάζειν τὴν δόξαν αὐτῶν ἐθέλοι, οὕτως ἂν καὶ θεῖντο καὶ ἐνεργοῦντες τοῦτο τῇ διανοίᾳ οὕτως ἀναπαύοιντο εἰς ἓν πως συνερείδοντες καὶ ταὐτόν, καὶ οὐδ' ἂν ἐθέλοιεν ταύτης τῆς ἑνότητος ἀποσχίζεσθαι. καὶ ἔστι πάντων βεβαιοτάτη ἀρχή, ἥν ὥσπερ αἱ ψυχαὶ ἡμῶν φθέγγονται, μὴ ἐκ τῶν καθέκαστα συγκεφαλαιωθεῖσα…[31]

Man is moved by a natural desire to believe that the One is immanent in himself. This belief is said to be prior to rational examination and irreducible to a particular thesis, because the desire in question is the motivating cause of philosophical inquiry. Thus understood, neither is the belief a propositional attitude, nor the immanence of the One reducible to a proposition about the One. Rather, it would be more appropriate to say that this belief is man's *vague, pre-reflective awareness* that the One is immanent.[32] Therefore, the One is immanent in the

---

31 VI.5.1.1–8.
32 Cf. V.3.14.8–19: "But just as those who have a god within them and are in the grip of divine possession may know this much, that they have something greater within them, even if they do not know what, and from the ways in which they are moved and the things they say get a certain awareness (αἴσθησίν τινα) of the god who moves them, though these are not the same as the mover; so we seem to be disposed towards the One, divining, when we have our intellect pure, that this is […] more and greater than anything said about It, because It is higher than speech and thought and awareness; It gives us these, but It is not these Itself." See also Chapter 1, passage (viii) and (ix) for the analysis of this passage.

motivating desire in the qualified sense that the desire which motivates philosophical inquiry is aroused not directly by the One, but only by man's vague awareness thereof. In other words, man is inspired to philosophical inquiry, because he desires to know more exactly that which he does not and cannot fully comprehend.

2.2 The Object of Philosophical Inquiry

What is the *object* of philosophical inquiry according to Plotinus? To explain this issue, we can start with Aristotle. For Aristotle, philosophy begins with the wonder about certain given *aporiai* or philosophical puzzles. Since the Aristotelian wonder concerns the problems passed down and not yet solved by previous philosophers, it is intrinsically philosophical and technical, and the philosophical inquiry which begins with such a wonder is situated within an already existent philosophical community.[33]

Plotinus' desire, by contrast, is pre-philosophical in that it gives rise to philosophical inquiry, and is irreducible to the curiosity aroused by certain philosophical puzzles. The very first sentence of III.8.1 reads: *"suppose we say* (εἰ λέγοιμεν), playing at first before we turn to serious inquiry, that all things desire contemplation."* That is to say, the desire motivates the philosopher to inquire into it and inspires in him certain *rational hypotheses* about it. Such a hypothesis is a natural expression of the motivating desire, and it is through the investigation of this hypothesis that the desire continues to inspire the philosopher. In this sense, desire is also constitutive of the object of philosophical inquiry. Plotinus explains the hypothetical nature of philosophical inquiry as follows:

(xiv) And this is *the firmest principle of all*, which our souls cry out, as it were, not summed up from individual instances, but preceding all the individuals and coming before *that principle which lays down and says that all things desire the good* [sic]. For this latter would be true if all things press on to the one [sic] and are one, and their desire is of this.

καὶ ἔστι πάντων βεβαιοτάτη ἀρχή, ἥν ὥσπερ αἱ ψυχαὶ ἡμῶν φθέγγονται, μὴ ἐκ τῶν καθέκαστα συγκεφαλαιωθεῖσα, ἀλλὰ πρὸ τῶν καθέκαστα πάντων

---

33   Cf. *Aristotle's Metaphysics*, tr. W. D. Ross, Clarendon Press, Oxford, 1953, Book I, 980a and III, 995a. See also Schaeffer, Denise, 'Wisdom and Wonder in Aristotle's Metaphysics', *The Review of Metaphysics*, vol. 52, 1999, 641–656; Benardete, Seth, 'On Wisdom and Philosophy: The First Two Chapters of Aristotle's Metaphysics A', *The Review of Metaphysics*, vol.32, 1978, 205–215.

προελθοῦσα καὶ πρὸ ἐκείνης τῆς τοῦ ἀγαθοῦ πάντα ὀρέγεσθαι τιθεμένης τε καὶ λεγούσης. οὕτω γὰρ ἂν αὕτη ἀληθὲς εἴη, εἰ τὰ πάντα εἰς ἓν σπεύδοι καὶ ἓν εἴη, καὶ τούτου ἡ ὄρεξις εἴη.[34]

This passage continues the discussion brought up in (xiii) and draws the important distinction between "the firmest principle of all" and "that principle which lays down and says that all things desire the good". The former is the *fact* that the One is immanent in all beings, whereas the latter is the *claim* that all beings desire the immanent One. There are two reasons why this claim is said to be "hypothetical", i.e. unable to *fully* explain the motivating desire. First, according to (xiii), the One is immanent even if no one wants to rationally examine It. Second, according to (xiv), the claim is true *only if* its content *corresponds* to what is the case about the One.

The Plotinian desire differs from the Aristotelian wonder also because it is not technical or sophisticated. "Could anyone endure the oddity of this line of thought (τὸ παράδοξον τοῦ λόγου)?" Plotinus asks himself in passage (xii), and explains as follows: "Well, as this discussion has arisen among ourselves (πρὸς ἡμᾶς), there will be no risk in playing with our own ideas." That is to say, the philosopher's claim is neither made about objective reality, nor intended to persuade peer philosophers. It is rather a rational expression of his own experience of desire which concerns nobody but himself, and he is concerned less with the *philosophical* problems which *other* philosophers have been studying, and more with the *existential* problems which inspire and matter to *him*, however paradoxical it might appear to others.

The personal and existential relevance of the desire for philosophical inquiry brings us to compare Plotinus with the Stoics. On the Stoic terminology, desire (ἐπιθυμία) is one of the four types of passions (πάθοι), the other three being pleasure, distress and fear. For the Stoics, they give rise to emotional agitations which impede man's sound judgment, and lead him finally to a tragic end. Seneca's play *Medea*, for instance, lively illustrates how passionate love, untamable by rational governance, oscillates between the extremities of anger, grief and murderous impulse. At the climax of the play, the pregnant Medea, infuriated because of her husband's betrayal, mutilates herself and kills their child. This is a symbolic act for the self-destruction of passionate love. Seneca's lesson is that once we submit to the tyranny of passions, they will drive us in all directions beyond ourselves and lead us to our own demise.

---

34   VI.5.1.8–14.

The Plotinian desire, by contrast, does not arouse in the philosopher a *non-rational* reaction such as blush or excitement, but is *intelligible* and inspires intellectual inquiry. Desire is ethically significant, not because man suffers from it emotionally, but because it inspires man to study it intellectually.

For Plotinus, then, the intrinsic relation between the motivating desire and the activity of philosophical inquiry is reciprocal: On the one hand, the motivating desire inspires the philosopher; on the other hand, the philosopher lays down certain hypotheses in order to explain this desire. From this reciprocal relation two points are to be noted: First, philosophical inquiry is not a theoretical "research" exercised for its own sake. Rather, the very fact that the philosopher begins to philosophize because something inspires and matters to him, indicates that philosophical inquiry is an ethical and spiritual "search" for the solution of practical problems arising from his own experience of desire. Second and more important, the original desire is an *inexhaustible* inspiration for the philosopher, and his hypothesis thereof *cannot* adequately explain it.

2.3 The Method of Philosophical Inquiry

Seneca writes: "The question has often been raised whether it is better to have moderate emotions, or none at all. *Philosophers of our school reject the emotions; the Peripatetics keep them in check.*"[35] For the Stoics, since true happiness is considered to be an impassionate state of mind called *ataraxy* (ἀταραξία), and since passions are emotional sufferings, there is no other way but to eradicate or exterminate them altogether.

Now, since Plotinus holds that desire is intelligible and inspires intellectual inquiry, he would encourage man not to be turned off by the apparently oddity of his hypothesis about desire, but to cherish it in a more affirmative light and to examine it more carefully. As he says in III.8.1: "Well, as this discussion has arisen among ourselves, there will be no risk in playing with our own ideas. Then are we now *contemplating as we play*? Yes, we and all who play are doing this, or at any rate this is what they aspire to as they play." That is to say, not only the origin and the object of philosophical inquiry, but also the very *process* thereof, are linked to desire, for the desire to be inquired into is not just any desire, but precisely that specific desire which motivates this very inquiry. Thus, we could say that

---

35   *Moral Letters to Lucilius* 3 vols., tr. Richard Mott Gumerre, Harvard University Press, Cambridge, 1917–1925, 116.1, my italics. See also Nussbaum, Martha C., *The Therapy of Desire: Theory and Practice in Hellenistic Ethics* (2nd edition), Princeton University Press, Princeton, 2009, 359–401.

philosophical inquiry is a *reflexive* undertaking, to the extent that desire pertains to both its subjective and objective aspect.

Furthermore, since desire is intelligible, there is no need to resort to the Stoics' radical solutions such as the eradication or extermination of desire; it is enough to weed out its undesirable and unintelligible parts, and preserve the intelligible ones. Consequently, for Plotinus the method of dealing with desire lies in the *purification* (κάθαρσις) thereof. To borrow a psychoanalytic jargon, the Stoics prefer the suppression of desire, whereas Plotinus privileges the *sublimation* of desire. Plotinus explains this point as follows:

(xv)   The soul then in her natural state is in love with God and wants to be united with It; it is like the noble love of a girl for her noble father. But when the soul has come into the world of becoming and is deceived, so to say, by the blandishments of her suitors, she changes, bereft of her father, to a mortal love and is shamed; but again she comes to hate her shames here below, and purifies herself of the things of this world and sets herself on the way to her father and fares well. And if anyone does not know this experience, let him think of it in terms of our loves here below, and what it is like to attain what one is most in love with, and that these earthly loves are mortal and harmful and loves only of images, and that they change because it was not what is really and truly loved nor our good nor what we seek.

ἐρᾷ οὖν κατὰ φύσιν ἔχουσα ψυχὴ θεοῦ ἐνωθῆναι θέλουσα, ὥσπερ παρθένος καλοῦ πατρὸς καλὸν ἔρωτα. ὅταν δὲ εἰς γένεσιν ἐλθοῦσα οἷον μνηστείαις ἀπατηθῇ, ἄλλον ἀλλαξαμένη θνητὸν ἔρωτα ἐρημίᾳ πατρὸς ὑβρίζεται· μισήσασα δὲ πάλιν τὰς ἐνταῦθα ὕβρεις ἁγνεύσασα τῶν τῇδε πρὸς τὸν πατέρα αὖθις στελλομένη εὐπαθεῖ. καὶ οἷς μὲν ἄγνωστόν ἐστι τὸ πάθημα τοῦτο, ἐντεῦθεν ἐνθυμείσθω ἀπὸ τῶν ἐνταῦθα ἐρώτων, οἷόν ἐστι τυχεῖν ὧν τις μάλιστα ἐρᾷ, καὶ ὅτι ταῦτα μὲν τὰ ἐρώμενα θνητὰ καὶ βλαβερὰ καὶ εἰδώλων ἔρωτες καὶ μεταπίπτει, ὅτι οὐκ ἦν τὸ ὄντως ἐρώμενον οὐδὲ τὸ ἀγαθὸν ἡμῶν οὐδ' ὃ ζητοῦμεν.[36]

The claim that "these earthly loves are mortal and harmful and loves only of images" seems to indicate that Plotinus despises ordinary experiences of desire, but this is not the case. The message of (xv) is rather that these experiences provide the philosopher a rough idea of what the desire which inspires him is like. They serve, so to speak, as the imperfect images or signs of henosis for the philosopher to study. The same point is restated in another passage:

---

36   VI.9.9.33–44.

(xvi) And just as here below those who are in love shape themselves to the like-ness of the beloved, and make their bodies handsomer and bring their souls into likeness, since as far as they can they do not want to fall short of the integrity and all the other excellence of the loved [sic] one—if they did they would be rejected by loved ones like these—and these are the lovers who are able to have intercourse; in this way the soul also loves that Good, moved by It to love from the beginning.

ὥσπερ δὲ ἐνταῦθα σχηματίζονται εἰς ὁμοιότητα τῷ ἐραστῷ οἶ ἂν ἐρῶσι, καὶ τὰ σώματα εὐπρεπέστερα καὶ τὰς ψυχὰς ἄγοντες εἰς ὁμοιότητα, ὡς μὴ λείπεσθαι κατὰ δύναμιν θέλειν τῇ τοῦ ἐρωμένου σωφροσύνῃ τε καὶ ἀρετῇ τῇ ἄλλῃ—ἢ ἀπόβλητοι ἂν εἶεν τοῖς ἐρωμένος τοῖς τοιούτοις—καὶ οὗτοί εἰσιν οἱ συνεῖναι δυνάμενοι, τοῦτον τὸν τρόπον καὶ ψυχὴ ἐρᾷ μὲν ἐκείνου ὑπ᾽ αὐτοῦ ἐξ ἀρχῆς εἰς τὸ ἐρᾶν κινηθεῖσα.[37]

In passage (xv) and (xvi) Plotinus introduces a new concept, namely *the Good* as the *end* of philosophical inquiry. It is to this issue that we shall now turn.

2.4 The End of Philosophical Inquiry

Overall, we can discern in the *Enneads* three senses in which the end of philo-sophical inquiry is described in terms of desire. According to the basic sense, the end of philosophical inquiry is simply the ultimate *goal* which the philosopher desires:

(xvii) So we must ascend again to the good [sic], which every soul desires. Any-one who has seen It knows what I mean when I say that It is beautiful. It is *desired as good*, and *the desire for It is directed to good*, and the attainment of It is for those who go up to the higher world and are converted and strip off what we put on in our descent; [...] until, passing in the ascent all that is alien to the God, one sees with one's self alone That alone, simple, single and pure, from [sic] which all depends and to which all look and are and live and think: for It is cause of life and mind and being.

Ἀναβατέον οὖν πάλιν ἐπὶ τὸ ἀγαθόν, οὗ ὀρέγεται πᾶσα ψυχή. Εἴ τις οὖν εἶδεν αὐτό, οἶδεν ὃ λέγω, ὅπως καλόν. Ἐφετὸν μὲν γὰρ ὡς ἀγαθὸν καὶ ἡ ἔφεσις πρὸς τοῦτο, τεῦξις δὲ αὐτοῦ ἀναβαίνουσι πρὸς τὸ ἄνω καὶ ἐπιστραφεῖσι καὶ ἀποδυομένοις ἃ καταβαίνοντες ἡμφιέσμεθα· [...] ἕως ἄν τις παρελθὼν ἐν τῇ ἀναβάσει πᾶν ὅσαν ἀλλότριον τοῦ θεοῦ αὐτῷ μόνῳ

---

37   VI.7.31.11–19.

αὐτὸ μόνον ἴδῃ εἰλικρινές, ἁπλοῦν, καθαρόν, ἀφ᾿ οὗ πάντα ἐξήρτηται καὶ πρὸς αὐτὸ βλέπει καὶ ἔστι καὶ ζῇ καὶ νοεῖ.[38]

Previously the philosopher desired to know about his own experience of desire. It is not until now that the Good is brought up for the first time in Plotinus' discussion of the practice of philosophy, and described as that which "every soul desires", namely the intentional object of philosophical inquiry. The reason is that since the Good is the ultimate reality of all beings, It must also be manifest in the original desire as that which the philosopher *really desires to know*.[39] For this reason, it is crucial to note that what Plotinus is describing here is not henosis or the philosopher's mystical "vision" of the Good *as such*, but *the philosopher's ascent* to the Good from his own subjective point of view. The expression "one sees with one's self alone that Good alone" has to be understood accordingly. It suggests to the effect that the philosopher "sees" nothing but the Good, in the same way the archer focuses single-mindedly on the target.

So far in our discussion, Plotinus' basic insight is that since the philosopher is by nature a "desirer of knowledge", he must *always remain desiring* throughout the activity of his inquiry—not only when he is inspired to begin to philosophize, but also when he is in the process of doing philosophy with his ultimate goal in mind. Thus, it is reasonable that the philosopher's desire will intensify when he is getting close to the goal, and that when he finally attains knowledge of his experience of desire, his desire will be the strongest. Accordingly, there is yet another sense in which the end of philosophical inquiry is related to desire, namely when the inquiry culminates or *ends* in a desirous state. Thus Plotinus writes:

(xviii) If anyone sees It, what passion will he feel, what longing in his desire to be united with It, what a shock of delight! The man who has not seen It may desire It as good, but he who has seen It glories in Its beauty and is full of wonder and delight, enduring a shock which causes no hurt, loving with true passion and piercing longing; he laughs at all other loves and despises what he thought beautiful before; it is like the experience of those who have met appearances of gods or spirits and do not any more appreciate as they did the beauty of other bodies.

Τοῦτο οὖν εἴ τις ἴδοι, ποίους ἂν ἴσχοι ἔρωτας, ποίους δὲ πόθους, βουλόμενος αὐτῷ συγκερασθῆναι, πῶς δ᾿ ἂν οὐκ ἐκπλαγείη μεθ᾿

---

38 I.6.7.1–12.
39 Cf. Introduction, Section 3 and Chapter 1, Section 3.

ἡδονῆς; Ἔστι γὰρ τῷ μὲν μήπω ἰδόντι ὀρέγεσθαι ὡς ἀγαθοῦ· τῷ δὲ ἰδόντι ὑπάρχει ἐπὶ καλῷ ἄγασθαί τε καὶ θάμβους πίμπλασθαι μεθ᾽ ἡδονῆς καὶ ἐκπλήττεσθαι ἀβλαβῶς καὶ ἐρᾶν ἀληθῆ ἔρωτα καὶ δριμεῖς πόθους καὶ τῶν ἄλλων ἐρώτων καταγελᾶν καὶ τῶν πρόσθεν νομιζομένων καλῶν καταφρονεῖν· ὁποῖον πάσχουσιν ὅσοι θεῶν εἴδεσιν ἢ δαιμόνων προστυχόντες οὐκέτ᾽ ἂν ἀποδέχοιντο ὁμοίως ἄλλων κάλλη σωμάτων.[40]

Armstrong translates τῷ δὲ ἰδόντι ὑπάρχει ἐπὶ καλῷ ἄγασθαί τε into "but he who has seen It glories in Its beauty". But the keyword in this passage should be ὑπάρχει ("begins"). That is to say, in (xvii) the soul is *striving* to see, but in (xviii) the soul *begins* to see (ὑπάρχει ὁράω) for the first time. As in (xvii), what is described here is not henosis as such, but the philosopher's personal experience of desire, and indeed his cognitive representation thereof. He is said to "love with true passion and piercing longing" on the one hand, and "laugh at all other loves and despise what he thought beautiful before" on the other, because *he thinks* the One which he sees is far more desirable than all desirable objects.

However, it should be noted from (xviii) that the philosopher has this "piercing longing" only when he *begins* to see the One. But such a desire is transitory, not because the philosopher will get used to the mystical vision after he sees the One. Quite the contrary, the reason is that the very transitoriness in question is due to the *illusive* nature of the philosopher's vision of the One. The reason is stated below:

(xix) For to say that It *[the One]* is the cause is not to predicate something incidental of It but of us, because we have something from It while that One is in Itself; but one who speaks precisely should not say "that" or "is"; but we run round It outside, in a way, and want to explain our own experiences of It, sometimes near It and sometimes falling away in our perplexities about It.

ἐπεὶ καὶ τὸ αἴτιον λέγειν οὐ κατηγορεῖν ἐστι συμβεβηκός τι αὐτῷ, ἀλλ᾽ ἡμῖν, ὅτι ἔχομέν τι παρ᾽ αὐτοῦ ἐκείνου ὄντος ἐν αὐτῷ· δεῖ δὲ μηδὲ τὸ "ἐκείνου" μηδὲ "ὄντος" λέγειν ἀκριβῶς λέγοντα, ἀλλ᾽ ἡμᾶς οἷον ἔξωθεν περιθέοντας τὰ αὐτῶν ἑρμηνεύειν ἐθέλειν πάθη ὁτὲ μὲν ἐγγύς, ὁτὲ δὲ ἀποπίπτοντας ταῖς περὶ αὐτὸ ἀπορίαις.[41]

---

40   I.6.7.12–19.
41   VI.9.3.49–54.

Since the One is the cause which is beyond all beings, It cannot be adequately explained in terms of them. To do so, only leads to perplexities. For the same reason, the One cannot really be seen as an object of vision, be it physical or intellectual. Thus, when the philosopher claims that he sees the One and experiences a "piercing longing", his claim is false and his desire is an illusion. On the whole, the second sense in which desire is related to the end of philosophy is ambiguous, and can be summed up as follows. On the one hand, philosophical inquiry culminates in a state of piercing longing in which the philosopher beholds the mystical vision of the One. But on the other hand, since the philosopher does not really see the One, his inquiry ends up immediately in perplexity and his desire turns into an illusion.

The last sense in which desire is related to the end of philosophical inquiry is the negation or *renunciation* of desire. Since philosophical inquiry ends up in perplexity, the philosopher realizes that it is but a futile business. He should not study the One *as an intelligible being*, but should ascend to the next stage of negative theology and study It *as that which is beyond all beings*. To this end, first he has to end or suspend his philosophical inquiry, put to rest the desire to know the One as an intelligible being, and forget about that illusive desire which he wrongly believed to have experienced. This negation of desire is expressed by the phrase "ἔφεσις πρὸς ἀφὴν" from a famous passage of VI.9.11:

(xx)   But that other *[mystical vision of the One]*, perhaps, was not a contemplation but another kind of seeing, a being out of oneself and simplifying and giving oneself over and pressing towards contact and rest and a sustained thought leading to adaptation, if one is going to contemplate what is in the sanctuary.

τὸ δὲ ἴσως ἦν οὐ θέαμα, ἀλλὰ ἄλλος τρόπος τοῦ ἰδεῖν, ἔκστασις καὶ ἅπλωσις καὶ ἐπίδοσις αὐτοῦ καὶ ἔφεσις πρὸς ἀφὴν καὶ στάσις καὶ περινόησις πρὸς ἐφαρμογήν, εἴπερ τις τὸ ἐν τῷ ἀδύτῳ θεάσεται.[42]

In his commentary, P. A. Meijer remarks that these descriptions "are all aporetic terms, merely approximately correct, for ultimately it is impossible to describe the activities on the part of the soul."[43] I agree with Meijer's comment, but would like to add that the *aporiai* surrounding these descriptions are not so much due to the inaccessibility of the soul's private experience, as to the very ineffability of

---

42   VI.9.11.23–26.
43   Meijer, P. A., *Plotinus on the Good or the One (Enneads VI, 9): An Analytical Commentary*, J. C. Gieben, Amsterdam, 1992, 280.

the One. It is because the soul is united with the ineffable One that her experience or state of unification must also be properly ineffable and hence intelligible only approximately. For this reason, the best we exegetes can do is to decipher the descriptions in (xx) in terms of the negation on the part of the soul. Accordingly, "being out of oneself", "simplifying", and "giving oneself over" summarily refer to both the "radical laying aside of any quality or activity" and the "unfolding of oneself" and "making oneself open for" the One.[44] "Rest" refers to the immediate result of this radical laying aside.

It is in the above context that the expression ἔφεσις πρὸς ἀφὴν is to be understood. Armstrong's and Harder's respective translations are "pressing towards contact" and "Hinstreben zur Berührung". However, at this point the soul's active striving for contact has already been put to rest. In specific, πρός in this case does not designate the *movement* towards, for or against an intentional object. Rather, it refers to an abstract relation of *accord* or *proportion* between ἔφεσις and ἀφή, such that the soul's desire is not so much *seizing* (ἅπτουσα) the One as *seized* (ἁπτομένη) by It. In this sense, it might be more appropriate to understand ἔφεσις πρὸς ἀφὴν as the desire for and open toward seizure, namely the desire to be seized, overwhelmed and overcome. It is a state in which the ordinary, active desire comes to rest.

To sum up, for Plotinus the end of philosophical inquiry consists of three stages. In the first stage, the end is understood as the ultimate *goal* which the philosopher desires to attain. In the second stage, the end is understood as the culmination and *cessation* of philosophical inquiry in which the philosopher experiences a piercing yet illusive desire. In the final stage, the end is understood as the negation or *renunciation* of philosophical inquiry in which the desire to know the One as an intelligible being is given up altogether. As we see, in each stage desire plays an indispensable role; and this is so especially in the last stage, for without negating the desire to know the One as an intelligible being, it is impossible for the philosopher to ascend to the second stage of Plotinus' mystical teaching, namely negative theology.

Before concluding this chapter, I would like to reconsider a scholarly debate over the nature of henosis in Plotinus' mysticism. The debate is framed in terms of R. C. Zaehner's distinction between *theistic* and *monistic* mysticism: very roughly, in Plotinus' case, theistic union refers to the state in which the soul is united with the One but somehow preserves her own identity, and monistic identity designates the state in which the soul is united with the One and her

---

44   Cf. ibid., 280–282.

distinction from the One is overcome.[45] I shall take the summary above as a clue to tackle this issue from a more specific perspective.

To start with, since we are directly investigating the *Enneads* rather than Plotinus' personal experience, all that we can examine are his descriptions of henosis, rather than the nature thereof. So the debate should be modified as follows: are the descriptions found in the *Enneads* more in agreement with the notion of theistic union, or with that of monistic identity? Now, as I have just explained in this sub-section, since philosophical inquiry has intelligible beings as its proper object, it is unable to attain henosis. In accordance with the different stages of the end of philosophical inquiry, consequently, the union in question can be described in *different* senses. In particular, the second and the third stage seem similar to the theistic union and the monistic identity, respectively. To wit, in the second stage when the philosopher sees the One, it is still possible for him to "laugh at all other loves and despise what he thought beautiful before" (cf. (xviii)). This is evidence that, in spite of his vision of the One, the philosopher still retains memory, emotion, and judgment, and hence possesses personal identity to a certain degree. Following passages, furthermore, can also be taken as approximate descriptions of this stage.

(xxi)   There one can see both It and oneself as it is right to see: *the self glorified*, full of intelligible light, [...] having become—but rather, being—a god; ...

       ὁρᾶν δὴ ἔστιν ἐνταῦθα κἀκεῖνον καὶ ἑαυτὸν ὡς ὁρᾶν θέμις· ἑαυτὸν μὲν ἠγλαϊσμένον, φωτὸς πλήρη νοητοῦ, [...] θεὸν γενόμενον, μᾶλλον δὲ ὄντα, ...[46]

(xxii)   When therefore the seer sees *himself*, then when he sees, he will see *himself* as like this, or rather he will be in union with *himself* as like this and will be aware of *himself* like this since he has become single and simple.

       ἑαυτὸν μὲν οὖν ἰδὼν τότε, ὅτε ὁρᾷ, τοιοῦτον ὄψεται, μᾶλλον δὲ αὐτῷ τοιούτῳ συνέσται καὶ τοιοῦτον αἰσθήσεται ἁπλοῦν γενόμενον.[47]

(xxiii) [...] *she [the soul]* sees It *[the One]* in herself suddenly appearing (for there is nothing between, nor are there still two but *both* are one; nor

---

45   Cf. Arp, Robert, 'Plotinus, Mysticism and Mediation', *Religious Studies* 40, 2004, 145–163; Bussanich, John, 'Plotinian Mysticism in Theoretical and Comparative Perspective', *American Catholic Philosophical Quarterly* 71, 1997, 339–365.

46   VI.9.9.55–58.

47   VI.9.10.9–11.

could you still make a distinction while it is present; lovers and their beloveds here below imitate this in their will to be united)...

[...] ἰδοῦσα δὲ ἐν αὐτῇ ἐξαίφνης φανέντα (μεταξὺ γὰρ οὐδὲν οὐδ᾽ ἔτι δύο, ἀλλ᾽ ἓν ἄμφω· οὐ γὰρ ἂν διακρίναις ἔτι, ἕως πάρεστι· μίμησις δὲ τούτου καὶ οἱ ἐνταῦθα ἐρασταὶ καὶ ἐρώμενοι συγκρῖναι θέλοντες)...[48]

In the third stage, the philosopher is out of himself and gives himself up. The union with the One thus attained must exclude any remnant of personal identity. In this sense, the description of the third stage is more consistent with *monistic* identity. The passages below, all of which center around the theme of renunciation or negation, also suggest similarity to monistic identity:

(xxiv) So then the seer *does not see and does not distinguish and does not imagine* two, but it is as if he had become someone else and he is not himself and does not count as his own there, but has come to belong to that and so is one, having joined, as it were, center to center. For here too when the centers have come together they are one, but there is duality when they are separate.

τότε μὲν οὖν οὔτε ὁρᾷ οὐδὲ διακρίνει ὁ ὁρῶν οὐδὲ φαντάζεται δύο, ἀλλ᾽ οἷον ἄλλος γενόμενος καὶ οὐκ αὐτὸς οὐδ᾽ αὑτοῦ συντελεῖ ἐκεῖ, κἀκείνου γενόμενος ἕν ἐστιν ὥσπερ κέντρῳ κέντρον συνάψας. καὶ γὰρ ἐνταῦθα συνελθόντα ἕν ἐστι, τό τε δύο, ὅταν χωρίς.[49]

(xxv) Since, then, *there were not two*, but the seer himself was one with the seen (for it was not really seen, but united to him), if he remembers who he became when he was united with that, he will have an image of that in himself. He was one himself, with *no distinction* in himself either in relation to himself or to other things....

ἐπεὶ τοίνυν δύο οὐκ ἦν, ἀλλ᾽ ἓν ἦν αὐτὸς ὁ ἰδὼν πρὸς τὸ ἑωραμένον, ὡς ἂν μὴ ἑωραμένον, ἀλλ᾽ ἡνωμένον, ὃς ἐγένετο ὅτε ἐκείνῳ ἐμίγνυτο εἰ μεμνῷτο, ἔχοι ἂν παρ᾽ ἑαυτῷ ἐκείνου εἰκόνα. ἦν δὲ ἓν καὶ αὐτὸς διαφορὰν ἐν αὑτῷ οὐδεμίαν πρὸς ἑαυτὸν ἔχων οὔτε κατὰ ἄλλα...[50]

---

48 VI.7.34.13–14; this passage seems to me more like a description of theistic union than of monistic identity, because the unification in question is described from the perspective of the soul as something which she sees and which involves a minimal degree of duality (cf. "*both* are one").

49 VI.9.10.14–18.

50 VI.9.11.4–9.

Thus, in response to the debate over the description of Plotinian mysticism, I suggest that both the theistic union interpretation and the monistic identity interpretation are partially correct but not entirely accurate. For man's ascent to the One in the stage of philosophy is a dynamic process which is not only irreducible to a particular phase, but also incapable of reaching complete unity with the One Itself.

2.5 Section Summary

For Plotinus, the intrinsic structure of desire consists in the self-relation of the desiring agent, and desire is a certain reflexive attitude by which the agent relates toward his own desire (Section 1). This attitude can be properly called philosophical, insofar as it is that by which the philosopher regards his own desire as the origin, object, method and end of his philosophical inquiry. Reflexive desire, or desire for knowledge, is therefore constitutive of philosophical inquiry. By locating the desire for knowledge as the vantage point for our investigation, we have indirectly shown that Plotinus' psychological analysis of desire can also be understood as the practical guidance of doing philosophy. For to "do" philosophy just is to take on the philosophical attitude of desire for knowledge, to know oneself as one who desires to know, and to clarify to oneself what one's own experience of desire is about.

Chapter Summary

The notion of desire for knowledge provides us a vantage point to grasp the essential message behind Plotinus' practice of philosophy. According to Section 1, desire for knowledge is the intrinsic structure of all modes of desire. To base the practice of philosophy upon desire for knowledge, consequently, renders the ascent to the One universally accessible to every human being as long as he or she is endowed with the faculty of reason and moved by the experience of desire. According to Section 2, desire for knowledge is constitutive of philosophical inquiry: desire not only arouses intellectual curiosity about one's own desire to search for the truth behind it, but also intensifies itself to such an extent that it ultimately pushes one beyond philosophy to search for that which lies beyond the intelligible, namely the One.

Chapter 3 The Practice of Negative Theology

For Plotinus, the philosopher desires to know the One but only ends up reducing It to an intelligible being. This problem is overcome when the philosopher realizes that the One is far more original and desirable than the intelligible beings which he is able to know. Enflamed by the more intense desire to know the One insofar as It is beyond all beings, the philosopher will be transformed into a "dialectician" or negative theologian. Such is the background from which Plotinus' practice of negative theology (henceforth *negative theology* in short unless otherwise noted) comes into play, which can be roughly characterized as the intellectual inquiry into the One insofar as It is beyond all beings.

This sketch of negative theology helps to bring to light one of its distinctive features to be studied in this chapter. Like philosophy, negative theology is an intellectual inquiry and rests upon the experience of desire to know the One, which is itself *unknowable*. Therefore, although negative theology does not reduce the One into an intelligible being but rather seeks to know It insofar as It transcends all beings, it fails to realize that the One, in reality, must also transcend the confinement of negative theology. For this reason, negative theology runs into the *same problem* just like philosophy does, namely reducing the One into an object of knowledge. However, negative theology stands out because its *solution* is radically different from that of philosophy. Philosophy, let us recall, is overcome and develops into negative theology when the philosopher realizes that there is something more original and desirable to be known. However, since there is nothing beyond the One which is beyond all beings, there is nowhere for negative theology to go, and the negative theologian has to realize that there is nothing to be known. In this sense, negative theology is not simply an intellectual inquiry into the One like philosophy is, but rather the praxis of *abandonment* (τὸ ἐᾶν) which *dissolves* (ἀφανίζει) itself by means of this inquiry.[1] The self-dissolution of negative theology will be the focus of this chapter.

This feature of Plotinus' negative theology, I suggest, becomes most distinctive when contrasted against the thought of Pseudo-Dionysius the Areopagite (henceforth Dionysius) in his *De Mystica Theologia*. Thus, in Section 1 I will outline the basic ideas of Dionysius' negative theology of *unknowing* (ἀγνωσία). Against this background, I offer in Section 2 a detailed exegesis of VI.7.36 in

---

1   These two keywords appear in VI.7.36.15 and VI.7.41.13 respectively, and will be clarified in the following sections.

which Plotinus' negative theology of abandonment is set forth. In Section 3, its central tenet will be examined more closely in the light of other passages from the *Enneads*.

Section 1 Dionysius' Negative Theology of Unknowing

The profound influence of Dionysius' thought is beyond question: it can be seen not only in Christian spirituality of the Catholic and the Orthodox Church, but also throughout the history of Western philosophy.[2] His contemporary relevance, on the other hand, owes a lot to the theological writings of the French phenomenologist, Jean-Luc Marion.[3] More recently, Eric Perl tries to demonstrate the Neoplatonic philosophical elements underlying Dionysius' mystical thought.[4] In this and the next section, I shall set aside historical issues and theological

---

2   For Dionysius' influence on Christian spirituality, see Louth, Andrew, 'The Reception of Dionysius up to Maximus the Confessor', *Re-Thinking Dionysius the Areopagite*, ed. Sarah Coakley and Charles M. Stang, Blackwell Publishing, Malden 2009, 43–53; idem., 'The Reception of Dionysius in the Byzantine World: Maximus to Palamas', ibid., 43–53; McGinn, 1991, 157–185. For a synopsis of the Western Dionysian commentators see Rorem, Paul, *Pseudo-Dionysius: A Commentary on the Texts and an Introduction to Their Influence*, Oxford University Press, New York, 1993, 29–38, 73–83, 118–126, 167–175, 214–225, 237–240. For Thomas Aquinas' appropriation of Dionysius' negative theology, see his *Summa Theologica* I, q.12–13 and O'Rourke, Fran, *Pseudo-Dionysius and the Metaphysics of Aquinas* (2nd edition), University of Notre Dame Press, Notre Dame, 2005, 22–61, 85–113, 133–187, 225–274.

3   See Marion, Jean-Luc, *The Idol and Distance: Five Studies*, tr. Thomas A. Carlson, Fordham University Press, New York 2001, 139–196; idem., *In Excess: Studies of Saturated Phenomena*, tr. Robyn Horner and Vincent Berraud, Fordham University Press, New York, 2002, 128–162; Jones, Tamsin, *A Genealogy of Marion's Philosophy of Religion*, Indiana University Press, Bloomington, 2011. For the influence and relevance of Dionysius' Neoplatonism in contemporary Continental philosophy, see Hankey, Wayne, 'French Neoplatonism in the 20th century', *Animus* 4, 1999, 135–167; idem., 'Neoplatonism and Contemporary Constructions and Deconstructions of Modern Subjectivity', *Philosophy and Freedom: The Legacy of James Doull*, ed. David G. Peddle and Neil G. Robertson, University of Toronto Press, Toronto, 2003, 250–278; idem., 'Neoplatonism and Contemporary French Philosophy', *Dionysius* 23, 2005, 161–190; and idem., 'Jean-Luc Marion's Dionysian Neoplatonism', *Perspectives sur le neoplatonisme, International Socicety for Neoplatonic Studies, Actes du colloque de 2006*, ed. Martin Achard, Wayne Hankey, and Jean-Marc Nabonne, Les Presses de L'Universite Laval, Quebec, 2009, 267–280.

4   Cf. Perl, Eric D., *Theophany: The Neoplatonic Philosophy of Dionysius the Areopagite*, State University of New York Press, Albany, 2007.

interpretations, and focus mainly on extracting the main argument from a key passage of Dionysius' original *De Mystica Theologia*; reference to Perl's interpretation will be made when necessary.

To start with, the comparison between Plotinus, the non-theistic thinker, and Dionysius, the Christian theologian, calls for some explanation. My basic reason is simply that they use similar terminologies, with reference to which their respective connotations and context can be mapped out. Instead of giving in-depth explanation beforehand, here I shall simply point to the two most important concepts which Dionysius shares with Plotinus, namely union or *henosis*, and God as that which transcends or is *beyond all beings*, as we can see from the basic thesis of Dionysius' negative theology:

> [...] with your understanding laid aside, [you have] to strive upward as much as you can toward union with him who is beyond all beings and knowledge.
>
> πρὸς τὴν ἕνωσιν, ὡς ἐφικτόν, ἀγνώστως ἀνατάθητι τοῦ ὑπὲρ πᾶσαν οὐσίαν καὶ γνῶσιν.[5]

As Dionysius makes clear in this passage, it is by *unknowing* (ἀγνωσία) or "laying aside the understanding" that we ascend to henosis. Here ἀγνωσία refers not merely to the state of ignorance or the absence of knowledge, but more technically to *the method of putting to rest the activity of intellect*. But why does it lead to henosis? As Dionysius explains:

> What has actually to be said about the Cause of everything is this. Since it is the Cause of all beings, we should posit and ascribe to it all the affirmations we make in regard to beings, and, more appropriately, we should negate all these affirmations, since it surpasses all beings. Now we should not conclude that the negations are simply the opposites of the affirmations, but rather that *the cause of all is considerably prior to this, beyond privations, beyond every denial, beyond every assertion.*
>
> Δέον ἐπ' αὐτῇ καὶ πάσας τὰς τῶν ὄντων τιθέναι καὶ καταφάσκειν θέσεις, ὡς πάντων αἰτίᾳ, καὶ πάσας αὐτὰς κυριώτερον ἀποφάσκειν, ὡς ὑπὲρ πάντα ὑπερούσῃ, καὶ μὴ οἴεσθαι τὰς ἀποφάσεις ἀντικειμένας εἶναι ταῖς καταφάσεσιν, ἀλλὰ πολὺ πρότερον αὐτὴν ὑπὲρ τὰς στερήσεις εἶναι τὴν ὑπὲρ πᾶσαν καὶ ἀφαίρεσιν καὶ θέσιν.[6]

Dionysius distinguishes three ways of knowing God in ascending order. On the positive way, we first ascribe to God attributes of beings insofar as He is their cause. But since the cause of all beings is itself not a being, we then take on the negative way and deny that these attributes apply to Him exactly. However, since the cause of all beings is not the opposition or privation of beings, but eminently

---

5   *MT*, 1000A.
6   *MT*, 1000B, my italics.

transcends them, we shall assume the eminent way of *unknowing* and no longer know God either positively or negatively.

Although Dionysius is addressing a central issue of the Christian theology, the *philosophical* presupposition which underlies his account is especially noteworthy. According to Perl,

> Neoplatonic and Dionysian 'negative theology' and 'mysticism' is [sic] an aspect of rational metaphysics… in the Greek philosophical tradition that Dionysius draws on and continues. The foundational principle of Neoplatonic thought is the doctrine that to be is to be intelligible. *The identification of being… as that which can be apprehended by intellection is the basis not only for the Platonic and Neoplatonic identification of being as form or idea… but also for the Neoplatonic insistence that the One or Good, the source of reality, is itself "beyond being".*[7]

The philosophical tradition to which Perl refers can be traced back to Parmenides, who is arguably the first Western philosopher to claim that thinking and being are one and the same:

> Denken und des Gedankens Ziel ist eins; denn nicht ohne das Seiende, in dem es sich ausgesprochen findet, kannst Du das Denken antreffen.
>
> ταὐτὸν δ᾿ ἐστὶ νοεῖν τε καὶ ὅυνεκέν ἐστι νόημα. οὐ γὰρ ἄνευ τοῦ ἐόντος, ἐν ὧι πεφατισμένον ἐστίν, εὑρήσεις τὸ νοεῖν.[8]

After Parmenides, Plato propounds a similar thesis in *Phaedrus*:

> What is in this place is without color and without shape and without solidity, a being that really is what it is, the subject of all true knowledge, visible only to intelligence, the soul's steersman.[9]

Now Dionysius' own thesis runs as follows:

> And if all knowledge is of that which is and is limited to the realm of the existent, then whatever transcends being must also transcend knowledge.
>
> Εἰ γὰρ αἱ γνώσεις πᾶσαι τῶν ὄντων εἰσὶ καὶ εἰς τὰ ὄντα τὸ πέρας ἔχουσιν, ἡ πάσης οὐσίας ἐπέκεινα καὶ πάσης γνώσεως ἐστιν ἐξῃρημένη.[10]

The intellect is correlated to the intelligible beings as its proper object. From this claim Dionysius draws a thesis fundamental for his negative theology: that which

---

7   Perl, 2007, 5, my italics.
8   Diels, H. and Kranz, W., *Die Fragmente der Vorsokratiker*, 2nd edition, Weidmannsche Buchhandlung, Berlin, 1906, fr. 8.34–36.
9   *Phaedrus*, 247c6–8.
10   *DN* 593A.

is beyond intelligible beings is correlated not to the intellect, but to that which is beyond the intellect. In particular, when Dionysius claims that "we should not conclude that the negations are [...] but rather [conclude] that the cause of all is..." (μὴ οἴεσθαι τὰς ἀποφάσεις... εἶναι... ἀλλὰ πολὺ πρότερον αὐτὴν... εἶναι), he is asking us to treat God as a peculiar object of reasoning in the eminent way of unknowing. Accordingly, unknowing is not just about *not knowing God* as a being or non-being, but about "*knowing* beyond the mind by knowing nothing" (τῷ μηδὲν γινώσκειν ὑπὲρ νοῦν γινώσκων).[11] This eminent way does not lead to the complete cessation of the mind and sheer ignorance, but is rather a method of properly knowing God by *not knowing Him as a being*. For Dionysius, therefore, mystical knowledge of God is indeed possible, as long as God is not treated as a being and knowledge is not understood in the ordinary sense. For this reason, Dionysius likens the result of unknowing not to total darkness, but paradoxically to "the ray of the divine shadow (τοῦ θείου σκότους ἀκτῖνα)",[12] and "the divine ray (τὴν θεαρχικὴν ἀκτῖνα) [which] enlightens us only by being upliftingly concealed (ἀναγωγικῶς περικεκαλυμμένην) in a variety of sacred veils".[13]

In the last analysis, then, for us human to know God is just to know that we cannot know Him as a being and hence to put to rest our activity of intellect:

> We leave behind us all our own notions of the divine. We call a halt to the activities of our minds and, to the extent that is proper, we approach the ray which transcends being. Here, in a manner no words can describe, preexisted all the goals of all knowledge and it is of a kind that neither intelligence nor speech can lay hold of it nor can it at all be contemplated since it surpasses everything and is wholly beyond our capacity to know it.

> [...] καὶ μετὰ πᾶσαν τὴν καθ᾽ ἡμᾶς τῶν θεοειδῶν νόησιν ἀποπαύοντες ἡμῶν τὰς νοερὰς ἐνεργείας εἰς τὴν ὑπερούσιον ἀκτῖνα κατὰ τὸ θεμιτὸν ἐπιβάλλομεν, ἐν ᾗ πάντα τὰ πέρατα πασῶν τῶν γνώσεων ὑπεραρρήτως προϋφέστηκεν, ἣν οὔτε ἐννοῆσαι δυνατὸν οὔτε εἰπεῖν οὔτε ὅλως πως θεωρῆσαι διὰ τὸ πάντων αὐτὴν ἐξηρημένην εἶναι καὶ ὑπεράγνωστον...[14]

---

11 Cf. *MT*, 1001A: "Here, renouncing all that the mind may conceive, wrapped entirely in the intangible and the invisible, he [Moses] belongs completely to him who is everything. Here, being neither oneself nor someone else, one is supremely united to the completely unknown by an inactivity of all knowledge, and knows beyond the mind by knowing nothing.".

12 *MT*, 1000A.

13 *CH*, 121B.

14 *DN*, 592C-D: see also *DN*, 593C: "[...] the union of divinized minds with the Light beyond all deity occurs in the cessation (ἀπόπαυσιν) of all intelligent activity..." See also Perl, 2007, 12–14,104–108and Rorem, 1993, 187–189.

From the above analysis we can sum up three points. First, Dionysius' negative theology of unknowing is not merely the *negative propositional knowledge* that God cannot be known and is not a being, but mainly the *intellectual exercise* by which the mind knows God by not knowing Him as a mere being. Second and more important, the *mystical knowledge* thus engendered is understood as the unification with God or *henosis*. Hence third, for Dionysius, negative theology and henosis are *correlated* to each other like the act of knowing and the corresponding knowledge: the former is what the negative theologian does, and the latter is what he thereby attains. In specific, although henosis does not depend on unknowing as its cause, still the former would not exist without the latter. This is why Dionysius sometimes refers to such mystical unification simply in terms of unknowing. For example, in his exegesis of Deut. 24,12–18 it is said that Moses "plunges into the truly mysterious darkness of unknowing" (τὸν γνόφον τῆς ἀγνοσίας εἰσδύνει τὸν ὄντως μυστικόν) and "is supremely united to the completely unknown by an inactivity of all knowledge" (τῷ παντελῶς δὲ ἀγνώστῳ τῇ πάσης γνώσεως ἀνενεργησίᾳ κατὰ τὸ κρεῖττον ἑνούμενος).[15] The upshot is that Dionysian mysticism amounts, so to speak, to a mysticism mediated by and actualized in the intellect. As Albert the Great, one of the most prominent Dionysian commentators in the Latin West, remarks:

> But God is what is best and he is the ultimate perfection of our intellects, so for our intellect, being united with Him is for the very best. [...] our minds receive a certain divine light, which [...] raises them above all their natural ways of seeing things, and this is how our minds come to see God, though only in a *blurred and undefined knowledge* "that" He is.[16]

Section 2 Plotinus' Negative Theology according to VI.7.36

In this section I analyze Plotinus' account of the practice of negative theology presented in VI.7.36. I do not aim at a detailed exposition of Plotinus' negative theology in its entirety; my intention is rather to highlight its unique features which distinguish it from Dionysius' version. Therefore, my explanation will be relatively brief when it comes to those parts similar to Dionysius'. The main theses in this section, to anticipate, run as follow: Unlike Dionysius' negative theology, Plotinus' negative theology does not take an epistemic approach to acquiring

---

15   *MT* 1001A.
16   *Commentary on Dionysius' Mystical Theology*, in *Albert and Thomas: Selected Writings*, ed. and tr. Simon Tugwell, Paulist Press, New York. 1988, 164 and 172, my italics.

mystical knowledge about the One. Furthermore, unlike Dionysius, for Plotinus negative theology is not correlated to henosis.

2.1 VI.7.36.3–5: Introduction

Before elaborating his negative theology, Plotinus presents a more detailed explanation of the goal of his mystical teaching:

(i) The knowledge or touching of the Good is the greatest thing, and Plato says it is the "greatest study"…

ἔστι μὲν γὰρ ἡ τοῦ ἀγαθοῦ εἴτε γνῶσις εἴτε ἐπαφὴ μέγιστόν, καὶ μέγιστόν φησι τοῦτ εἶναι μάθημα, …[17]

The goal, "knowledge of the Good", is mentioned in connection with "touching of the Good", which is a metaphor for henosis. According to Pierre Hadot, "knowing" and "touching" refer in the quoted passage to two distinct things: the former refers to the rational theology about the One based on the power of *discursive* intellect, while the latter to the ineffable mystical contact based on the power of *loving* intellect.[18] This amounts to the distinction between intellect and desire in Plotinus' thought.

However, as far as exegesis is concerned, this interpretation is not convincing, because the expression εἴτε…εἴτε usually indicates cases which are equally possible or equivalent, rather than opposed to or different from each other. Without hastening to any pre-mature determination, we could at least ascertain that "knowledge" and "touch", whatever they could be, are *not* distinct from each other. A more philosophical explanation, based upon Plotinus' metaphysics, is that the One is absolutely simple and that the One which is really "known" cannot be distinct from the One which is really "touched".

On this interpretation, when it comes to Plotinus' teaching of henosis, "knowledge" is not simply a representation of objective facts detached from human concern, and "touch" is far more than an expression of subjective attitude toward matters of fact. The notion of "mystical" or "religious experience" as understood in contemporary philosophy of religion is irrelevant to Plotinus. According to Ludwig Wittgenstein, the mystical shows itself but cannot be expressed in descriptive language.[19] Keith Yandell, among others, argues that

---

17   VI.7.36.3–5.
18   Hadot, Pierre. *Plotin, Traité 38*. Les Editions du Cerf, Paris, 1987, 346–348.
19   Cf. *Tractatus* 6.522: "There are, indeed, things that cannot be put into words. They make themselves manifest. They are what is mystical."

religious experience provides cognitive evidence for God because of its similarity to perceptual experience.[20] Both of them presuppose the dualism between belief and desire, and the distinction between world-to-mind mind-to-world direction of fit. For Plotinus, by contrast, such a dualism not only drives man's practical life into discord, but is also in conflict with the ultimate reality which is absolutely simple.

Through comparison with contemporary philosophy, therefore, the least thing we can gather from (i) is that it is incorrect to reduce Plotinus' "touch" of the Good to a kind of passion (πάθος), sentiment or drive which is either opposed or irrelevant to the intellect and reason (νοῦς, λόγος). Likewise, "knowledge" of the Good is not a proposition abstracted from real-life experience; it is rather situated within, and constantly interacts with, the concrete life-world of the negative theologian. These points also explain why Plotinus does not refer to "the greatest study" with the term ἐπιστήμη, meaning *science* or a systematic body of objective knowledge. Rather, Plotinus' technical term is μάθημα, which means learning experience, and even "learning by experience" or experiential learning. As such, this term gives us a further clue to understand the expression "the knowledge and touch of the Good": it does not describe the content of the "greatest study", but simply prescribes the methods by which the "greatest study" should be carried out.

2.2 VI.7.36.5–8: the Indirect Study

After laying down the task of the "greatest study" and affirming the possibility of attaining "knowledge" and "touch" of the One, Plotinus proceeds to outline three ways of knowing the One which comprise the "indirect study":

(ii) [...] and Plato says it is the "greatest study", not calling the looking at It *[the One]* a "study", but learning about It beforehand. We are taught about It by comparisons and negations and knowledge of the things which come from It and certain methods and ascent by degrees, ...

καὶ μέγιστόν φησι τοῦτ᾽ εἶναι μάθημα, οὐ τὸ πρὸς αὐτὸ ἰδεῖν μάθημα λέγων, ἀλλὰ περὶ αὐτοῦ μαθεῖν τι πρότερον. διδάσκουσι μὲν οὖν ἀναλογίαι τε καὶ ἀφαιρέσεις καὶ γνώσεις τῶν ἐξ αὐτοῦ καὶ ἀναβασμοί τινες, ...[21]

---

20   Cf. Yandell, Keith E., *The Epistemology of Religious Experience*, Cambridge University Press, Cambridge, 1993, 33–57, 256–275; Swinburne, 2004, 293–298.

21   VI.7.36.5–8

Literally, "τὸ πρὸς αὐτὸ ἰδεῖν" means *the direct vision of the One*, while "περὶ αὐτοῦ μαθεῖν" *the indirect study* which consists of the positive, negative and eminent ways of knowing the One. According to Plotinus, "the One is all things and not a single one of them: it is the principle of all things, not all things."[22] Thus we should first understand the One on the positive way, namely by the "knowledge of the things which come from it" (γνώσεσι τῶν ἐξ αὐτοῦ) and the "comparisons" (ἀναλογίαις) with them.[23]

But to know the One insofar as It is the cause of all beings already implies that the One *as such* is not thereby known. Therefore we have to take on the second, negative way of "negations" (ἀφαιρέσεις) and emphasize that the One is not a being and cannot be known as such. As Plotinus explains:

(iii) Since the substance which is generated [from the One] is form [...] the One must be without form. But if It is without form It is not a substance; for a substance must be some one particular thing, something, that is, defined and limited; but it is impossible to apprehend the One as a particular thing: for then It would not be the principle, but only that particular thing which you said It was. But if all things are in that which is generated [from the One], which of the things in It are you going to say that the One is?

τῆς δὲ γενομένης οὐσίας εἴδους οὔσης [...] ἀνάγκη ἀνείδεον ἐκεῖνο εἶναι. ἀνείδεον δὲ ὂν οὐκ οὐσία· τόδε γάρ τι δεῖ τὴν οὐσίαν εἶναι· τοῦτο δὲ ὡρισμένον· τὸ δὲ οὐκ ἔστι λαβεῖν ὡς τόδε· ἤδη γὰρ οὐκ ἀρχή, ἀλλ᾽ ἐκεῖνο μόνον, ὃ τόδε εἴρηκας εἶναι. εἰ οὖν τὰ πάντα ἐν τῷ γενομένῳ, τί τῶν ἐν τούτῳ, ἐκεῖνο ἐρεῖς;[24]

However, that the One is not a being and cannot be known as such is itself a negative *attribute*, and to ascribe such an attribute to the One still imposes on It a certain limitation and multiplicity, which is absurd. For this reason, the eminent way of "ascents" (ἀναβασμοί) is needed to *transcend* both the affirmative and the negative way of knowing the One:

(iv) Since It is none of them, it can only be said to be beyond them. But these things are beings, and being: so It is "beyond being". This phrase "beyond being" does not mean that It is a particular thing—for it makes no positive statement about It—and it does not say Its name, but all it implies is that It

---

22   V.2.1.1–2.

23   Cf. V.3.14.1–8, VI.8.7.31–32, VI.8.7.42–45, VI.8.8.1–7, VI.8.13.47–50; see also Gerson, 1994, 15–16, Bussanich, 1996, 45 and Perl, 2007, 12–14.

24   V.5.6.2–9.

is "not this". But if this is what the phrase does, it in no ways comprehends the One:...

οὐδὲν δὲ τούτων ὂν μόνον ἂν λέγοιτο ἐπέκεινα τούτων. ταῦτα δὲ τὰ ὄντα καὶ τὸ ὄν· ἐπέκεινα ἄρα ὄντος. τὸ γὰρ ἐπέκεινα ὄντος οὐ τόδε λέγει—οὐ γὰρ τίθησιν—οὐδὲ ὄνομα αὐτοῦ λέγει, ἀλλὰ φέρει μόνον τὸ οὐ τοῦτο. τοῦτο δὲ ποιοῦν οὐδαμοῦ αὐτὸ περιλαμβάνει·[25]

Plotinus' eminent way, like Dionysius' unknowing, also aims at the cessation of the intellect's activity in approaching the One. However, there is an important difference between these two approaches. For Dionysius, the cessation is correlated to the mystical knowledge of God identified as henosis. For Plotinus, by contrast, the cessation amounts to sheer intellectual darkness; indeed, for reasons that will be clarified in more detail in the sections below, he emphasizes that the eminent way only makes up the *indirect* study about the One. Relatedly, although both Dionysius and Plotinus claim that God or the One is beyond all beings and cannot be known as such, the former understands this claim as equivalent to the mystical knowledge of God, whereas the latter treats it simply as a cautious *forewarning* that our thought and language in no way comprehend the One.

2.3 VI.7.36.8–15: the Direct Vision

Plotinus is in agreement with Dionysius that man can possess some kinds of knowledge of the ultimate reality. But he also goes farther than Dionysius, because such knowledge is only the *preliminary* stage of his negative theology as a whole and should be superseded by the "direct vision" (τὸ πρὸς ἰδεῖν) whereby man "*is put on the way*" to the One:

(v)   *We are taught about It* by comparisons and negations and knowledge of the things which come from It and certain methods and ascent by degrees, *but we are put on the way to It* by purifications and virtues and adorning and by gaining footholds in the intelligible [sic] and settling ourselves firmly there and feasting on its contents.

δίδάσκουσι μὲν οὖν ἀναλογίαι τε καὶ ἀφαιρέσεις καὶ γνώσεις τῶν ἐξ αὐτοῦ καὶ ἀναβασμοί τινες, πορεύουσι δὲ καθάρσεις πρὸς αὐτὸ καὶ ἀρεταὶ καὶ κοσμήσεις καὶ τοῦ νοητοῦ ἐπιβάσεις καὶ ἐπ᾽ αὐτοῦ ἱδρύσεις καὶ τῶν ἐκεῖ ἑστιάσεις.[26]

---

25   V.5.6.9–15.
26   VI.7.36.5–10.

The textual evidence that this passage is discussing the "direct vision" is that it is contrasted against the "indirect" study about the One explained in Section 2.2. On this interpretation, it is important to note that this second stage is called direct not because it is immediately united with the *One* without any distinction, but because it concerns the negative theologian's ascetical trainings of *himself* (ἄσκησις) which lead him to the world of the intelligible beings. Hadot has pointed out that the terms *purifications, adornments* and *feast* refer back to Platonic dialogues and stem from Plato's practical philosophy.[27] But why are they relevant in the "greatest study", and indeed more advanced than the indirect study? The reason, I suppose, might be as follows:

To start with, it is noteworthy that the first stage is characterized as indirect not because it does not comprehend the One as such. Rather, the fact that in the second stage the negative theologian becomes relevant suggests that a *personal* or *existential* element is missing in the first approach. Just as biology, the science of life, does not directly contribute to the biologist's good life, so the theoretical knowledge about the One at most satisfies the negative theologian's curiosity but remains indirect or *indifferent* to his personal concern. The abstract and impersonal character of such knowledge seems especially problematic in the "greatest study", because that which does not in one way or another answer to the mystic's personal concern cannot be called "the greatest".

However, as Plotinus argues below, because the mystic can acquire the theoretical knowledge about the One only by means of *his own* inquiry and understanding, he cannot really know anything about the One without first preparing himself for the mindsets and methods proper for such an inquiry.

(vi) For that which investigates is the soul, and she should know what she is as an investigating soul, so that she may learn first about herself, whether she has the power to investigate things of this kind, and if she has an eye of the right kind to see them, and if the investigation is suitable for her. For if the objects are alien, what is the point? But if they are akin, the investigation is suitable and discovery is possible.

τὸ γὰρ ζητοῦν ἐστι ψυχή, καὶ τί ὂν ζητεῖ γνωστέον αὐτῇ, ἵνα αὐτὴν πρότερον μάθῃ, εἰ δύναμιν ἔχει τοῦ τὰ τοιαῦτα ζητεῖν, καὶ εἰ ὄμμα τοιοῦτον ἔχει, οἷον ἰδεῖν, καὶ εἰ προσήκει ζητεῖν. εἰ μὲν γὰρ ἀλλότρια, τί δεῖ; εἰ δὲ συγγενῆ, καὶ προσήκει καὶ δύναται εὑρεῖν.[28]

---

27   Cf. Hadot, *Traité 38*, p.348–349 and *Phaedo*, 67c-d, 69b, 114e; *Timaeus*, 90c5 and *Phaedrus* 247e4.

28   V.1.1.32–35; see also V.3.6, V.8.11 and VI.9.5.

Note that the point is not to search for or invent a proper *method* for the inquiry, but to prepare the *soul* herself for mastering such a method, for the method does not work by itself but must always depend on someone who knows how to use it well. Consequently, although the *content* of the knowledge about the One remains indifferent to the negative theologian, the *formation* or *acquisition*-process thereof is always directly based upon his ascetical trainings by which he works upon and transforms *himself*. The upshot is that the dynamic conversion (ἐπιστροφή) of ascetical trainings brings the negative theologian to the One closer than the theoretical knowledge about the One does, because the latter is necessarily grounded upon or conditioned by the former. It is in this sense that ascetical trainings are rightly considered to be elemental for Plotinus' negative theology.

Among all the trainings, including moral purifications and contemplation of natural beauties, it is through *self-contemplation* that the negative theologian acts upon and transforms himself most completely:

(vii) But whoever has become at once contemplator and all the rest and object of his contemplation, and, since he has become substance and intellect and "the complete living being", no longer looks at it from outside—when he has become this he is near, and that Good is next above him, and already close by, shining upon all the intelligible world.

> ὅστις δὲ γεγένηται ὁμοῦ θεατής τε καὶ θέαμα αὐτὸς αὑτοῦ καὶ τῶν ἄλλων καὶ γενόμενος οὐσία καὶ νοῦς καὶ ζῷον παντελὲς μηκέτι ἔξωθεν αὐτὸ βλέποι—τοῦτο δὲ γενόμενος ἐγγύς ἐστι, καὶ τὸ ἐφεξῆς ἐκεῖνο, καὶ πλησίον αὐτὸ ἤδη ἐπὶ παντὶ τῷ νοητῷ ἐπιστίλβον.[29]

Plotinus has already introduced his doctrine of self-contemplation in the practice of philosophy (cf. Chapter 2). There the point is to contrast it against the desire for objects: man's desire is "actualized" not when an object gratifies him, but when he becomes content and puts down his desires for the object through the practice of contemplation. In explaining Plotinus' basic intention, it is suggested in Chapter 2 that the Plotinian contemplation is a kind of meditation rather than cognition, and that it is attained precisely when nothing is known in an ordinarily cognitive sense. Here, in the second stage of negative theology, Plotinus' point is to highlight the intimacy between self-contemplation and the

---

29   VI.7.36.10–15. Plotinus also discusses other ascetic praxes, such as moral purifications (I.2), dialectics (I.3) and contemplation of nature (III.8) and of beauty (I.6 and V.8).

One: self-contemplation brings the contemplator or the negative theologian closest to the One than does any other self-training, such as moral purifications and contemplation of natural beauties. While the focus is now different, the reason remains the same: for Plotinus, self-contemplation is not a piece of information about oneself but a technique of meditation to be performed, and its goal is not to acquire knowledge about oneself in the ordinary sense, but to attain self-control and forestall mental distraction. And in the second stage of negative theology, this practice becomes all the more relevant, precisely because it helps the negative theologian to prepare for an appropriate attitude toward the inquiry into the One: the attitude that his inquiry should neither attend to nor be distracted by any *being*, because what it searches for is *beyond* all beings.

2.4 VI.7.36.15–21: the Abandonment of Contemplation

Since the One is beyond all beings, It does not think Itself like the intellect does. After VI.7.36, Plotinus devotes several chapters to emphasize exactly this point.[30] Therefore, through the practice of self-contemplation the negative theologian can at best "become substance, intellect and complete life",[31] but he is still unable to attain the unification with the One. This is why Plotinus says in (vii) that when the negative theologian contemplates himself, the One is not united with him, but only "next above him and already close by, shining upon the intelligible world." So what should the negative theologian do now? At this point, Plotinus introduces his unique method, namely *abandonment* (τὸ ἐᾶν). Since this is the most crucial part in Plotinus' entire negative theology, I shall examine its descriptions more carefully.

(viii)   It is there that one lets all study go; up to a point one has been led along and settled firmly in beauty and as far as this one thinks that in which one is, but is carried out of it by the surge of the wave of Intellect itself...

   ἔνθα δὴ ἐάσας τις πᾶν μάθημα, καὶ μέχρι του παιδαγωγηθεὶς καὶ ἐν καλῷ ἱδρυθείς, ἐν ᾧ μέν ἐστι, μέχρι τούτου νοεῖ, ἐξενεχθεὶς δὲ τῷ αὐτοῦ τοῦ νοῦ οἷον κύματι...[32]

A few clarifications of the text are in order. First, "all study" refers to the indirect study and the direct vision explained in Section 2.2 and 2.3, but the constant references to the negative theologian himself indicate that the emphasis is placed

---

30   Cf. VI.7.37–42.
31   VI.7.36.12.
32   VI.7.36.15–18.

upon the latter. The phrase "one lets all study go" (ἐάσας τις πᾶν μάθημα) there-fore introduces the method of *abandonment* which surpasses the practice of self-contemplation and approaches the One more closely.

Second, because the negative theologian thinks as far as (μέχρι) he is led and settled in the beauty of *intelligible* objects, and because it is precisely at this point that he is said to be "carried out of it by the surge of the wave of Intellect itself" (ἐξενεχθεὶς δὲ τῷ αὐτοῦ τοῦ νοῦ οἷον κύματι), the phrase "surge of the wave of Intellect itself" should refer to the intellect's *proper function* of contemplating intelligible objects. The "of" is an appositive genitive by which "intellect itself" is used to explain "surge": the intellect itself is likened to the powerful movement of surge, because the negative theologian contemplates the intelligible objects "as far as possible". For this reason, we should emphasize that the surge is not a metaphor of an ecstatic feeling or hyper-noetic intuition which transcends the normal operation of intellect, but rather symbolizes the radical actualization of the intellect's proper function.

Finally, the usage of δὲ ("and then") rather than ἀλλὰ ("but") indicates that the phrases thus connected do not oppose to each other but have a certain degree of coherence, continuity or dependency.

Accordingly, we can abbreviate the long-winding sentence "as far as this one thinks that in which one is, but is carried out of it by the surge of the wave of Intellect itself" (μέχρι τούτου νοεῖ ἐξενεχθεὶς δὲ τῷ αὐτοῦ τοῦ νοῦ οἷον κύματι) as follows: when the negative theologian is absorbed *in* con-templation, he is elevated *from* contemplation and elevated *by* contempla-tion. From this follow two consequences the significance of which cannot be overstated. First, abandonment is neither an exalted emotion nor a hyper-noetic intuition, but consists in *the radical actualization of the intellect's own power*. Second, the act of abandonment described here contains an unusual double moment: *abandoning oneself to* or concentrating on contemplation, while *abandoning it* or disregarding it altogether. Therefore, abandonment is neither just a passive withdrawal from contemplation nor an active involve-ment in it, but the *synthesis* of both.

We will have to examine more closely in the sections below why the negative theologian could concentrate on contemplation while disregarding it altogether. Here I shall only emphasize that the abandonment of all study and the end of the second stage of Plotinus' mystical teaching are two sides of the same coin. For this reason, when Plotinus proceeds from VI.7.36.18 onward, he is no longer giv-ing any substantial instruction, but instead digresses to descriptions of subjective experience about what it is like to "see" the One and metaphysical explanation of Its causality:

(ix) *[He is]* lifted on high by a kind of swell and sees suddenly, not seeing how, but the vision fills his eyes with light and does not make him see something else by it, but the light itself is what he sees. For there is not in that Good something seen and Its light, nor intellect and object of intellect, but a ray which generates these afterwards and lets them be beside It; but It Itself is the ray which only generates Intellect and does not extinguish Itself in the generation, but It Itself abides, and that Intellect comes to be because this Good exists. For if this was not of the kind It is, that would not have come into existence.

[...] καὶ ὑψοῦ ὑπ᾽ αὐτοῦ οἷον οἰδήσαντος ἀρθεὶς εἰσεῖδεν ἐξαίφνης οὐκ ἰδὼν ὅπως, ἀλλ᾽ ἡ θέα πλήσασα φωτὸς τὰ ὄμματα οὐ δι᾽ αὐτοῦ πεποίηκεν ἄλλο ὁρᾶν, ἀλλ᾽ αὐτὸ τὸ φῶς τὸ ὅραμα ἦν. οὐ γὰρ ἦν ἐν ἐκείνῳ τὸ μὲν ὁρώμενον, τὸ δὲ φῶς αὐτοῦ, οὐδὲ νοῦς καὶ νοούμενον, ἀλλ᾽ αὐγὴ γεννῶσα ταῦτα εἰς ὕστερον καὶ ἀφεῖσα εἶναι παρ᾽ αὐτῷ· αὐτὸς δὲ αὐγὴ μόνον γεννῶσα νοῦν, οὔτι σβέσασα αὐτῆς ἐν τῷ γεννῆσαι, ἀλλὰ μείνασα μὲν αὐτή, γενομένου δ᾽ ἐκείνου τῷ τοῦτο εἶναι. εἰ γὰρ μὴ τοῦτο τοιοῦτον ἦν, οὐκ ἂν ὑπέστη ἐκεῖνο.[33]

Plotinus' account of mystical vision will be explained in greater detail in the next chapter; now let us highlight only this point: Strictly speaking, since the core of Plotinus' mystical teaching consists of instructions and exercises, descriptions about the (so to speak) "mystical qualia" need not play any substantial role. And because we cannot suppose all the readers to have a mystical experience similar to Plotinus', there is no point for us to examine these descriptions in our present context. With the exercise of abandonment, the second stage of Plotinus' teaching already comes to an end.

2.5 Section Summary

In the light of the comparison with Dionysius, Plotinus' practice of negative theology can be summed up as follows:

First, Dionysius' negative theology takes an epistemic approach to God, and his unknowing is a cognitive activity of the intellect which brings about the mystical knowledge that God is beyond beings. Plotinus' ascetical approach, on the

---

33   VI.7.36.18–26.

other hand, deepens the epistemic approach by highlighting the contemplator's constitutive role in his intellectual inquiry into the One. In emphasizing the mystic's personal engagement, Plotinus' negative theology does not resort to magic, theurgy and secret rites, but remains consistently *rational*, for the practice not only resides in contemplation, but also radicalizes the intellect's proper function. Since this approach contains the negative element of abandonment, we can rightly call it Plotinus' unique version of negative theology.

Second, Dionysius' method of unknowing consists in the cessation of the intellect's proper activity, namely comprehending intelligible beings. But Plotinus' method of abandonment is more sophisticated, for it is about suspending the intellect's proper activity *by means of the same activity*.

Finally, Dionysius' unknowing leads to the mystical knowledge of God identified as henosis. But as we shall explain in the next chapter, Plotinus' abandonment of contemplation does not lead to henosis.

Section 3 Plotinus' Negative Theology of Abandonment

One of the most crucial questions concerning Plotinus' negative theology is why the negative theologian can concentrate on contemplation while disregarding it altogether. Plotinus addresses this question in two passages: the shorter one is found in VI.7.41, and the more elaborate one from V.3.17 is put in the context of his entire mystical teaching. However, the practice of abandonment has not received much scholarly attention. Major commentators, including A. H. Armstrong and Pierre Hadot, subscribe to the so-called doctrine of two intellects which seems to render our present discussion irrelevant and the practice of abandonment pointless. In view of this, it is incumbent on us to look into this doctrine before examining VI.7.41 and V.3.17.

3.1 The Doctrine of Two Intellects in VI.7.35.19–33

Many Plotinian commentators subscribe to the doctrine of two intellects based on the following passage in VI.7.35.

(x)   Intellect also, then, has one power for thinking, by which it looks at the things in itself, and one by which it looks at what transcends it by a *direct awareness and reception*, by which also before it saw only, and by seeing acquired intellect and is one. And that first one is the contemplation of Intellect in its right mind, and the other is Intellect in love, when it goes out of its mind "drunk with the nectar"; then it falls in love, simplified into happiness by having its fill; and it is better for it to be drunk with a drunkenness like this than to be more respectably sober. But does that Intellect see in part, at one time some things and at another others? No, but our rational discourse instructing us makes them come to be, but Intellect always has its thinking and always its not thinking, but looking at that god in another way. For when it saw him it had offspring and was intimately aware of their generation and existence within it; and when it sees these it is said to think, but it sees that by the power by which [later] it was going to think.

καὶ τὸν νοῦν τοίνυν τὴν μὲν ἔχειν δύναμιν εἰς τὸ νοεῖν, ᾗ τὰ ἐν αὐτῷ βλέπει, τὴν δέ, ᾗ τὰ ἐπέκεινα αὐτοῦ ἐπιβολῇ τινι καὶ παραδοχῇ, καθ᾽ ἣν καὶ πρότερον ἑώρα μόνον καὶ ὁρῶν ὕστερον καὶ νοῦν ἔσχε καὶ ἕν ἐστι. καὶ ἔστιν ἐκείνη μὲν ἡ θέα νοῦ ἔμφρονος, αὕτη δὲ νοῦς ἐρῶν, ὅταν ἄφρων γένηται μεθυσθεὶς τοῦ νέκταρος· τότε ἐρῶν γίνεται ἁπλωθεὶς εἰς εὐπάθειαν τῷ κόρῳ· καὶ ἔστιν αὐτῷ μεθύειν βέλτιον ἢ σεμνοτέρῳ εἶναι τοιαύτης μέθης. παρὰ μέρος δὲ ὁ νοῦς ἐκεῖνος ἄλλα, τὰ δὲ ἄλλοτε ἄλλα ὁρᾷ; ἢ οὔ· ὁ δὲ λόγος διδάσκων γινόμενα ποιεῖ, τὸ δὲ ἔχει τὸ νοεῖν ἀεί, ἔχει δὲ καὶ τὸ μὴ νοεῖν, ἀλλὰ ἄλλως ἐκεῖνον βλέπειν. καὶ γὰρ ὁρῶν ἐκεῖνον ἔσχε γεννήματα καὶ συνῄσθετο καὶ τούτων γενομένων καὶ ἐνόντων· καὶ ταῦτα μὲν ὁρῶν λέγεται νοεῖν, ἐκεῖνο δὲ ᾗ δυνάμει ἔμελλε νοεῖν.[34]

According to Armstrong,

Intellect [...] is eternally and unchangingly in two simultaneous states, one "sober" and one "drunk", one knowing and one loving. It eternally pursues its activity of knowing while it is eternally raised above itself in the union of love. The soul of the individual mystic in its ascent to the mystical union is raised first to one and then to the other of these states. [The mystical] contact, vision or union with the One is identical with Intellect's contact, vision or union.[35]

Similarly, Hadot remarks that

The intellect thus has a double rapport with the Good: a mediated rapport when it contemplates the refraction of the power of the Good in the system of Ideas; an unmediated rapport when it tries to remain in contact with the Good from which it emanates, by trying not to be caught up in the multiplicity of Ideas.[36]

---

34   VI.7.35.19–33.
35   Armstrong, A. H., 'Plotinus', *The Cambridge History of Later Greek and Early Medieval Philosophy*, ed. A.H. Armstrong, Cambridge University Press, Cambridge, 1967, 262–263.
36   Hadot, Pierre, 'Neoplatonist Spirituality: Plotinus and Porphyry', *Classical Mediterranean Spirituality*, ed. A.H. Armstrong, Routledge, London, 1986, 243.

In short, it is held that the intellect has two simultaneous states: in the thinking states it contemplates intelligible beings, while in the loving states it is immediately united with the One.[37] If this interpretation is correct, the question concerning the abandonment of contemplation would be trivial. For what leads to henosis is no longer the radicalization of the intellect's proper function (the thinking intellect), but rather the loving intellect (νοῦς ἐρῶν); and the mystical union would be a union actualized by the loving intellect, rather than a union which is somehow mediated through the abandonment of contemplation.

But there are several reasons why I think the passage (x) is irrelevant for our present issue. To start with, the "direct awareness" (ἐπιβολή) and the "reception" (παραδοχή) by which the loving intellect "looks at what transcends it" are two different acts. Ἐπιβολή is a cognate of ἐπιβάλλειν, which means *to throw upon* or *to turn one's attention to*, and ἐπιβολή usually means *an application of the mind to a thing*, or *an act of direct apprehension*. Armstrong's translation of this term in the *Enneads* is usually *intuition*.[38] However, the directness of this act has nothing to do with its lack of distinction from its object, but rather highlights the fact that its movement is straightforward and uninterrupted. So if in passage (x) ἐπιβολή is translated into *direct awareness*, it should refer to the mental act which

---

37 For other similar accounts see Beierwaltes, Werner, *Denken des Einen*, Vittorio Klostermann, Frankfurt am Main, 1985, 141–142; Bussanich, 1996, 56–57; Corrigan, 2005, 32–33; O'Meara, Dominic, 'Plotinus', *The Cambridge History of Philosophy in Later Antiquity*, ed. Lloyd Gerson, Cambridge University Press, Cambridge, 2010, 322–323. For a criticism of this interpretation see Gerson, 1994, 223.

38 In these four passages Armstrong translates ἐπιβολή into *intuition*: "For, again, since knowledge of other things comes to us from intellect, and we are able to know intellect by intellect, by what sort of *simple intuition* (ἐπιβολῇ ἀθρόᾳ) could one grasp this which transcends the nature of intellect?" (III.8.9.19–21) "What then prevents the soul too from having a *unified intuition* of all her objects in one? (τί οὖν κωλύει καὶ ταύτην τὴν ἐπιβολὴν ἀθρόαν ἀθρόων γίγνεσθαι;)" (IV.4.1.19–20) "[...] a man in this state, by his *intuition* of himself (τῇ μὲν εἰς ἑαυτὸν... ἐπιβολῇ) [...] has everything included in this seeing..." (IV.4.2.12) "[...] the thing itself when it is without matter is object of thought and thought, not thought in the sense of being a definition of the thing or an *intuition* of it (οὐχ οἵαν λόγον εἶναι πράγματος οὐδ᾽ ἐπιβολὴν πρὸς αὐτὸ)..." (VI.6.2.24–25) In other passages, however, ἐπιβολή is translated into *quick glance* (cf. II.8.1.40), *application* (cf. III.7.1.4, VI.2.4.23), *attention* (cf. IV.4.8.6), *notion* (cf. IV.6.3.73), *act of attention* (cf. VI.3.18.12), *intuitive conception* (cf. VI.6.9.14), *concentration of attention* (cf. VI.7.39.2), and *concentrated gaze* (cf. VI.8.11.23). In II.4.10.2–3, Καὶ τίς ἡ νόησις καὶ τῆς διανοίας ἡ ἐπιβολή; is translated into "What is the act of thought, and how do you apply your mind to it?"

is directed toward its intentional object in a straightforward and uninterrupted way. Παραδχή, on the other hand, refers to the mind's receiving of that which it is directly aware. Now Plotinus does not simply speak of the loving intellect's "unification with the One" or "henosis", but rather of its "direct awareness *and* reception", precisely in order to emphasize that the loving intellect is not altogether simple, but still entangled in multiplicity. A similar distinction between direct awareness and reception is highlighted twice in V.3.11:

(xi) [...] it *[the intellect] desired one thing*, having vaguely in itself a kind of image of it, but *came out having grasped something else* which it made many in itself.

ὥστε ἄλλου μὲν ἐπεθύμησεν ἀορίστως ἔχουσα ἐπ᾽ αὐτῇ φάντασμά τι, ἐξῆλθε δὲ ἄλλο λαβοῦσα ἐν αὐτῇ αὐτὸ πολὺ ποιήσασα.[39]

(xii) So this Intellect had *an immediate apprehension of the One*, but by grasping it became Intellect, perpetually in need [of the One] and having become at once *Intellect and substance and intellection* when it thought;

οὗτος οὖν ὁ νοῦς ἐπέβαλε μὲν ἐκείνῳ, λαβὼν δὲ ἐγένετο νοῦς, ἀεὶ δὲ ἐνδεόμενος καὶ γενόμενος καὶ νοῦς καὶ οὐσία καὶ νόησις, ὅτε ἐνόησε.[40]

Now since the direct awareness is distinct from reception and hence not simple, and since that which is not simple cannot be united with what is absolutely simple, it follows that the intellect's direct awareness and reception of the One cannot be the immediate or non-distinct *unification* with the One.

Furthermore, even if the gist of this passage can be interpreted as an explanation of the intellect's ascent to the One, this interpretation is still inadequate. For what it claims is only that henosis is to be found in the "direct awareness and reception". But beside this claim, nothing informative is given in passage (x); all we are told is that the intellect has a normal state of thinking and a mystical state of union. Just how its normal state of thinking is transformed into the mystical state of union, remains unexplained.

Finally, it seems that passage (x) is not concerned with the intellect's (per impossibile) unification with the One in the first place, but rather with the *generation* of the act of intellection. According to line 30–33, "when it saw him it had offspring and was intimately aware of their generation and existence within it; and when it sees these it is said to think, but it sees that by the power by which

---

39   V.3.11.6–8.
40   V.3.11.12–15.

[later] it was going to think." That is to say, the intellect in its loving state desires to see the One; but since the One itself is unknowable, what the intellect actually sees is only the images thereof. Thus understood, the message of (x) is similar to that of V.6.5, where Plotinus explains as follows:

(xiii) And this is what thinking is, a movement towards the Good in its desire of that Good; for the desire generates thought and establishes it in being along with itself: for desire of sight is seeing.

καὶ τοῦτό ἐστι νοεῖν, κίνησις πρὸς ἀγαθὸν ἐφιέμενον ἐκείνου· ἡ γὰρ ἔφεσις τὴν νόησιν ἐγέννησε καὶ συνυπέστησεν αὐτῇ· ἔφεσις γὰρ ὄψεως ὅρασις.[41]

That is to say, the intellect is motivated by its desire for the Good or the One. The intellect's desire for the One, however, is the desire to know the One as an intelligible being. Therefore what it knows is not the One as such, but a mere image thereof.[42]

To sum up, the doctrine of two intellects is irrelevant for our present discussion, because the loving intellect is not united with the One by its "direct awareness and reception".

3.2 The Explanation of the "Dissolution" of the Intellect in VI.7.41.12–14

Why can the negative theologian concentrate on contemplation while disregarding it altogether? According to VI.7.41, this is because the intellect by which he contemplates *dissolves itself* when it unites with the intelligible objects.

(xiv) But if intellect, thinking, and object of thought are the same, if they become altogether one, they will make themselves disappear in themselves; but if they are distinguished by being other they will, again, not be that Good.

εἰ δὲ ταὐτὸν νοῦς, νόησις, νοητόν, πάντη ἓν γενόμενα ἀφανιεῖ αὐτα ἐν αὐτοῖς· διακριθέντα δὲ τῷ ἄλλο πάλιν αὖ οὐκ ἐκεῖνο ἔσται.[43]

This passage is a further development of the identity thesis introduced in V.3.5 and V.5.1 (cf. Chapter 2). According to those two chapters, true knowledge (or

---

41 V.6.5.8–10.
42 See also Chapter 1, passage (xi) and the analysis thereof.
43 VI.7.41.12–14.

rather meditation, as we have explained in Chapter 2) is possible only if the intellect is identical to the intelligible object. For the intellect to be identical to the intelligible object, they must unite together in and through the act of intellection; otherwise the intellect would not know what the case really is, but merely know what resembles it. Now in passage (xiv), Plotinus goes on to claim that when the intellect, thinking, and the intelligible object become altogether one (πάντη ἓν γενόμενα), they will "make themselves disappear" or dissolve (ἀφανιεῖ) in themselves. Note that the intellect's becoming one with its object and thinking is not the same as the One Itself: the former is described as "One-Many" (ἓν-πολλά), in contradistinction to the latter as the *first One* (τὸ πρῶτον ἕν) and the One Itself (τὸ αὐτὸ ἕν), and to the soul as "One and Many" (ἓν καὶ πολλά).[44] For this reason, "becoming *altogether* one" (πάντη ἓν γενόμενα) should not be confused with "becoming *perfectly* one", which would be an oxymoron according to Plotinus' metaphysics. On the other hand, the original meaning of ἀφανίζειν is a strongly negative one, meaning *to conceal, destroy*, or *make disappear*, rather than to create, accomplish or perfect. Now it is clear that for Plotinus the intellect's actuality consists in the identity between the intellect and the intelligible object, rather than in the One Itself or henosis. However, why does he go so far as to say that this identity amounts to their *dissolution*? Let us attempt an explanation.

For Plotinus, since the intellect's actuality consists in its identity to the intelligible object, the intellect already contains within itself an element of becoming-other or self-alienation:

(xv) For one must always understand intellect as otherness and sameness if it is going to think. For [otherwise] it will not distinguish itself from the intelligible by its relation of otherness to itself, and will not contemplate all things if no otherness has occurred to make all things exist: for [without otherness] there would not even be two.

δεῖ γὰρ τὸν νοῦν ἀεὶ ἑτερότητα καὶ ταὐτότητα λαμβάνειν, εἴπερ νοήσει. ἑαυτόν τε γὰρ οὐ διακρινεῖ ἀπὸ τοῦ νοητοῦ τῇ πρὸς αὐτὸ ἑτέρου σχέσει τά τε πάντα οὐ θεωρήσει, μηδεμίας ἑτερότητος γενομένης εἰς τὸ πάντα εἶναι· οὐδὲ γὰρ ἂν οὐδὲ δύο.[45]

---

44 For the description of the One as the first One, the intellect as "One-Many" and the soul as "One and Many" see V.1.8.25–27. For the emphatic characterization of the One as "the One itself" see VI.7.1.39, VI.8.21.32–33, and VI.9.6.20.

45 VI.7.39.5–10; on the intellect's essential otherness see also V.1.4.3441; V.3.10.24; and VI.7.13.12.

The intellect's becoming identical to the intelligible object implies its becoming other than itself; likewise, the intelligible object's becoming identical to the intellect also implies its becoming other than itself. Thus, more precisely speaking, in becoming identical to the intelligible object, the intellect does not simply become it *once and for all*, but rather becomes that object which turns into the intellect and is therefore *no longer* itself. And this intellect which then appears is not the intellect itself, but rather becomes yet again that intelligible object which becomes once again other than itself. And so *ad infinitum*. This interplay between reflexivity and negativity underlies the intellect's actuality. Since everything within this process is turning into something other than itself, it lacks an *independent and permanent* nature of its own. Hence the intellect and the intelligible object are said to "dissolve" themselves in themselves, not because they are *without* any nature or even *inexistent*, but because they are by nature impermanent, insubstantial, and dependent on one another.

3.3 The Transition from the "Dissolution" of the Intellect to Henosis: V.3.17

The second passage to examine is V.3.17 in its entirety. In this last chapter of one of the most important treatises in the *Enneads*, Plotinus recapitulates the thesis of VI.7.41.12–14 and uses it to explain why and how we can go beyond the intellect to "ascend" to the One. What follows is an analytic exegesis of this chapter.

(xvi) *What* then *is* better than the wisest life, without fault or mistake, and than Intellect which contains all things, and than universal life and universal intellect? If we say "that which made them"—well, how did it make them? And, in case *something better* may appear, our train of thought will not go on to something else but will stop at Intellect.

> Τί οὖν ἐστι κρεῖττον ζωῆς ἐμφρονεστάτου καὶ ἀπταίστου καὶ ἀναμαρτήτου καὶ νοῦ πάντα ἔχοντος καὶ ζωῆς πάσης καὶ νοῦ παντός; ἐὰν οὖν λέγωμεν "τὸ ποιῆσαν ταῦτα," καὶ πῶς ποιῆσαν; καί, μὴ φανῇ τι κρεῖττον, οὐκ ἄπεισιν ὁ λογισμὸς ἐπ᾽ ἄλλο, ἀλλὰ στήσεται αὐτοῦ.[46]

These opening lines from V.3.17 do not repeat the thesis from previous chapters that the One transcends or is "better than" the intellect. On the contrary, in order to refine this familiar thesis, (xvi) raises the doubt that the One could be *something* (τι) to which transcendence can be ascribed. It also cautions us that,

---

46   V.3.17.1–5.

in order not to posit any *being* which exceeds the intellect's comprehension, our rational inquiry into the One should be confined within the intellect's proper domain and constrained by its proper function. Plotinus' main concern here, obviously, is methodological and epistemological rather than metaphysical. For there is no denying that the ultimate reality is beyond all beings; but it is not immediately clear how *the intellect*, which can only know intelligible beings, should deal with this fact consistently. Consequently, from the metaphysical principle that the ultimate reality transcends all beings, one cannot draw the epistemological thesis that the intellect can know the ultimate reality by transcending intelligible beings. This is why Plotinus warns us that "our reasoning will stop at the intellect and not go on to something else".

According to Beierwaltes' comment on this passage, "man's *consciousness* of the presence of the Good (or the One) in him becomes for him the impulse to ascend toward this very origin."[47] It is assumed that the presence of the One can be made conscious by the intellect, thereby suggesting that henosis is to be reached via intellectual reflection. However, the intellect's proper function just is to comprehend intelligible beings, rather than the One which is beyond all beings. Therefore its attempt to unite with the One does not lead to henosis, but only reduces the One to an intelligible being.

But does this mean that the intellect cannot ascend to the One by its proper function, and that a rational teaching of henosis is impossible? No; as Plotinus explains:

(xvii) But there are many reasons for going higher, particularly the fact that the self-sufficiency of Intellect which results from its being composed of all things is something which comes to it from outside: each of the things of which it is composed is obviously insufficient; and because each of them has participated in the absolute One and continues to participate in It, it is not the One Itself.

ἀλλὰ δεῖ ἀναβῆναι διά γε ἄλλα πολλὰ καὶ ὅτι τούτῳ τὸ αὔταρκες ἐκ πάντων ἔξω ἐστίν· ἕκαστον δὲ αὐτῶν δηλονότι ἐνδεές· καὶ ὅτι ἕκαστον τοῦ αὐτοῦ ἑνὸς μετείληφε καὶ μετέχει τοῦ αὐτὸ ἑνός, οὐκ αὐτὸ ἕν.[48]

We should "go beyond" (ἀναβῆναι) or higher than the intellect, because the self-sufficiency actualized by its proper function is "external" (ἔξω). But what do

---

47   Beierwaltes, 1991, 162–163, my translation.
48   V.3.17.5–9.

"external" and "go beyond" mean respectively? Let us first consider Beierwaltes' explanation:

> Just as there are two kinds of unity—on the one hand, the absolute unity, whereby the One as the grounding origin is everything and is, precisely for this reason, nothing determined; on the other hand, the image-like unity of the intellect which is in itself relational and merely analogous to the One, and which in its self-reflection unifies all beings in itself as the objects of thought and lets them exist all at once—so there are (at least) two kinds of self-sufficiency. The self-sufficiency of the intellect is due to the presence of the One to the intellect itself, such that the intellect is present to its own relational reflexive unity and always already possesses what it can seek and find. For this reason, the intellect does not possess and should not develop any inclination toward any further multiplicity—*except toward the upward movement* through which the intellect becomes consciouss of its own ground and thereby fulfills its essence in the first place. The dependency of the individual objects of thought will then be fulfiiled and overcome through the unity established in the intellect and by its absolute ground. But if the form of a self-sufficiency which is in itself thinking and living is generated *from the "outside", that is to say, from "above" or from the One*, then this One Itself should be undertood as absolutely self-sufficient.[49]

According to Beierwaltes, the intellect's self-sufficiency is called external, because the intellect depends on the One which is, as its ultimate principle, "from the outside". Therefore "external" refers to the intellect's *dependence* upon the One, and "going beyond" refers to the intellect's *ascent* toward the One: "The intellect's intrinsic self-sufficiency, which consists in the self-reflection upon its own being and can also be understood as the structure that dynamically unifies its multiple components, [...] is due to "the outside". That is to say, it is grounded in the One to which it must ascend."[50] Both "external" and "going beyond" designate the way in which the intellect relates to the One: the former points to the intellect's intrinsic condition, while the latter stands for its dynamic movement.

There are, however, two issues which call for reconsideration. The first is that the interpretation of "go beyond" as the intellect's ascent *toward the One* is inconsistent with the warning issued in (xvi) that the One is *not* a certain thing (τι) for the intellect to *go to*. To be sure, the One cannot be such a thing, because It is beyond beings. A more consistent reading of "go beyond", in my opinion, should be "going beyond", "leaving behind", or simply "*abandoning* the intellect". The point is not where the intellect should go *to*, but that its attempt to comprehend the One as an intelligible being should go *away*.

---

49   Beierwaltes, 1991, 165, my translation.
50   Cf. ibid., 246, my translation.

The second issue is that, according to the phrase "τὸ αὔταρκες ἐκ πάντων ἔξω ἐστίν", ἔξω is related to "τὸ αὔταρκες ἐκ πάντων". That is to say, the externality in question pertains to the self-sufficient intellect's *intrinsic structure*, rather than its extrinsic relation to the One. As Plotinus clarifies in the same passage, this is not only because the intellect's self-sufficiency is composed and hence dependent on its components, but also because its components themselves are "obviously insufficient". Here the argument from VI.7.41 comes into play: the components of the self-sufficient intellect are the intellect, the act of intellection and the intelligible objects; and the intellect's self-sufficiency is said to be external and its components insufficient, because they lack self-identity, alienate themselves, become one another and thereby dissolve themselves into one another.

The gist of our interpretation of (xvi) and (xvii) is this: the intellect does not ascend toward that which is beyond all beings, but simply dissolves in its actuality. It is noteworthy that since the intellect's self-dissolution is the radical actualization of its proper function, all that is needed to overcome the intellect's deficiency is the *intense concentration of intellectual contemplation*. This point fills in a missing link in our explanation of Plotinus' doctrine of contemplation. According to the analysis of VI.7.36.8–15 (Section 2.3), the practice of contemplation helps the negative theologian to withdraw from distraction, increase concentration and gain self-control, but does not lead him straight to henosis. However, this does not mean that this practice fails or is useless. As we now see, the aim of contemplation is neither self-control nor henosis, but simply the dissolution of the contemplator's self-identity. When the contemplator is fully immersed in contemplation and becomes united with the contemplated, he is unable to divert his attention to tell whether he is the one who is contemplating or the one who is contemplated; and it is at this point that he is said to lose self-identity and to dissolve himself.

It is noteworthy that, unlike Dionysius' method of unknowing, there is no need for Plotinus' technique of abandonment to appeal to a *non-* or *extra-* intellectual faculty, for a negative moment is already built into the very structure of the intellect. Therefore we can point out two peculiar features in Plotinus' case. First, the transcendence of the One remains intact and is not reduced to the status of mere being. Second, the intellect does not transgress its legitimate domain, but maintains its proper function of uniting with the intelligible objects. These two points combine to strike a healthy balance among rational metaphysics, common sense, and mysticism. Thus, after emphasizing once again that the

One transcends even the intellect's external or self-dissolving self-sufficiency,[51] Plotinus goes on to tackle the issue of henosis in the second half of V.3.17:

(xviii) Is that enough *[to conclude that the One is beyond the intellect and that the intellect dissolves itself]*? Can we end the discussion by saying this? No, my soul is still in even stronger labor. Perhaps she is now at the point when she must bring forth, having reached the fulness of her birth-pangs in her eager longing for the One. But we must sing another charm to her, if we can find one anywhere to allay her pangs. Perhaps there might be one in *what we have said already*, if we *sang* it *over and over again*. And what other charm can we find which has a sort of newness about it?

Ἀρκεῖ οὖν ταῦτα λέγοντας ἀπαλλαχθῆναι; ἢ ἔτι ἡ ψυχὴ ὠδίνει καὶ μᾶλλον. ἴσως οὖν χρὴ αὐτὴν ἤδη γεννῆσαι ἀίξασαν πρὸς αὐτὸ πληρωθεῖσαν ὠδίνων. οὐ μὴν ἀλλὰ πάλιν ἐπαστέον, εἴ ποθέν τινα πρὸς τὴν ὠδῖνα ἐπῳδὴν εὕροιμεν. τάχα δὲ καὶ ἐκ τῶν ἤδη λεχθέντων, εἰ πολλάκις τις ἐπάδοι, γένοιτο. τίς οὖν ὥσπερ καινὴ ἐπῳδὴ ἄλλη;[52]

The point at issue is how to ascend from the intellect to the One, considering that the One is beyond the intellect and the intellect dissolves itself. Both Armstrong's translation and Beierwaltes' version[53] suggest that *no new spell* can be found; that is, *no other way than the intellect* is needed to go beyond the intellect itself. Thus understood, "perhaps" (τάχα) must be taken in the affirmative sense: there is indeed one way toward henosis to be found in "what we have said already" (τῶν ἤδη λεχθέντων), *if we "sang it over and over again"* (ἐπάδοι πολλάκις).

But what is this "spell" which is supposed to lead the negative theologian to henosis? The answer is to be found in what "what we have said already" and "sang over and over again" means respectively. According to Beierwaltes:

If one considers closely the basic insights developed in the preceding passage, then it is clear that a new charm for the pregnant soul's birth-pangs is hardly conceivable and quite unnecessary. Now that these insights have been unfolded, it is clear—and we should recall—that what is capable of uniting with the absolutely simple One is not the

---

51 V.3.17.9–14: "What then is that in which it *[the intellect]* participates, which makes it exist, and all things along with it? If It makes each individual thing exist, and it is by the presence of the One that the multitude of individual things in Intellect, and Intellect itself, is self-sufficient, it is clear that It, since It is the cause of existence and self-sufficiency, is not Itself existence but beyond it and beyond self-sufficiency."

52 V.3.17. 15–20, my italics.

53 Beierwaltes, 1991, 65: "Hätten wir denn einen irgendwie neuen Zauberspruch?"

discursive thought that always aims at a being other than itself, but only the intuitively thinking "touch" which is free from difference and without distance.[54]

The intellect is no longer thinking and opposed to any object of thought, but is transformed into an identificatory seeing of the One as God, in which seeing "the seer and the object seen become one", and where there is "nothing 'seen' but only something 'united'". This leads to the attainment of ecstasy (ἔκστασις), i.e. the radical ascent from all relations, made familiar and expressed by speech, between oneness and multiplicity, identity and difference, being and non-being, movement and rest. This very transformation is the consummation of a complete and radical movement of abstraction, which Plotinus urgently teaches: "Take away everything!"[55]

On Beierwaltes' interpretation, the spell is an intuitive "touch" without distinction and distance, and this "touch" is attained via the "complete and radical movement of abstraction". According to his exegesis of V.3.14, this movement consists in the intellectual negation whereby the intellect "says not what the One is, but what the One is not."[56] Thus understood, "what we have said already" refers to the exercise of intellectual negation outlined in V.3.14.

However, it seems quite implausible that the phrase "what we have said already" should refer to an exercise discussed in V.3.14 but mentioned not even once in V.3.17. Contra Beierwaltes, I would suggest that this phrase refers back to the phrase "τὸ αὔταρκες ἐκ πάντων ἔξω ἐστίν" in (xvii), by which Plotinus explains that we should go beyond the intellect because it dissolves itself. Accordingly, "sang over and over again" should refer to the radicalization of the intellect's proper function, and the intense concentration upon self-contemplation.

There is another reason why I disagree with Beierwaltes' interpretation: from the perspective of Plotinus' metaphysics of the One, the exercise of saying what the One is *not* is not the most appropriate way to approach the One; rather, it would be more appropriate *not to think and speak of* the One at all. As explained in Chapter 1, this is because cognitive and linguistic representation about the One, however appropriate it might be, is not the One Itself but remains a representation.[57] In this context, the method of abandonment introduced in VI.7.36 can be understood as a further explanation why the intellect can, in and through its proper activity, consistently *not* think and speak the One at all: the intellect

---

54   Ibid., 166, my translation.
55   Ibid., 167, my translation. See also 168ff.; see also Beierwaltes, Werner, *Denken des Einen*, Vittorio Klostermann, Frankfurt am Main, 1985, 130–131 and idem., *Das Wahre Selbst*, Vittorio Klostermann, Frankfurt am Main, 2001, 104–105.
56   Cf. V.3.14; see also Beierwaltes, 1991, 149–154.
57   Cf. Perl, 2007, 12–14.

no longer thinks and speaks the One, because it dissolves itself in its actuality in which it unites with its intelligible objects (cf. Section 3.1).

In the remaining part of V.3.17, Plotinus emphasizes again that, in order to go beyond the intellect itself, complete silence is more appropriate than intellectual negation.

(xix) The soul runs over all truths, and all the same shuns the truths we know if someone tries to express them in words and discursive thought; for discursive thought, in order to express anything in words, has to consider one thing after another: this is the method of description; but how can one describe the absolutely simple? But it is enough if the intellect comes into contact with *It*; but when it has done so, while the contact lasts, it is absolutely impossible, nor has it time, to speak; but it is afterwards that it is able to reason about it.

ἐπιθέουσα γὰρ πᾶσι τοῖς ἀληθέσι καὶ ὧν μετέχομεν ἀληθῶν ὅμως ἐκφεύγει, εἴ τις βούλοιτο εἰπεῖν καὶ διανοηθῆναι, ἐπείπερ δεῖ τὴν διάνοιαν, ἵνα τι εἴπῃ, ἄλλο καὶ ἄλλο λαβεῖν· οὕτω γὰρ καὶ διέξοδος· ἐν δὲ πάντη ἁπλῷ διέξοδος τίς ἐστιν; ἀλλ᾽ ἀρκεῖ κἂν νοερῶς ἐφάψασθαι· ἐφαψάμενον δέ, ὅτε ἐφάπτεται, πάντη μηδὲν μήτε δύνασθαι μήτε σχολὴν ἄγειν λέγειν, ὕστερον δὲ περὶ αὐτοῦ συλλογίζεσθαι.[58]

Discursive thought (διάνοια) includes not simply the intellect's analogical description of what the One is like, but above all else its description of what the One is not (cf. Section 2.2). But as Plotinus emphasizes here, no discursive thought can describe "the absolutely simple" or the One, but the "intellectual contact" (νοερῶς ἐφάψασθαι) is enough for It. Consequently, this "intellectual contact" must be opposed to the discursive thought, and by extension connected to the silence or dissolution of intellect brought about by the method of abandonment. Thus understood, the translation of ἀλλ᾽ ἀρκεῖ κἂν νοερῶς ἐφάψασθαι into "but it is enough if the intellect comes into contact with It"[59] is inappropriate for two reasons. First, there is no accusative neutral pronoun in the original sentence; literally, it only reads "but it is enough to *touch intellectually*". Second, it is impossible for the intellect to come into contact with the One, because its proper objects are the intelligible objects. Rather, what is intellectually touched should be the intellect itself when it becomes united with its intelligible object and dissolves

---

58   V.3.17.21–28.
59   Beierwaltes has a similar translation: "Es genügt, wenn man Es denkend berührt." (cf. Beierwaltes, 1991, 65)

itself. For the same reason, the immediacy of the intellectual touch pertains not to the identity between the intellect and the One in mystical union (which would be absurd), but to the identity of the intellect and its intelligible object. The upshot is that, when Plotinus says that "it is enough to touch intellectually", he does not mean that the intellectual touch is enough for unification with the One. The point is rather the same as VI.7.41.12–14: the intellectual touch, namely the intellect's unification with its intelligible object in the act of intellection, is *enough for its self-dissolution*, and this self-dissolution is enough for the purpose of Plotinus' teaching of henosis.

However, if the practice of negative theology ends in the intellects' dissolution and does *not* lead to henosis, what is the negative theologian supposed to do? A more extensive explanation will be given in the next chapter, where various passages from the *Enneads* are brought into considerations to form a consistent presentation of Plotinus' mystical teaching. For now let us turn to the finishing lines of V.3.17 to see how Plotinus addresses this issue.

(xx) One must believe one has seen, when the soul suddenly takes light: for this is from It *[the One]* and It is it; we must think that It is present when, like another god whom someone called to his house, It comes and brings light to us: for if It had not come, It would not have brought the light. So the unenlightened soul does not have It as god; but when she is enlightened she has what she sought, and this is the soul's true end, to touch that light and see it by itself, not by another light, but by the light which is also her means of seeing. She must see that light by which she is enlightened, for we do not see the sun by another light than its own. How can this happen? Take away everything!

τότε δὲ χρὴ ἑωρακέναι πιστεύειν, ὅταν ἡ ψυχὴ ἐξαίφνης φῶς λάβῃ· τοῦτο γὰρ τοῦτο τὸ φῶς παρ' αὐτοῦ καὶ αὐτός· καὶ τότε χρὴ νομίζειν παρεῖναι, ὅταν ὥσπερ θεὸς ἄλλος ὅταν εἰς οἶκον καλοῦντος τινος ἐλθὼν φωτίσῃ· ἢ μηδ' ἐλθὼν οὐκ ἐφώτισεν. οὕτω τοι καὶ ψυχὴ ἀφώτιστος ἄθεος ἐκείνου· φωτισθεῖσα δὲ ἔχει, ὃ ἐζήτει, καὶ τοῦτο τὸ τέλος τἀληθινὸν ψυχῇ, ἐφάψασθαι φωτὸς ἐκείνου καὶ αὐτῷ αὐτὸ θεάσασθαι, οὐκ ἄλλου φωτί, ἀλλ' αὐτό, δι' οὗ καὶ ὁρᾷ. δι' οὗ γὰρ ἐφωτίσθη, τοῦτό ἐστιν, ὃ δεῖ θεάσασθαι· οὐδὲ γὰρ ἥλιον διὰ φωτὸς ἄλλου. πῶς ἂν οὖν τοῦτο; ἄφελε πάντα.[60]

According to the interpretation above, "take away" does not refer to the exercise of intellectual negation, but rather to the method of abandonment; and this

---

60   V.3.17.28–38.

imperative does not demand the intellect *per impossibile* to unite with the One by means of negation, but simply to let itself dissolve in its actuality. That which "sees the light by the light itself" and unites with the One immediately, therefore, must be something other than the intellect (this will be explained in the next chapter). Thus understood, the gist of (xx) is not that the soul should take away everything in order to see the light or the One Itself by Itself, as the latter half of this passage might suggest. Rather, as the first half of this passage explains, man does not need the intellect to unite with the One, for he "has already seen" (ἑωρακέναι) the One which "has already come" (ἐλθὼν), and the light by which his soul is illuminated is from the One and the One Itself (παρ' αὐτοῦ καὶ αὐτός). Here Plotinus introduces a new doctrine concerning the One' *mystical presence*, and we shall look more closely into it in the next chapter.

Chapter Summary

Plotinus' and Dionysius' negative theology both stem from Platonic philosophy. However, they appropriate in different ways the idealistic doctrine that to be is to be intelligible. Dionysius adheres closely to this doctrine and draws from it the consequence that God, being that which is beyond all beings, must also transcend the intellect. The upshot for his method of unknowing is that, in order to acquire the mystical knowledge of God, one has to "know beyond the mind by knowing nothing."[61] On the other hand, although Plotinus propounds a similar doctrine that the intellect is identical to its objects, he also draws from it the more radical consequence that such an intellect must necessarily dissolve itself. Whereas Dionysius follows the classical Platonic tradition, Plotinus shows a more critical attitude by *renovating* the old doctrine.

But more important, it is also due to their disagreement over the *nature of intellect* that Plotinus and Dionysius will part company on their respective approach to henosis. For Dionysius, since the proper function of intellect consists simply in the intellectual apprehension of intelligible objects, the unification with that which is *beyond* them must be mediated by a *different* function which is not intellectual in the strict sense. On Dionysius' epistemic approach, this function is identified as unknowing, and henosis is thereby *correlated* to it like ordinary knowledge is to the intellect. For Plotinus, because the intellect already contains within itself the moment of self-dissolution, the negative theologian does *not* have to appeal to another faculty in order to transcend the realm of mere beings.

---

61   *MT*, 1001A.

However, the *lack* of a mediating faculty which leads the intellect to the One, together with the very dissolution of the intellect itself, imply that it is impossible for the negative theologian to relate to the One in any way other than via the dissolution of intellect. Thus, whereas Dionysius' method of unknowing paves a straight road to the knowledge of God, Plotinus' method of abandonment leads to nowhere, and in the end, the One becomes elusive for him and vanishes from his sight.

Chapter 4   The Relation between Negative Theology and Henosis

Plotinus' negative theology is a rational inquiry into knowledge of the One insofar as It is beyond all beings. The main contention of Chapter 3 is that while Dionysius' negative theology of unknowing leads directly to henosis as mystical "knowledge",[1] Plotinus' negative theology of abandonment leads only to its own dissolution. His famous catchword, "Take away everything," sums it up in a nutshell. However, it would not be correct to conclude from this that Plotinus' emphasis on abandonment and dissolution drives his teaching of henosis into nihilism. If we turn to John of the Cross, we will find a similar *night of the spirit* described and explained in *The Dark Night*:

> My intellect departed from itself, changing from human and natural to divine. For united with God through this purgation it no longer understands by means of its natural vigor and light, but by means of the divine wisdom to which it was united. And my will departed from itself and became divine. United with the divine love, it no longer loves in a lowly manner, with its natural strength, but with the strength and purity of the Holy Spirit; and thus the will does not operate humanly in relation to God.[2]

For John, since the intellect lies at the threshold between the natural and the divine, one must go beyond it to reach for the divine; and once this threshold is crossed, the rest is to be done by the grace of God.[3] The key is to renounce one's own will completely, thereby becoming receptive to God's will.

Without suggesting that Plotinus should adopt the doctrines of God and of contemplation similar to the Carmelite mystic, the above allusion is intended to assuage the worry that Plotinus' negative theology of abandonment should be a self-defeating project. Furthermore, it also helps to remind us that "Take away everything" cannot be Plotinus' last words about his teaching of henosis, and that more attention is needed to look through the *Enneads* for the relation between

---

1   Here *henosis* or union is Dionysius' own technical term; cf. *De Mystica Theologia*, 1000A: "with your understanding laid aside, [you have] to strive upward as much as you can toward union (ἕνωσιν) with him who is beyond all beings and knowledge."

2   *The Dark Night*, in *The Collected Works of St. John of the Cross*, tr. Kieran Kavanaugh, O.C.D. and Otilio Rodriguez, O.C.D., Institute of Carmelite Studies, Washington, 1991, 400.

3   Cf. Mondello, Geoffrey K., *The Metaphysics of Mysticism: Commentary on the Mystical Philosophy of St. John of the Cross*, www.johnofthecross.com, 2010, 170–174.

negative theology and henosis. In my opinion, the following passage highlights such a transition most pointedly:

(i) But if because It *[the One]* is none of these things you become indefinite in your thought of It, stand fast on these and contemplate It from these. But contemplate It without casting your thought outwards. For It does not lie somewhere leaving the other things empty of It, but is always present to anyone who is able to touch It, but is not present to the one who is unable.

Εἰ δ᾽ ὅτι μηδὲν τούτων ἐστίν, ἀοριστεῖς τῇ γνώμῃ, στῆσον σαυτὸν εἰς ταῦτα, καὶ ἀπὸ τούτων θεῶ· θεῶ δὲ μὴ ἔξω ῥίπτων τὴν διάνοιαν. οὐ γὰρ κεῖταί που ἐρημῶσαν αὐτοῦ τὰ ἄλλα, ἀλλ᾽ ἔστι τῷ δυναμένῳ θιγεῖν ἀεὶ παρόν, τῷ δ᾽ ἀδυνατοῦντι οὐ πάρεστιν.[4]

Both "your thought of It" (τῇ γνώμῃ) and "your thought" (τὴν διάνοιαν) refer to man's attempt to know the One as an intelligible being; and he is said to become indefinite or uncertain about what he is doing, because the One is beyond intelligible beings. So far these points only repeat Plotinus' negative theology and are nothing new. But why does Plotinus, in spite of all these, insist that man should "stand fast" on the intelligible beings which he contemplates and "not cast outward" his thought of them? Plotinus' insistence would make more sense if repeated contemplation would finally lead to the attainment of henosis. But as we explained in the previous chapter,[5] this is simply not the case: repeated contemplation only leads to its own dissolution. And this point is not forgotten in (i), for as Plotinus claims, the One is absent from those who cannot "touch" It but merely contemplate It as an intelligible being, although It is present to those who can "touch" and do not contemplate It.

Since there is no good textual evidence that the "touch" (θιγεῖν) in question is not a metaphor for henosis,[6] I would simply interpret this term accordingly.

---

4   VI.9.7.1–5.
5   Cf. the analyses of quotations (viii) and (xviii) in Chapter 3.
6   See also VI.9.4.24–27: "[…] for that One is not absent from any, and absent from all, so that in Its presence It is not present except to those who are able and prepared to receive It, so as to be in accord with It and as if grasp It and touch It in their likeness (ἐναρμόσαι καὶ οἷον ἐφάψασθαι καὶ θιγεῖν ὁμοιότητι) by their affinity to It…". The synonyms more often used in the *Enneads* are ἐπαφή and ἐφάπτεσθαι, which generally describe *touch* or *contact* of any kind, including the touch of the body, of the intelligible forms, of the beloved person, and of the One. For instances of the last case see V.1.11.13, V.3.17.25–26, V.6.6.35, VI.5.10.27–28, VI.5.10.41, VI.7.30.3, VI.8.21.29, VI.9.4.27, VI.9.9.19, VI.9.9.55.

So the message of (i) boils down to this: On the one hand, we should focus on contemplating the One; but on the other, our effort is in vain because the One is present to those who do not contemplate. These apparently conflicting claims generate following questions:

(A) Who is in the presence of the One, if not the contemplator?
(B) Why does Plotinus maintain that we have to cling to contemplation, in spite of the fact that this will only bring about uncertainty?
(C) Is there any way for those unable to touch the One to free themselves from uncertainty, and to become capable of uniting with It?

Since answers to (A), (B) and (C) could summarily explain the relation between negative theology and henosis, in the following three sections I will look into these questions in turn. One issue to be noted in advance is that, since the chapter from which (i) is quoted does not directly answer these questions, we have to look elsewhere in the *Enneads* more carefully.[7] The texts I shall adduce are relatively sketchy and cry out for more elaboration when compared to other passages in the *Enneads* such as those concerning the doctrines of the One and of the intellect. However, as I try to make clear, this is no reason to underestimate their relevance to Plotinus' thought as a whole. Instead of just making wild speculations over these scant remarks, I shall take a systematic and comparative approach to cope with them. The systematic analysis, based on Plotinus' basic theses concerning the transcendence and negativity of the One,[8] helps to fill in the information missing from the texts in a way consistent with Plotinus' philosophical argumentations. On top of this, the comparative analysis takes as its point of departure certain general similarities between Plotinus and other more well-known theologians and philosophers, and proceeds to highlight the distinctive features in Plotinus' case, thereby gaining a more sympathetic and perceptive understanding thereof.

---

7   See van Winden, J. C. M., 'Das ἐκεῖ in Plotin Enneaden VI.9.7.4' in *Museum Helveticum* 37, 1980, 62 and Meijer, 1992, 216–217. According to their interpretation of passage (i), "the One is to be found somewhere in the 'other things' [intelligible beings]. [...] Indeed, one need not go to a place beyond the world: the One is present to be touched by him who can touch It, because It is there (ἐκεῖ). We shall see that ultimately we must also leave 'die Dinge' [these other things]." Although this interpretation is correct, it does not confront the apparent inconsistency in passage (i). It is this very inconsistency which I shall seek to explain in the present section.

8   Cf. Chapter 1, Section 2 and 3 of this dissertation.

Section 1 The One's Mystical Presence

The first issue to investigate is the mystical presence of the One. As is indicated by the claim from passage (i) that the One "is always present to anyone who is able to touch It, but is not present to the one who is unable", the notion of mystical presence whereby man "touches" the One cannot be *simply* a metaphysical one, because the One is metaphysically present to all beings as their cause, *whether or not* they can unite with It. Reversely, this means that the notion of the One's mystical presence presupposes that of Its metaphysical presence. This gives us a clue as to how our explanation should proceed: we will explain the One's mystical presence in man in light of the metaphysical presence of the One.

1.1 The Metaphysical Presence of the One

In the *Ennead* VI.5, Plotinus argues that the absolute simplicity of the One entails Its indivisibility.[9] But to say that the One is indivisible only says of what the One lacks or is not, and this negative way of speaking should be completed by the eminent characterization that the One is *omnipresent* (πανταχοῦ).[10] That is to say, the One is called un-divided and un-"spaced", not in the sense that It is absent from any place, but—to the contrary—in the sense that It is in every place as the *cause of all beings*. This, roughly, is his notion of the One's metaphysical presence. In the closing chapter of that same treatise, he deepens his reflections upon this notion as follows:

(ii) How then is It [*the One*] present? As one life: for life in a living being does not reach only so far, and then is unable to extend over the whole, but it is everywhere.

Πάρεστιν οὖν πῶς; ὡς ζωὴ μία· οὐ γὰρ μέχρι τινὸς ἐν ζῴῳ ἡ ζωή, εἶτ᾽ οὐ δύναται εἰς ἅπαν φθάσαι, ἀλλὰ πανταχοῦ.[11]

It is suggested that the One is not just omnipresent, but omnipresent as *life*, in the sense of "extending over the whole living being". But just what this means, remains unexplained in VI.5. A clue to this question can be found in VI.9.9,

---

9   Cf. VI.5.3.
10   Cf. VI.5.7.13–17, VI.5.9.31–42, VI.5.10–11; see also VI.8.16.1–2: "But since we maintain, and it appears to be so, that this [the One] is everywhere and again is nowhere (πανταχοῦ... καὶ οὐ οὐδαμοῦ)...".
11   VI.5.12.1–3.

according to which for the One to extend over the whole living being is to *sustain* or *preserve* it:

(iii) For we are not cut off from It *[the One]* or separate, even if the nature of body has intruded and drawn us to itself, but we breathe and are preserved because that Good has not given Its gifts and then gone away but is always bestowing them as long as It is what It is.

οὐ γὰρ ἀποτετμήμεθα οὐδὲ χωρίς ἐσμεν, εἰ καὶ παρεμπεσοῦσα ἡ σώματος φύσις πρὸς αὐτὴν ἡμᾶς εἵλκυσεν, ἀλλ᾽ ἐμπνέομεν καὶ σῳζόμεθα οὐ δόντος, εἶτ᾽ ἀποστάντος ἐκείνου, ἀλλ᾽ ἀεὶ χορηγοῦντος ἕως ἂν ᾖ ὅπερ ἐστί.[12]

The notion of preservation is explained in terms of χορηγοῦντος. Armstrong's English translation is *bestowing*, Richard Harder's German translation is *spendet*, and Pierre Hadot's French translation is *procure*.[13] All three translations suggest that the One is an abundant giver who is always generously sustaining the taker with his gifts. But there are two difficulties about these translations. First, Plotinus expressly states here that the One "has not given Its gifts and then gone away (οὐ δόντος, εἶτ᾽ ἀποστάντος)." This can be read either in the strong sense that the One does not give any gift whatsoever in the first place, or in the weaker sense that the One does bestow gifts but does not go away once the gifts are given. Other passages from the *Enneads*, however, indicate that the former should be the more appropriate interpretation. For instance, according to VI.5.10, the lover "does not receive (οὐ δεχόμενος)".[14] And in V.5.12, it is also said that the One does not give or "arouse pain" (ὀδύνας δίδωσιν) like beauty does. I shall look into this second instance later; for now let us consider the more important, systematic reason why the One cannot be a giver. The most straightforward explanation is that the act of giving is always relative to a certain receiver and a certain gift, for it is counterintuitive just to give without giving anything to anyone. So if the One were to be a giver, then, It would be relative to other beings

---

12 VI.9.9.7–11.
13 For Hadot's translation see Hadot, Pierre, *Plotin, Traité 9*, Edition du Cerf, Paris, 1994, 104.
14 Cf. VI.5.10.1–5: "It [the One] has the good sense, then, to remain in itself, and would not come to be in another; but those other things hang from It as if by their longing they had found where It is. And this is "Love camping on the doorstep", even coming from outside into the presence of beauty and longing for it, and satisfied if in this way he can have a part in it; since the lover here below as has beauty in this way, *not by receiving it [into himself] but by lying with it* (οὐ δεχόμενος τὸ κάλλος, ἀλλὰ παρακείμενος οὕτως ἔχει)."

(the gift and the receiver). But this is impossible, because the One is beyond all beings. Other related explanations, abundant throughout the *Enneads*, are to the effect that the One "does not make plan", "does not act", "does not desire", "does not think", and so on.

Still another reason why we should be more cautious when translating χορηγοῦντος into *bestowing* is that this translation insinuates the Christian notion of χαρίσμα (charity, gift, grace). Now it is always a tricky business to draw connection between the different notions of God and ultimate reality. Indeed, for both Plotinus and Christianity, the name "God" can refer to the first cause, the ultimate reality, or something to that effect. And at least in the face of it, both parties speak of the creation, production, or making (τὸ ποιεῖν) of all beings by this first cause. Besides, since they both hold that the making bears upon *all* beings, it would be inaccurate to say that creation *ex nihilo* must be a strictly Christian doctrine and that whoever maintains the first cause's creation *ex nihilo* must be a Christian theologian. However, all these considerations give us no reason to suppose that Plotinus might subscribe unbeknownst to a quasi-Christian notion of God. The benchmark by which we tell whether Plotinus (or anyone else) counts as a Christian theologian, in my opinion, should be whether his thought is consistent with the doctrine of *trinity*. On the doctrine of trinity, it is not absurd that the God remains absolute while being related to the created beings. For Christian theologians it makes perfect sense to say that God is a giver. But Plotinus, as a non-Christian, does not understand the mystery of the Triune God. He cannot but deny that the One, being absolutely simple, should be also a giver.

For an alternative translation of χορηγοῦντος, let us consider its literal meaning, namely *conducting the choir*. The One is likened to a choirmaster who leads and directs the choir. Although the choirmaster is *unlike* any other member of the choir due to his role of conducting, he can conduct the choir only because he is *present* to it. The same metaphor also appears in VI.9.8: "And we are always around It *[the One]* but do not always look to It; it is like a choral dance (χορὸς): in the order of its singing the choir keeps round its conductor (κορυφαῖον) but may sometimes turn away, so that he is out of their sight, but when it [sic] turns back to him it sings beautifully and is truly with him; so too we are always around (περὶ) It—and if we were not, we should be totally dissolved and no longer exist..."[15] This literal translation of χορηγοῦντος also explains why Plotinus says

---

15   VI.9.8.37–43.

in passage (iii) that "that Good has not given Its gifts and then gone away," and in VI.5.10 that the lover of the One "does not receive" It.[16]

Now what does the metaphor of choir-leading tell us about the One's presence? My suggestion is that, just as the choirmaster conducts and directs the choir, so the omnipresent One sustains or preserves all beings as their *efficient cause*. Plotinus does not apply this term to the One in the *Enneads* and prefers σῴζειν (to preserve) over κινεῖν (to move), mainly because the One is not involved in any physical motion. But the One can be said to be an efficient cause in the sense that It is the *metaphysical* cause of oneness and being of all things.[17] Just as the physical mover directly works upon the thing it moves and does not "give" motion to something which has to first "receive" the motion so as to be moved, so too the One qua metaphysical mover does not just "give" oneness and being to all things, but is rather directly present in all of them. Accordingly, John Bussanich explains,

> In bringing things into existence and sustaining them the One's efficient causality differs from Aristotelian efficient causality among sensible substances, with its more limited focus on (i) initiating motion or (ii) explaining how an object or event gives rise to another that is numerically distinct from it, but which is like it in kind. The One, in sharp contrast, is the ultimate ground being of all things.[18]

1.2 The One's Mystical Presence in Man's Innate Desire

To see how Plotinus' notion of metaphysical presence qua efficient cause relates to his doctrine of *mystical* presence, we can compare it with the case of Thomas Aquinas. For Aquinas, God is also said to be in all things as their efficient cause:

> God is in all things [...] as an agent is present to that upon which it works. For an agent must be joined to that wherein it acts immediately and touch it by its power, hence it is proved in Phys. vii that the thing moved and the mover must be joined together. Now since God is very being (ipsum esse) by His own essence, created being must be His proper effect [...] Now God causes this effect in things not only when they first begin to be, but as long as they are preserved in being [...] Therefore as long as a thing has being, God must be present to it, according to its mode of being.[19]

Both Aquinas and Plotinus understand the metaphysical presence of the first cause (God or the One) to be efficient cause. Now Aquinas goes on to claim that

---

16   VI.5.10.5.
17   Cf. VI.9.1–2.
18   Bussanich, 1996, 46.
19   *ST* I, q.8, a.1, c.

[…] God is said to be in a thing in two ways: in one way after the manner of an efficient cause, and thus He is in all things created by Him; in another way He is in things *as the object of operation is in the operator*; and this is proper to the operations of the soul, *according as the thing known is in the one who knows, and the thing desired in the one desiring*. In this second way God is especially in the rational creature which knows and loves Him actually or habitually. And because the rational creature possesses this prerogative by grace. […] He is said to be thus in the saints by grace.[20]

God is not only metaphysically present in all beings as their efficient cause, but also present in *man* as the object of his knowledge and desire.[21] And God is said to be an object of man's knowledge and desire, because, for Aquinas, it is natural for man's desire for knowledge to seek knowledge of the first cause.[22] God, therefore, is present in man as his *knowledge* of the first cause, including His efficient causation.

By contrast, Plotinus does not hold the desire for knowledge in such a high place in his teaching of henosis, for he lays more stress than Aquinas does on the *transcendence* and *negativity* of the ultimate reality. Therefore, for Plotinus, man would be present to the One more intimately, when he abandons the desire to know the One and realizes that the One transcends all beings. If Aquinas ascribes to the notion of divine presence in man by his *knowledge* of God, then we can say that Plotinus upholds a notion of divine presence by man's *unawareness* of the One. Just what this presence by unawareness is, is explained as follows:

(iv)   But the Good *[the One]*, since It was there long before to arouse an *innate desire*, is present even to those asleep and does not astonish those who at any time see It, because It is always there and there is no recollection of It; but people do not see It, because It is present to them in their sleep. But the passionate love of beauty, when it comes, causes pain, because one must have seen it to desire it.

τὸ δ᾽ ἀγαθὸν, ἅτε πάλαι παρὸν εἰς ἔφεσιν σύμφυτον, καὶ κοιμωμένοις πάρεστι καὶ οὐ θαμβεῖ ποτε ἰδόντας, ὅτι σύνεστιν ἀεὶ καὶ οὔποτε ἡ

---

20   *ST* I, q.8, a.3, c., my italics.
21   Cf. Niederbacher, Bruno, 'Ist Gott in allen Dingen?", *Gott suchen und finden nach Ignatius von Loyola* , ed. Josef Thorer, Echter Verlag, Würzburg, 2013, 54–58.
22   Cf. *ST* I-II, q.3, a.8; see also Feingold, Lawrence, *The Natural Desire to See God according to St. Thomas and His Interpreters*, The Catholic University of America Press, Washington, 2004, 11–26.

ἀνάμνησις· οὐ μὴν ὁρῶσιν αὐτό, ὅτι κοιμωμένοις πάρεστι. τοῦ δὲ καλοῦ ὁ ἔρως, ὅταν παρῇ, ὀδύνας δίδωσιν, ὅτι δεῖ ἰδόντας ἐφίεσθαι.²³

Armstrong's translation of ἅτε πάλαι παρὸν εἰς ἔφεσιν σύμφυτον is "since It was there long before to *arouse* an innate desire", which suggest that the One actively "arouses" this innate desire as a stimulus which is either logically extrinsic or temporally anterior to it.²⁴ However, if the One *arouses* an innate desire in such a way, then It would relate to it like the motivating cause does to its effect. But this is at odds with the basic thesis of Plotinus' metaphysics, according to which the One is simple and hence without relation. Furthermore, from an exegetical perspective, this translation also runs counter to the passage immediately following it, where Plotinus says that the One "is *present* even to those asleep" (κοιμωμένοις πάρεστι) and "does not astonish". Thus, in my opinion, it might be more appropriate to stick to the literal translation of παρὸν, namely being *present*.

Plotinus explains the causality of the One indirectly in contrast to that of beauty. For beauty to be efficiently present is to "cause" (διδόναι) or arouse in the patient a conscious desire which, having first seen (ἰδόντας) beauty, pursues it as its desired object. Desire is then said to be passive and painful in the sense that it must first suffer the "shock" (θάμβος) of beauty and then hang on the uncertainty of attaining it.²⁵ The presence of the One, by contrast, is such that It does not arouse any conscious reaction, but is always present in man's *innate desire* (ἔφεσιν σύμφυτον). That the One qua efficient cause does not arouse any conscious reaction should be clear, given Plotinus' non-theistic position and his extensive arguments that the One is unknowable and does not make plans;²⁶ at present, we shall therefore focus on explaining Plotinus' notion of *innate desire* in which the One is always already present without man's awareness thereof.

Before we start, an exegetical reminder is in order: since the direct object of our inquiry is Plotinus' *text*, we are not directly dealing with the *ontological* question concerning the reality of innate desire, but primarily with the *semantic* question concerning the meaning and reference of the technical term *innate desire* according to Plotinus. The reason is very simple: the ontological question presupposes an acquaintance and knowledge of the reality of innate desire, but the reality of innate desire must first be picked out by the term *innate desire*. Now

23   V.5.12.11–15.
24   Richard Harder's German translation reads similarly: "welches uns ja seit je bei-
      wohnt als Gegenstand unseres angeborenen Trachtens".
25   Cf. V.5.12.20–26 and V.5.12.34–37.
26   Cf. III.8.10, VI.8.17, and VI.8.19–21. See also Chapter 1 of this dissertation.

since this term is used by Plotinus in a particular way, we should not confuse its reference with what it might refer to in another context, for example man's natural desire for preservation and pleasure, his natural desire for knowledge (according to Aquinas), his unconscious libido, and the like.

Now the first thing to note from passage (iv) is that, although the innate desire would not exist without the presence of the One, it does not exist as an effect passively motivated by the One. That is to say, neither does the One attract man to come into Its presence, nor does man has an innate desire for the One in the hope that It would come to his presence, for as long as man has an innate desire *for the One*, the One is *already* present there.[27] Consequently, the preposition "for" does not designate a relation to an object to be obtained, as in the expression "working for money", but the mode in which the subject is appropriate, proportional or adapted to the object, as in the expression "wage for the work". Therefore, to avoid unnecessary confusion and emphasize that the One is not an object of desire, it might be better to shorten "innate desire for the One" simply to "innate desire" when we talk about the presence of the One *in* man. This, of course, is just an exegetical makeshift, and does not yet impose any determination on the nature of innate desire.

So far we can only ascertain that Plotinus' technical term *innate desire* does not refer to an object-related activity such as wish, desire or longing. To what activity it refers, or whether it refers to something else, is a question which we have to look further into. Another clue can be found in the following passage:

(v) And we shall no longer be surprised if that which produces these strangely powerful longings is altogether free from even intelligible shape; since the soul also, when she gets an intense love of It *[the One]*, puts away all the shape which she has, even whatever shape of the intelligible there may be in her.

Καὶ οὐκέτι θαυμάσομεν τὸ τοὺς δεινοὺς πόθους παρέχον εἰ πάντη ἀπήλλακται καὶ μορφῆς νοητῆς· ἐπεὶ καὶ ψυχή, ὅταν αὐτοῦ ἔρωτα σύντονον λάβη, ἀποτίθεται πᾶσαν ἣν ἔχει μορφήν, καὶ ἥτις ἂν καὶ νοητοῦ ᾖ ἐν αὐτῇ.[28]

Since the "strangely powerful longings" (το δεινὸς πόθος) and "intense love" (ἔρως σύντονος) are free even from intellectual limitations, they, like the innate desire in (iv), are that in which the One is present without man's awareness

---

27   Cf. VI.5.12.26–27: "It [the One] does not come in order to be present (οὐκ ἦλθεν, ἵνα παρῇ)."

28   VI.7.34.1–5.

thereof. For consistency's sake I shall take them to refer to the same thing. According to Hadot's French translation, τὸ τοὺς δεινοὺς πόθους παρέχον reads "the object which provokes (provoque) the ardent desires", and ὅταν αὐτοῦ ἔρωτα σύντονον λάβῃ is "when she feels and reacts with (ressent) an ardent love for it". Accordingly, as Hadot goes on to remark, "Si l'âme se dépouille de tout forme, c'est précisément parce que le Bien qu'elle recherche est lui-même libre de tout forme."[29] That is to say, because the infinite One first provokes man's innate desire, therefore man must become infinite in order to unite with the One, and his innate desire for the One is like a *reaction* to Its provocation.

However, this interpretation is incoherent with Plotinus' subsequent description that the soul which has this innate desire sees the One "suddenly appearing" (ἐξαίφνης φανέντα) and "could not make a distinction while It is present" (οὐ γὰρ ἂν διακρίναις ἔτι, ἕως πάρεστι).[30] To wit, if the soul must first become infinite in order to unite with the One, then such unification must be conditioned and hence mediated, which is absurd because the One appears immediately. Reversely, if the presence of the One is immediate, there would be no need for the soul to "react" in order that the One could be present, which contradicts Hadot's interpretation.

There is another problem about translation. The literal meaning of παρέχον is "showing" or "presenting as"; in our current context, it can be interpreted as *presenting what is present* in itself, in a similar way in which a substance (οὐσία) manifests its disposition (ἕξις) or possession (ἔχειν).[31] Therefore τὸ δεινοὺς πόθους παρέχον should mean "that which presents the strange longings", "the phenomena of strange longings", or simply "*strange longings*". In passage (v), there is neither explicit reference nor implicit allusion to any alleged causality from the part of the One; the whole message is simply that *man himself* "puts away all the shape" and is infinite, "when he has an intense love" (ὅταν αὐτοῦ ἔρωτα σύντονον λάβῃ). As Plotinus says elsewhere, "the soul then *in her natural state* (κατὰ φύσιν ἔχουσα) is in love with God and wants to unite with It."[32] Here, as well as in (v), man's "natural state" is not identified as an *anterior* event which brings about the innate desire, but only the *concurrent* condition together with which the innate desire is present. Therefore, it would be more accurate to interpret the "since" (ἐπεὶ) in passage (v) as "to the extent that" or "insofar as", rather

---

29   Cf. Hadot, 1987, 171 and 336, my italics.
30   VI.7.34.13–14.
31   Note the semantic connection between παρέχον and ἔχειν on the one hand, and παρόν, ὄν and οὐσία on the other.
32   Cf. VI.9.9.33–34.

than "as a result of". Thus construed, in (v) Plotinus is claiming to the effect that *man's innate desire is as infinite as his nature.*

Leaving aside for the moment the issue concerning man's "infinite nature", let us pause to consider the precise meaning of the last thesis. I think there are two options to interpret it. First, the term "man's innate desire" refers to an activity which is as infinite as his nature. Second, the term "man's innate desire" is co-extensive with the term "man's nature". The first option is clearly untenable, for none of man's activity, no matter how great it is, can be as infinite *as his nature,* because man must first exist or "be" before he can be active at all. Thus we are left with the second option: the technical term *innate desire,* for Plotinus, refers to man's nature.

Thus understood, in passage (v) the term "innate desire" has the same reference as the term "man's nature". In saying that innate desire is infinite, what is meant is simply that the reference of this term is infinite. This interpretation also helps to explain why, in (iv), Plotinus specifically adopts the expression *"innate desire"* (ἔφεσις σύμφυτον). This expression does not imply that there should be a desire which is "unnatural" or "cultivated"; its point is simply to emphasize that such an innate desire pertains to human nature. Consequently, what appeared in passage (iv) as an observation of psychological experience, then, turns out to be an anthropological thesis of the nature of man: the One is always present in man's innate desire, not because man has a psychological *power* which is infinite, but rather insofar as the One is always present in his "infinite nature", which is also why the One is said to be "indistinct" and "suddenly appear" to him.[33]

This brings us to consider in what sense man's nature is infinite. A comparison with Gregory of Nyssa can help us specify what Plotinus might think. The point of contrast is Gregory's doctrine that man's natural desire (ἐπιθυμία) is infinitely progressing (συνεπιτείνειν, ἐπέκτασις) toward God.

And so the desire for the Beautiful (πρὸς τὸ καλὸν ἡ ἐπιθυμία) which is drawn to that ascent constantly progresses (ἀεὶ... συνεπιτείνεται) in the course of pressing toward the Beautiful. And this is the real meaning of seeing God: never to find satisfaction for this desire. But one must always, by looking at what he can see, kindle his desire to see more. Thus, no limit can interrupt the growth of ascent toward God, because neither can any limit be imposed upon the Beautiful (τὸ μήτε τοῦ καλοῦ τι πέρας εὑρίσκεσθαι), nor can any growth of desire for the Beautiful be cut off (μήτε τινὶ χόρῳ τὴν πρόοδον τῆς πρὸς τὸ καλὸν ἐπιθυμίας ἐκκόπτεσθαι).[34]

---

33   Cf. VI.7.34.13–14.
34   *De Vita Moysis,* from *Patrologia Graeca,* vol.44, ed. J. P. Migne, Imprimerie Catholique, Paris, 1863, 404–405, my translation.

The use of correlative conjunction "neither... nor..." (μήτε...μήτε) indicates that "the Beautiful" and "the desire for the Beautiful" are neither equivalent nor synonymous, but rather refer to two distinct entities. Therefore, with his doctrine of progress Gregory is implicitly endorsing a *distinction between two infinities*: on the one hand, the infinity of the "Beautiful" or God; on the other hand, the infinity of man's "growing desire" for the Beautiful. The former has no limit of any kind whatsoever, whereas the latter, defined in terms of movement and finitude, remains somehow distinct from the former and progresses toward it from a given point onward indefinitely. For Gregory, human nature is infinite in the sense that his desire is infinitely progressing toward the infinite God.[35]

For Plotinus, however, distinction implies multiplicity and finitude, and is incoherent with infinity.[36] For this reason, he cannot subscribe to Greogory's distinction between two infinities. If the claim that the nature of man is infinite should cohere with Plotinus' doctrine of simplicity, then a slight modification of this claim is in order. We can do this by attending to the ambiguity of the term "nature" and distinguishing the correct meaning from the wrong one. On the one hand, this term means the nature to which man ultimately belongs and on which he depends. Since this nature just is the One, it must be infinite. But on the other hand, this term can also mean man's *finite* nature, such as his mortality and individuality. For a more accurate understanding of the claim in question, we have to reject the second sense and embrace the first one. So the original claim is modified as follows: *that nature of man is infinite, which he ultimately belongs to and depends on.*

In the last analysis, therefore, Plotinus' doctrine of mystical presence boils down to a fairly ordinary intuition: The ultimate reality called "One" is present in man's nature, in the sense that man's true nature just is the ultimate reality of man. Consequently, what appeared in (v) to be an anthropological thesis about human nature turns out to be the corollary of Plotinus' metaphysics of the One. In particular, this doctrine is not intended to puff up, *per impossibile*, mere humanity to the status of the Absolute. Quite the contrary, it only emphasizes that

---

35   Cf. von Balthasar, Hans Urs, *Presence and Thought: Essay on the Religious Philosophy of Gregory of Nyssa*, tr. Mark Sebanc, Ignatius Press, San Francisco, 1995, 37–46. In particular, von Balthasar discerns *three* infinities in Gregory's thought: "[...] the infinity of the created spirit is ineluctably opposed to the infinity of matter, just as it is opposed to the infinity of God. It is ineluctably opposed to quantitative infinity, which is infinity of number, of emptiness, of time, and thereby of the finite itself, just as it is opposed to the uncreated infinite..." (ibid., 45).

36   Cf. V.5.10.19–21, VI.7.32.15 and VI.9.6.10.

man cannot set a definite limit upon his own nature from his restricted, anthropocentric point of view.

This roundabout interpretation helps us to differentiate Plotinus' notion of human infinity from Gregory's as follows. For Gregory, human infinity consists in man's *progress toward* God, whereas for Plotinus it consists in the One's *presence in* man. If the former is defined in terms of movement and with reference to God as its *terminus ad quem*, then the latter should be defined to the contrary: human infinity is a state rather than movement, and it neither reaches toward the One as its *terminus ad quem*, nor abides in the absence of the One. Positively speaking, for Plotinus, man is always already in the presence of the One and hence naturally divine, and human infinity consists in his *natural state of divinity*. As Bernard McGinn remarks:

> The essential root of this distance [between Plotinus and the Christian mystics] is that Plotinus had quite a different conception of the nature of the human person... [Plotinus'] true self was the undescended soul living in union with Nous, the divine transcendent I, not the reflexively conscious lower self. Where the soul is *naturally divine*, rather than a created spirit, the Christian concept of grace can have no real place. [37]

Plotinus' account of innate desire (that is, human nature) based on quotations (iv) and (v) can be restated as follows. First, the term *innate desire* refers neither to the natural desire for any object nor to the unconscious desire such as libido. To wit, all these desires pertain to man's doing. For man to do anything at all, however, presupposes that he must first *exist*—namely be preserved in the presence of the One. Now the fact that this preservation takes effect in man, or that the One comes to presence in man, is precisely what the term *innate desire* is used to designate. It refers not to man's activity of desire for an object, but to man's being or natural condition in which the One is present.

1.3 The Coherence between Metaphysical and Mystical Presence

By way of conclusion, let us bring together Plotinus' notions of metaphysical presence and of mystical presence of the One. On the one hand, the One is metaphysically present in man as the cause of his oneness and being. As long as man is aware of himself, has self-consciousness and knows that he exists, he is also indirectly aware of the metaphysical presence of the One. He can also become aware of it when he acquires certain metaphysical knowledge about the One— for example, the knowledge that the One is the cause of all beings and beyond

---

37   McGinn,1991, 54.

all beings. On the other hand, because the transcendent One cannot be reduced to an intelligible being, man is more intimately and more properly present to the One when he lays down the desire to know the One and has no more awareness thereof. The One is then said to be present not to man's knowledge, but to his nature to which he ultimately belongs.

Section 2 The Role of Negative Theology

According to Plotinus' doctrine of mystical presence, the One is always already present in man's nature; reversely, it means that man is also always already present to the One in his nature. This doctrine, we could say, is a natural extension of his metaphysics of the One. However, it seems to render Plotinus' negative theology entirely *useless*,[38] for if man is always already with the One in his nature, what is the point of practicing negative theology in order to "ascend" to the One?

Plotinus does not explicitly try to solve the apparent inconsistency between his doctrine of mystical presence and the role of his negative theology. However, he does address another issue which also appears to run counter to that bewildering doctrine, namely man's *fall* from the One. Therefore, I suggest that we digress a little bit to see how Plotinus deals with this issue, so as to get a clue to explaining the real function of negative theology.

2.1 The Consistency between the One's Presence in Man and Man's Fall from the One

The issue we shall examine is this: If man is always already united with the One, why does he fall from the One and not remain with It? This question is discussed in the following passage:

(vi)   How is it, then, that one does not remain there *[with the One]*? It is because one has not yet totally come out of this world. But there will be a time when the vision *[of the One]* will be continuous, since there will no longer be any hindrance by the body *(line 1–3)*. But it is not that which has seen which is hindered *(line 4)*, but the other part which, when that which has seen rests from vision, does not rest form the knowledge which lies in demonstrations and evidence and the discourse of the soul;…

---

38   Strictly speaking, this doctrine seems to render Plotinus' teaching of henosis as a whole useless. But since his negative theology is the last stage and hence the apex of the whole teaching, I will only focus on it for the sake of brevity and emphasis.

Πῶς οὖν οὐ μένει ἐκεῖ; ἢ ὅτι μήπω ἐξελήλυθεν ὅλος. ἔσται δὲ ὅτε καὶ τὸ συνεχὲς ἔσται τῆς θέας οὐκέτι ἐνοχλουμένῳ οὐδεμίαν ἐνόχλησιν τοῦ σώματος. ἔστι δὲ τὸ ἑωρακὸς οὐ τὸ ἐνοχλούμενον, ἀλλὰ τὸ ἄλλο, ὅτε τὸ ἑωρακὸς ἀργεῖ τὴν θέαν, οὐκ ἀργοῦν τὴν ἐπιστήμην τὴν ἐν ἀποδείξεσι καὶ πίστεσι καὶ τῷ τῆς ψυχῆς διαλογισμῷ.[39]

Note the apparent inconsistency between line 1–3 and line 4: on the one hand, man's "vision" or union with the One is interrupted; but on the other hand, his union with the One is not interrupted. This inconsistency can be found in other translations as well. For example, according to Richard Harder's version:

> Weshalb bleibt denn nun die Seele nicht oben? Nun, weil sie noch nicht gänzlich herausgelangt ist. Es wird aber eine Zeit kommen wo man ununterbrochen schauen wird, ohne daß der Leib einen noch irgend belästigt. Diese Belästigung trifft übrigens nicht das Schauende in uns, sondern das andere welches, während das Schauende die Schau ruhen läßt, nicht ruhen läßt die Wissenschaft die in Beweisen und Argumenten und einem Selbstgespräch der Seele sich vollzieht;…

According to Stephen MacKenna's translation:

> But how comes the soul not to keep that ground? Because it has not yet escaped wholly: but there will be the time of vision unbroken, the self no longer hindered by any hindrance of body. Not that those hindrances beset that in us which has veritably seen; it is the other phase of the soul that suffers, and that only when we withdraw from vision and take to knowing by proof…

Finally, according to Hadot:

> Pourquoi donc ne demeure-t-on pas là-haut? N'est-ce pas tout entier sorti d'ici? Il viendra un temps où il y aura continuité de la vision pour celui qui aura cessé de subir le moindre obstacle du corps. D'ailleurs ce n'est pas la partie qui a vu qui est gênée par le corps, mais l'autre, celle qui, au moment où la partie qui a vu est inactive pour ce qui est de la vision, n'est pas inactive, elle, pour ce qui est de la science, qui consiste dans les demonstrations…

A. E. Meijer complains that the apparent inconsistency between line 1–3 and line 4 makes hardly any sense. For clarity's sake, he suggests that we shift the position of οὐ from line 4. So the original text changes from "ἔστι δὲ τὸ ἑωρακὸς **οὐ** τὸ ἐνοχλούμενον, ἀλλὰ τὸ ἄλλο…" to "ἔστι δὲ τὸ ἑωρακὸς τὸ ἐνοχλούμενον, ἀλλ᾽ **οὐ** τὸ ἄλλο…", which Meijer translates into "And what has the vision is hindered,

---

39   VI.9.10.1–5.

but not the rest, which, when the vision stops the contemplation, does not stop knowledge... [sic]".[40]

Consistency, to my mind, needs not be bought at the price of violating the text. We can easily dispel the apparent inconsistency if passage (vi) is understood as an *exchange* of question and answers between teacher and students. Accordingly, a more elegant and sensible interpretation would read as follows:

(1) To start with, the teacher poses the question: *Why* does man not remain with the One? (line 1)

(2) Then follows the students' attempted answer: *Presumably*, it is because man is still hindered by his body (line 1–3).

(3) Finally, there is the teacher's reply, which does not answer anything so much as *dismisses* the question and the attempted answer altogether: *No*; for that which remains with the One is not prevented from remaining with It (line 4).

(3), when construed in light of the doctrine of mystical presence, will become more comprehensible: "to remain with the One" means "to be naturally divine" and refers to man's true nature. So the gist of (3) can be put this way: Because it pertains to man to be naturally divine and more than mere body, it is impossible for him *not to be so*. Overall, then, the entire passage (vi) is not intended to answer (1) seriously, as if a substantial theory about the fall were possible at all, but to show that (1) rests on mistaken presupposition and must be dispelled.

Now let us consider a similar passage, namely the famous autobiographical report of "mystical experience" from IV.8.1:

(vii) Often I have woken up out of the body to my self [sic] and have entered into myself, going out from all other things; I have seen a beauty wonderfully great and felt assurance that then most of all I belonged to the better part; I have actually lived the best life and come to identity with the divine; and set firm in it I have come to that supreme actuality, setting myself above all else in the realm of Intellect. Then after that rest in the divine, when I have come down from Intellect to discursive reasoning, I am puzzled how I ever came down, and how my soul has come to be in the body when she is what she has shown herself to be by herself, even when she is in the body.

Πολλάκις ἐγειρόμενος εἰς ἐμαυτὸν ἐκ τοῦ σώματος καὶ γινόμενος τῶν μὲν ἄλλων ἔξω, ἐμαυτοῦ δὲ εἴσω, θαυμαστὸν ἡλίκον ὁρῶν κάλλος, καὶ τῆς κρείττονος μοίρας πιστεύσας τότε μάλιστα εἶναι, ζωήν τε ἀρίστην

---

40   Meijer, 1992, 267–270.

ἐνεργήσας καὶ τῷ θείῳ εἰς ταὐτὸν γεγενημένος καὶ ἐν αὐτῷ ἱδρυθεὶς εἰς ἐνέργειαν ἐλθὼν ἐκείνην ὑπὲρ πᾶν τὸ ἄλλο νοητὸν ἐμαυτὸν ἱδρύσας, μετὰ ταύτην τὴν ἐν τῷ θείῳ στάσιν εἰς λογισμὸν ἐκ νοῦ καταβὰς ἀπορῶ, πῶς ποτε καὶ νῦν καταβαίνω, καὶ ὅπως ποτέ μοι ἔνδον ἡ ψυχὴ γεγένηται τοῦ σώματος τοῦτο οὖσα, οἷον ἐφάνη καθ᾽ ἑαυτήν, καίπερ οὖσα ἐν σώματι.[41]

As the first-person narrative indicates, the confidence about mystical experience and the subsequent puzzlement about the fall from it pertain *not* to the divine presence in man, but to the linguistic *mediation* and *representation* of what the imaginary author *believes* to have experienced. Similarly, what is really called into question in this passage is not man's fall from the divine presence in him, but the linguistic *mediation* and *representation* of it. Therefore, toward the end of the same treatise, Plotinus answers the puzzlement to the effect that there is no real fall from henosis, but only man's confusion of it: "[…] even our soul does not altogether come down, but there is always something of her in the intelligible; but if the part which is in the world of sense-perception gets control, or rather if it is itself brought under control and *thrown into confusion* [by the body] (θορυβοῖτο), it prevents us from perceiving the things which the upper part of the soul contemplates…"[42]

The basic intuitions behind (vi) and (vii) are the same: The self-evident fact that the ultimate reality subsists in man, or that he is in the presence of the One, appears *to man* to be dubious. However, if man were to judge the self-evident to be dubious, it is his judgment which is dubious, not the self-evident. What is self-evident and absolutely real does not depend on his judgment to be real, and his judgment which depends on it is not self-evident and absolutely real. Therefore, Plotinus does not take the doubt seriously, as if the self-evident could ever be in question in the first place. Rather, by dismissing the very question which he posited himself, Plotinus is alerting us to the *illusive* nature of such questioning.[43]

2.2 The Consistency between the One's Presence in Man and the Role of Negative Theology

The main question of Section 2, namely whether there is any point in practicing negative theology if the One is always already present in man's nature, can be explained in the light of our analysis of (vi) and (vii) to this effect: Plotinus

---

41   IV.8.1.1–11.
42   IV.8.8.2–6.
43   Cf. V.1.12.1–10 and VI.4.14.22–31. See also Gerson, 1991, 207.

supposes that the self-evident presence of the One appears to the students as questionable. Assuming that the One must be separate from themselves, that strenuous effort is required to attain henosis, and that this cannot be done without a proper method, they ask: What is henosis, and how is it attained? Underlying this questioning is the problematic preconception of unification as success, achievement, or perfection. However, since the One is present in man's nature, no extra work is to be done on his part. The reason why the students are still searching in vain for a method, therefore, is simply that they are *deluded* and fail to see the self-evident fact. Thus, if there is anything they *have* to do on their part, it is not to strive to attain henosis, but—as is suggested in (vi) and (vii)—to *dispel* the false opinion that such striving is needed at all, so as to remain in their original condition.

Plotinus' negative theology of abandonment serves as a peculiar method for this project. For when the students receive Plotinus' negative theology as something to be practiced, they have the illusory preconceptions that henosis were a human achievement and that the exercise of negative theology is a reliable method of attaining henosis. But as the students work through this exercise and see the intellect dissolve itself, they will discover by themselves that their preconceptions are illusory. At last, it would become natural for them to doubt their own preconceptions, and this is what Plotinus' mystical teaching is intended for: If the students are so obsessed with achieving henosis on their own, they should see for themselves that this obsession leads to nothing but illusion, and then they would be *disillusioned* by this illusion and liberated from it. In the end, there is no need for Plotinus to dispel the illusion for them as if he were their savior, because the students can free themselves from their illusion *by and through this very illusion*.

On this interpretation, the nature of Plotinus' negative theology is not so much explanatory as *performative*, for it seeks to effect the change—more precisely, to dissolve—of what the student thinks about henosis rather than describe and explain it to him. More important, its *modus operandi* is self-referential: the change occurs when the student becomes aware that this performative discourse instructs him to disregard itself. Herein lies the reason why Plotinus teaches a seemingly inconsistent negative theology that explicitly claims to lead man to "ascent" to the One but implicitly insinuates that the One is already present in man's nature. For what appears inconsistent from an allegedly certain point of view, becomes sensible when this point of view has been shown to be illusory.

In summary, we can identify four interrelated functions of Plotinus' negative theology. First, it fakes the appearance of teaching man a way to attaining henosis. Second, it uncovers the illusion inherent in this doctrine. Third, it liberates man from this illusion by exposing the illusion as such. Last not least, it justifies its cheating on account of its use and result: it is a good cheat because it cheats with good intention and yields desirable outcome. Irony, critique of illusion and self-critique lie in the heart of Plotinus' negative theology which rests upon an extreme optimism toward human nature and an equally extreme affirmation of the ultimate reality.

One might complain that all this is nothing but a hoax designed to ridicule the fanatics obsessed with the occult. There are, however, several senses in which Plotinus' negative theology is connected to Platonic philosophy. To start with, as Perl correctly points out, Plotinus draws from Plato the doctrine that thinking and being are one and the same.[44] We have further argued in Chapter 3 that Plotinus develops from this doctrine the radical thesis that the intellect necessarily dissolves itself. This thesis constitutes the *theoretical* foundation of his negative theology and testifies to its profoundly rational nature.

Another sense in which Plotinus' negative theology is connected to philosophy is a *practical* one, for philosophy also plays a practical role in the ascetic life of the Plotinian mystic. According to Dominic O'Meara,

> [...] in exploring philosophical problems, in reasoning through puzzles about the world and about soul, in providing arguments leading towards knowledge, Plotinus' texts help rational soul to set aside its confusion and error and reach a better understanding of itself and its origin (V.1.1.27–28). His arguments, in his texts, can function as a 'leading up' (ἀναγωγή) of soul (I.3.1.1–6) and his teaching and writing as a 'road' and a 'way' (VI.9.4.1–5) to the Good.[45]

Plotinus' conception of philosophy as a way to the Good is also in harmony with the Greeks' original understanding that philosophy (φιλο-σοφία) is a loving quest for wisdom (σοφία). In both cases, philosophy is treated neither as abstract theory nor as exegesis, but—as Hadot puts it—as a "*spiritual exercise*":

> It [philosophy] is a concrete attitude and determinate lifestyle, which engages the whole of existence. [...] It is a progress which causes us to be more fully, and makes us better. It is a conversion which turns our entire life upside down, changing the life of the person who goes through it. It raises the individual from an inauthentic condition of life, darkened by unconsciousness and harassed by worry, to an authentic state of life, in which he attains self-consciousness, an exact vision of the world, inner peace, and freedom.[46]

---

44   Cf. Perl, 2007, 5–13; see also the Chapter 3, Section 1.

45   O'Meara, 2010, 320–321; see also Armstrong, 1967, 262–263.

46   Hadot, Pierre, *Philosophy as a Way of Life: Spiritual Exercises from Socrates to Foucault*, tr. Michael Chase, Wiley, Malden, 1995, 83.

Plotinus' negative theology is philosophical in the practical or even "spiritual" sense that the use of it puts man on the "ascent" to the One. Now, since the climax of his negative theology lies in abandoning all illusive intellectual strivings, it also suggests a new way of doing philosophy: As a loving quest for wisdom, philosophy is not wisdom as such, but only a mean to it. The fundamental difference between wisdom as such and love for wisdom, as well as the irreducibility of the final end to the means, pertain to philosophy's *intrinsic condition* which it should constantly reflect upon. Therefore, philosophy is not about meticulously following a method in the vain hope of attaining wisdom; rather, it is about showing humility and realizing its weakness vis-à-vis wisdom, and discerning the right moment to stop philosophizing any longer.

2.3 Section Summary

To summarize: the ultimate reality called the One is naturally present in man's natural condition. Since man is already in Its presence, there is no need to strive to attain henosis. However, he does need to dispel the illusion that the One is separate from him and that labor is required in order to attain henosis. To this end, the practice of Plotinus' negative theology plays two roles. First, it highlights the illusive preconception that henosis can be attained by man's own striving. Second, it exposes the failure of man's striving, and thereby lets man dispel his illusive adherence to it.

By way of conclusion, we can compare Plotinus' negative theology with late Wittgenstein's notion of philosophy and specify its distinctive features, thereby gaining a more perceptive understanding of it. Wittgenstein is another obscure philosopher whose thought has been interpreted and evaluated in different ways, and I have no ambition to contribute yet another study on Wittgenstein by doubling the length of this dissertation. What I will do here is simply to point out several passages from *The Philosophical Investigations* concerning the task, problem and method of the practice of philosophy, thereby presenting a rough sketch of "metaphilosophy" as Wittgenstein might have conceived it.[47]

The basic point of comparison between Plotinus and Wittgenstein is that both thinkers understand their respective enterprise to be *therapeutic*, rather than constructive. Just as the doctor heals the patient not by grafting unto him a healthy body, but simply by removing the sick parts, so Plotinus and Wittgenstein

---

47   Cf. Wittgenstein, Ludwig, *Philosophical Investigations*, tr. G.E.M. Anscombe, Blackwell Publishing, Malden, 2001.

seek to enlighten us not by setting forth a theory about the ultimate reality, but by dispelling our misconceptions thereof. In specific, following points from Wittgenstein's part are to be noted:

First, like Plotinus, Wittgenstein aims at retrieving what is self-evident, which he calls the "clear view", "perspicuity", "perspicuous presentation" or "complete clarity".

> A main source of our failure to understand is that we do not *command a clear view* (übersehen) of the use of our words.—Our grammar is lacking in this sort of *perspicuity* (Übersichtlichkeit). A *perspicuous presentation* (übersichtliche Darstellung) produces just that understanding which consists in 'seeing connexions'. [...] The concept of a perspicuous representation is of fundamental significance for us. It earmarks the form of account we give, the way we look at things.[48]

> The aspects of things that are most important for us are hidden because of their *simplicity* and *familiarity*. (One is unable to notice something—because it is always before one's eyes.)[49]

> It is not our aim to refine or complete the system of rules for the use of our words in unheard-of ways. For the clarity that we are aiming at is indeed *complete clarity*.[50]

Second, like Plotinus, Wittgenstein seeks to achieve this task by dispelling our confusions about it; in particular, both hold that once the confusions are dispelled, man comes to see what is really self-evident.

> The results of philosophy are the uncovering of one or another piece of plain nonsense and of bumps that the understanding has got by running its head up against the limits of language. *These bumps make us see the value of the discovery.*[51]

Third, just as Plotinus' negative theology uses man's illusion to dispel his own illusion, so too the means by which Wittgenstein dispels confusions is of the same kind as the confusions themselves.

> Our investigation is therefore a *grammatical* one. Such an investigation sheds light on our problem by *clearing misunderstandings away*. Misunderstandings *concerning the use of words*, caused, among other things, by certain analogies between the forms of expression in different regions of language.[52]

> We must do way with all explanation, and description alone must take its place. And this description gets its light, that is to say its purpose, *from the philosophical problems.* [...] The problems are solved, not by giving new information, but by arranging what we have

---

48   *PI*, §122, my italics.
49   *PI*, §129, my italics.
50   *PI*, §133, my italics.
51   *PI*, §119, my italics.
52   *PI*, §90, my italics.

always known. Philosophy is a battle against the bewitchment of our *intelligence* [i.e. language] by means of *language*.[53]

> When I talk about language [...] I must speak the language of every day. Is this language somehow too coarse and material for what we want to say? Then how is another one to be constructed?—And how strange that we should be able to do anything at all with the one we have! [...] Yes, but then how can these explanations satisfy us?—Well, your very questions were framed in this language; they had to be expressed in this language, if there was anything to ask! [...] *Your questions refer to words; so I have to talk about words.* You say: the point isn't words, but its meaning [...] Here the word, there the meaning. The money, and the cow that you can buy with it. (But contrast: money, and its use.)[54]

However, given these loose similarities, it is precisely the difference between Plotinus and Wittgenstein which call for more attention. For Plotinus, the self-evident and the confusions about it are of different natures: the former is independent from linguistic representation, whereas the latter arises when man tries to confine the former within linguistic representation. By contrast, the "clear view" which Wittgenstein seeks to present is the grammar or "rule" of a language game, which is of the same linguistic nature as the confusions about it:

> Philosophy is a battle against the bewitchment of our *intelligence* by means of *language*.[55]

> *The fundamental fact here is that we lay down rules* [...] for a game, and that then when we follow the rules, things do not turn out as we had assumed. That we are therefore as it were *entangled in our own rules*.[56]

Confusions, therefore, are about the correct use of the grammar of language games. Thus, to the extent that the "clear view" which Wittgenstein seeks to present is also linguistic, it is not entirely free from confusions in the strict sense, but is itself that from which the confusions *arise*:

> The problems arising through a misinterpretation of our forms of language have the character of depth. They are deep disquietudes; *their roots are as deep in us as the forms of our language*...[57]

> A picture held us captive. And we could not get outside of it, for *it lay in our language and language seemed to repeat it to us inexorably*.[58]

---

53   *PI*, §109, my italics.
54   *PI*, §120, my italics.
55   *PI*, §109, my italics.
56   *PI*, §125, my italics.
57   *PI*, §111, my italics.
58   *PI*, §115, my italics.

Section 3 Plotinus on the Mystical Vision

In this chapter we set out to explain three questions: First, who is in the presence of the One, if not the contemplator? Second, why does Plotinus maintain that we have to cling to contemplation, in spite of the fact that this will only bring about uncertainty? Third, is there any way for those unable to touch the One to free themselves from uncertainty, and to become capable of uniting with It? According to the preceding sections, the first two questions can be explained shortly as follows: The One is always already present in man's nature, but man is unaware of this and strives to attain henosis by his own effort. So he has to "see" through his illusive striving and to "see" that the One is always already present in his nature. This explanation helps to specify the third question thusly: *How should we free ourselves from the illusive striving for henosis, and what is henosis when the illusion is dispelled?*

A clue to this question can be found in the above-mentioned term *seeing* and its cognate *vision*. Let us not confuse them with the *beatific vision* in Christian theology and wrongly suppose that Plotinus were talking about something in the afterlife. In the *Enneads*, "vision" is a metaphor often used for henosis.[59] On the other hand, in VI.9.8 Plotinus also provides a visual illustration to explain his teaching of henosis. In this section, therefore, I shall take "mystical vision" as a technical term to refer specifically to Plotinus' *visual illustration of henosis*,[60] propose an interpretation of it based on the exegeses of I.6.8 (Section 3.1) and VI.9.8 (Section 3.2), and then use the interpretation to explain the guiding question: How should we free ourselves from illusion, and what is henosis when the illusion is dispelled? (Section 3.3)

3.1 The Mystical Vision in I.6.8.21–27

The first key passage to examine where Plotinus discusses mystical vision is found in I.6.8.21–27:

---

59 Sometimes it stands for the act and object of intellectual contemplation as well (cf. III.8 and V.8), but this will not be the topic of our present discussion.

60 This is not to deny that certain passages in the *Enneads* can be construed as descriptions of mystical experience from a first-person point of view, i.e. of what it is like to "see" the One. But given their personal and private nature, it is unlikely for the interpreters to say anything certain about them. Therefore I shall restrict my present investigation to Plotinus' visual illustration of henosis, and leave open the question whether it corresponds to the real experience of henosis from a subjective perspective.

(viii)   This would be truer advice "Let us fly to our dear country." [...] How shall
         we travel to it, where is our way of escape? We cannot get there on foot;
         for our feet only carry us everywhere in this world, from one country to
         another. You must not get ready a carriage, either, or a boat. Let all these
         things go, and do not look. *Shut your eyes, and change to and wake an-
         other way of seeing*, which everyone has but few use.

Φεύγωμεν δὴ φίλην ἐς πατρίδα, ἀληθέστερον ἄν τις παρακελεύοιτο. [...]
Τίς οὖν ὁ στόλος καὶ ἡ φυγή; Οὐ ποσὶ δεῖ διανύσαι· πανταχοῦ γὰρ φέρουσι
πόδες ἐπὶ γῆν ἄλλην ἀπ᾽ ἄλλης· οὐδέ σε δεῖ ἵππων ὄχημα ἤ τι θαλάττιον
παρασκευάσαι, ἀλλὰ ταῦτα πάντα ἀφεῖναι δεῖ καὶ μὴ βλέπειν, ἀλλ᾽ οἷον
μύσαντα ὄψιν ἄλλην ἀλλάξασθαι καὶ ἀνεγεῖραι, ἣν ἔχει μὲν πᾶς, χρῶνται
δὲ ὀλίγοι.⁶¹

The term *feet* refers to the act of sensation that mediates between the sensible
object and the power of sensation. *Carriage* and *boat*, as means of transportation
more powerful than feet, are metaphors for the act of intellection. We are told to
abandon both of them and even to "close our eyes", namely to *go beyond the intellect*. In this context, what could be meant by the term *vision* (ὄψις) by which man
is united with the One? Let us first consider a few remarks from Pierre Hadot's
monograph, *Plotinus or the Simplicity of Vision*. According to his interpretation
of I.6.8:

> Plotinus [...] invites us to a conversion of attention [...] The method is seemingly sim-
> ple: "We must not look, but must, as it were, close our eyes and exchange our faculty
> of vision for another. We must awaken this faculty which everyone possesses, but few
> people ever use." (I.6.8.25–27) This process is all the more simple in that *consciousness*,
> in the last analysis, is a kind of *mirror*: it need only be polished and turned in a certain
> direction *for it to reflect the objects* that present themselves to it.⁶²

In his quotation of I.6.8, Hadot omits line 21–25, which is cited in passage (viii)
as follows: "How shall we travel to it, where is our way of escape? We cannot get
there on foot; for our feet only carry us everywhere in this world, from one country to another. You must not get ready a carriage, either, or a boat. Let all these
things go, and do not look." Here Plotinus emphasizes that *not only the body, but
also the intellect must be abandoned*. Omitting this claim leads Hadot to set forth

---

61   I.6.8.21–27.
62   Hadot, Pierre, *Plotinus or the Simplicity of Vision*, tr. Michael Chase, The University
     of Chicago Press, Chicago and London, 1993, 30, my italics.

his first main thesis: *the mystical vision is "mirroring", reflective and related to consciousness.* This point is restated in another remark:

> As we saw above, consciousness must stop splitting itself into two, and come to coincide with our true self, that higher level of tension and unity. We must learn to *look within* ourselves, in order to discover the *spiritual* world within us.[63]

"Spirit" is Hadot's translation of νοῦς, so the precise meaning of "spiritual", in line with his reasoning, should not be "mystical", but rather νοερός (intellectual) and νοητός (intelligible). Accordingly, to discover the spiritual world just is to comprehend the intelligible objects. Correlated to this interpretation is Hadot's second main thesis: man's true self resides not in the One which is beyond the intellect, but rather in *the divine Thought*:

> This true self—this self in God—is within ourselves. During certain privileged experiences, which raise the level of our inner tension, we can identify ourselves with it. We then become this eternal self [...] and when we identify ourselves with this self, *we identify ourselves with divine Thought* itself, within which it is contained.[64]

> This higher level is our "self" within divine Thought, or rather, it is the divine thought in our "self".[65]

To summarize these two theses with maximum brevity: for Hadot, the One is divine Thought, and the mystical vision consists in *the self-thinking of the divine Thought*:

> [...] when vision becomes spiritual, there is no longer any distinction between inner and outer light. Vision is light, and light is vision. There is a kind of *self-vision of light*, in which light is, as it were, transparent to itself. [...] In the mystical experience, the inner eye of the soul sees nothing but light [...] It is as if the soul were seeing the light at the very center of its own vision.[66]

Hadot's interpretation is not convincing for two related reasons. First, for Plotinus, the One does not think and is beyond the intellect, but Hadot identifies the One as divine *thought*.[67] Second, for Plotinus, man's nature is in the One's presence, but Hadot identifies man's true self as divine *thought*.

---

63   Ibid., 35, my italics.
64   Ibid., 27, my italics.
65   Ibid., 28.
66   Ibid., 62, my italics.
67   There are two passages from the *Enneads* where the One *appears* to be described in terms related to the self-thinking intellect. First, in VI.7.39.1–4: "Now nothing else is present to It *[the One]*, but It will have *a simple concentration of attention on Itself* (ἁπλῆ τις ἐπιβολὴ αὐτῷ πρὸς αὑτόν). But since there is no distance or difference in regard to Itself, what could Its attention (τὸ ἐπιβάλλειν ἑαυτῷ) be other than Itself?"

146

An interpretation similar to Hadot's can be found in Werner Beierwaltes' *Das wahre Selbst: Studien zu Plotins Begriff des Einen und des Geistes* (2001). This work is Beierwaltes' third and most recent study of Plotinus' mystical thought, following *Denken des Einen* (1985) and *Selbsterkenntnis und Erfahrung der Einheit* (1991). The thesis below captures the basic idea behind his interpretation:

> The intellect that unites with itself in its self-thinking can be understood as its own goal in thought (das Ziel seiner selbst im Denken), namely as man's authentic or true Self, or the living reference point that ensures the connection among the soul, the intellect and the One.[68]

In a way more explicitly than Hadot does, Beierwaltes claims that man's true self resides in the *intellect*. On the other hand, he is more evasive than Hadot when it comes to explaining mystical vision in terms of man's true self. I shall cite more than one passage to show that the vagueness is due neither to the author's oversight nor to my own misreading.

> The thought's return to itself is the condition for its transformation into the self-manifesting, eternal and absolute Intellect in the thought itself—namely into its "true self". But it is also the condition of a growing consciousness, such that the ground of this very self *goes beyond itself* in its "being" or its supra-being (Über-sein) which grounds and encompasses everything. This authentic "true self" guarantees *the consciousness of absolute transcendence* (das Bewußtsein absoluter Transzendenz) [which grows] out of the trace of the One/ the Good's existence and operation in it.[69]

> The second part of the title [of *Selbsterkenntnis und Erfahrung der Einheit*], namely "experience of union", is inspired by the idea which Plotinus develops mostly in the second part of the *Enneads* V.3 (V.3.10–17). The idea is that one's true self does not allow one to "remain idle", that the soul should *"ascend"* or *"advance" further* from the realm where

---

And in VI.8.16.30–37: "If then It *[the One]* did not come into being, but Its activity was always and a something like being awake, when the wakener was not someone else, *a wakefulness and a thought transcending thought* (ἐγρήγορσις καὶ ὑπερνόησις) which exists always, then It is as It woke Itself to be. But Its waking transcends substance and intellect and intelligent life; but these are Itself. It then is an active actuality *above* (ὑπέρ) intellect and thought and life; but these are from It and not from another." However, judging from the whole context, it is clear that in both cases the "simple concentration of attention on Itself", and the "thought transcending thought" are employed in order to emphasize that these terms in fact fall short of adequately describing the One, *precisely because the One is beyond the intellect.*

68 Beierwaltes, Werner, *Das wahre Selbst: Studien zu Plotins Begriff des Einen und des Geistes*, Vittorio Klostermann, Frankfurt am Main, 2001, 104, Beierwaltes' italics, my translation.

69 Ibid., 12, my translation and italics.

she becomes conscious of the self-thinking intellect which is at once present to itself and to her as her immediate ground and immediate goal, and that she should [transit] into the *"touch"* (Berührung) of and *unification* with the ultimate or "absolute" goal, which is at the same time the unsurpassable origin of the intellect's being and operation.[70]

Self-knowledge as the intellect's comprehending penetration into itself, as the intellectual inquiry into its purest form of being, or as the discovery of its own noetic ground which exists and operates "over" and "in" itself: this self-knowledge is the necessary and dynamic condition in man whereby he himself, through this very act of self-comprehending (Sich-sebst-Begreifen) and self-knowing (Sich-sebst-Wissen), and in the act of *self-transcendence* (in an active sense) into the intellect's ground of unity, transits into the One Itself while touching and uniting with It.[71]

If one considers closely the basic insights developed in the preceding passage [of V.3.17], then it is clear that a new charm for the pregnant soul's birth-pangs is hardly conceivable and quite unnecessary. Now that these insights have been unfolded, it is clear—and we should recall—that what is capable of uniting with the absolutely simple One is not the discursive thought that always aims at a being other than itself, but *only the intuitively thinking "touch" which is free from difference and without distance.*[72]

In short, to unite with the One, the intellect must go beyond itself and become an "intuitively thinking 'touch'". However, there are two difficulties in this interpretation. First, the insistence that the intellect must be transcended is already emphasized by Plotinus himself, so there is no need for the interpreters to go over this point again. For the interpreters, the task is rather to explain, in a way consistent to Plotinus' metaphysics of the One, *just how* this could be done. Second, regarding this point, Beierwaltes suggests that the intellect must become "free from difference" and somehow "touch" the One. But this suggestion raises more questions than it should have answered: For one, exactly what it this mysterious "touch"? More seriously, if the self-thinking intellect is really man's *true* self, isn't it absurd for man to go beyond this intellect?

Aside from a few minor details in their interpretations, both Hadot and Beierwaltes understand the *vision* (ὄψις) whereby man is united with the One as a *form* (εἶδος) or intelligible object, thereby reducing the One to a mere being. As an alternative, I suggest that we understand "vision" as the *perspective* or viewpoint from which the intellect contemplates intelligible beings. Accordingly, to "change to a vision" is not to contemplate the One *as another being*, but to contemplate beings *from another perspective, such that man can be united with the*

---

70   Ibid., 85, my translation and italics.
71   Ibid., 105, my translation and italics.
72   Beierwaltes 1991, 166, my translation and italics.

One. Just what this specific and privileged perspective is, will be explained in the exegesis of VI.9.8 below. For now let us point out a few reasons why this interpretation is recommended.

First, it prevents the intellect from reducing the One to an intelligible object, while manages to preserve for it an access into unification with the One. In this way, a balance is kept between rationality and mysticism. Second, as I shall show, it is capable of explaining what this access is by accommodating the crucial text in the *Enneads* where Plotinus explains mystical vision with the help of the visual illustration of the *circle*. The third reason is this: If we keep the notion of *perspective* wide open, we can take into account several thinkers (to be shown below) who conceive this notion in different ways but employ a similar technique of perspective-change to approach the divine (or the mystical). Now, if we regard Plotinus *mutatis mutandis* as another such thinker, we can embed his thought in a broader, more accessible context. In this sense, the merit of interpreting *vision* as *perspective* is not that it stays faithful to the author's intention (which is a point we interpreters cannot know too surely), but that it enriches the interpreter's understanding of the text. Below I shall briefly point out how the notion of perspective-change is used, in one way or another, to approach the divine or the mystical.

The first thinker that comes to mind is Wittgenstein, who claims that "astonishment is essential to a change of aspect. And astonishment is thinking", and that "what is incomprehensible is that nothing, and yet everything, has changed".[73] Recently, Peter Tyler argues in his comparative analysis that there is a "family resemblance" between Wittgenstein and Teresa of Avila: both thinkers seek to elicit a change of aspect in our way of seeing and acting in the world by means of their performative discourse.[74]

Because of Wittgenstein's elliptical style of writing, it is uncertain as to what he means by "*Aspekt*". In a narrow sense, it could be merely visual or aesthetical. But in the context of Wittgenstein's late thought as a whole, perhaps a change of aspect stands in a certain dependency relation to the transformation of language game or way of life, although we cannot be sure which term is prior. Furthermore, although Wittgenstein emphasizes the significance of aspect-seeing, he refrains from recommending a specific "religious point of view" as a theologian

---

73   *Last Writings on the Philosophy of Psychology, Vol. I,* ed. G.E.M. Anscombe and G. H. von Wright, Blackwell, Oxford, 1982, 565; and *Remarks on the Philosophy of Psychology, Vol.II,* ed. G.H. von Wright and H. Nyman, Blackwell, Oxford, 1980, 474.

74   Tyler, Peter, *The Return to the Mystical: Ludwig Wittgenstein, Teresa of Avila and the Christian Mystical Tradition,* Continuum, New York, 2011, ix-xix, 227–236.

would do.[75] These factors make it difficult for us to approach the divine with too much proximity via the Wittgensteinian perspective-change. For a specification of the notion of perspective, we can turn to Hans Urs von Balthasar's comment on Pseudo-Dionysius the Areopagite:

All theology for him [Dionysius] is a glorious celebration of the divine mysteries and therefore has its archetype and pattern in the liturgical songs of heaven [...] The 'hymnic' is therefore for [Dionysius] a methodology of theological thinking and speaking.[76]

Jean-Luc Marion's remark is similar but more explicit:

[...] Denys tends to substitute for the *to say* of predicative language another verb, ὑμνεῖν, to praise. What does this substitution signify? It no doubts indicates the passage from discourse to prayer, for 'prayer is a λόγος but neither true nor false' (Aristotle, *De Interpretatione*, 17a 2–4).[77]

Both authors note that Dionysius elicits a change in the mode of *speech act* in speaking about God: from unknowingly (ἀγνώστως) *knowing* God's eminent nature to *praising* God's absolute transcendence.[78]

In addition to this *illocutionary* approach, there is another way to articulate perspective-change, namely Thomas Aquinas' *semantic* distinction between *res significata* and *modus significandi*, or between that which a name is imposed to signify and that from which it is derived.[79] As such, what a name signifies can be understood from three perspectives depending on which one of the three elements of signification is emphasized: (P1) the context or source from which the

---

75   For a survey of Wittgenstein's influence on recent theologians see Ashford, Bruce R., 'Wittgenstein's Theologians? A Survey of Ludwig Wittgenstein's Impact on Theology', *The Journal of Evangelical Theological Society* 50/2, 2007, 357–375.

76   Cf. von Balthasar, Hans Urs, *The Glory of the Lord, vol.2: Studies in Theological Styles: Clerical Styles*, tr. Andrew Louth, Francis McDonagh and Brian McNeil C. R. V., ed. John Riches, Ignatius Press, San Francisco, 1984, 160.

77   Cf. Marion, 2001, 184.

78   Dionysius discusses how we know God by unknowing in *De Mystica Theologia*, but it should be noted that even this treatise is prefaced with a praise of God as *God beyond God* (ὑπέρθεε), (cf. 997A-997B).

79   For discussions of Thomas' discussion of divine names see Aertsen, Jan, *Medieval Philosophy and the Transcendentals: The Case of Thomas Aquinas*, Brill, Leiden, 1996, 378–387; Rocca, Gregory P., *Speaking the Incomprehensible God: Thomas Aquinas on the Interplay of Positive and Negative Theology*, Catholic University of America Press, Washington, 2004, 334–352; Torrell, Jean-Pierre, *Saint Thomas Aquinas: Spiritual Master*, tr. Robert Royal, Catholic University of America Press, Washington, 2003, 25–52; Shanley, 2006, 324–354 and te Velde, 2005, 95–121.

signification is derived, (P2) the thing which the speaker intends to refer to, and (P3) the signification as such or the surface meaning of the word.[80] From this distinction, it follows that although all divine names are man-made, they can be made under either one of these three perspectives, and hence that God can be designated under three difference aspects. For example, on (P1), God is called *lion*, to the extent that He is powerful and because the speaker learns from his experience that a lion is powerful;[81] on (P2), God is called *being, good, life*, etc. properly, because the term is imposed in order to signified His perfections;[82] and on (P3), the proper name of God is HE WHO IS (qui est), because this name signifies existence itself (ipsum esse).[83] More important, these perspectives are *integrated* in light of the relation of metaphysical causality between God and created beings. Since God is the cause of all beings, the source man draws on to designate Him is none other than His created effects by which He can be known. Consequently, there is an analogical relation among (P1), (P2) and (P3); that is, (P1) and (P2) are viewed in relation or proportion to (P3), the *primum analogatum*.[84] Overall, then, Thomas not only maintains that God can be designated by man from different perspectives, but also recommends us to see Him from an *analogical perspective*.[85]

3.2 The Visual Illustration of Henosis in VI.9.8.13–22

As the preceding examples indicate, different thinkers understand the notion of *perspective* in different ways. Plotinus' own version is set forth in VI.9.8 with a visual illustration of the circle. My aim in this section is to pinpoint a few critical details of this illustration; how this illustration helps to explain henosis or the mystical vision will be treated in the next section.

(ix) For the soul is not a circle in the same way as a geometrical figure, but because there is in her and around her the ancient nature, and because she comes from an origin of this kind, and because souls are wholly separated.

---

80   *ST* I, q.13, a.2, ad.2; q.13, a.3, c.; q.13, a.11, c.
81   *ST* I, q.13, a.6, c.
82   *ST* I, q.13, a.2, c.; q.13, a.3, ad.1; q.13, a.6, c.
83   *ST* I, q.13, a.11, c.
84   *ST* I, q.13, a.5, c.
85   For a similar interpretation of Thomas' approach to divine names via perspective-change see Burrell, John, *Aquinas: God and Action*, University of Notre Dame Press, Notre Dame, 1979, 9–11, 66–71.

οὐδὲ γὰρ οὕτω κύκλος ἡ ψυχὴ ὡς τὸ σχῆμα, ἀλλ᾽ ὅτι ἐν αὐτῇ καὶ περὶ αὐτὴν ἡ ἀρχαία φύσις, καὶ ὅτι ἀπὸ τοιούτου, καὶ ἔτι μᾶλλον καὶ ὅτι χωρισθεῖσαι ὅλαι.[86]

Plotinus restates here the doctrine that the One is present in man's nature: just as all the points on the circle are at equal distance from the center, so everything she (the soul) does depends on and leads back to her primordial nature, i.e. the One. With this analogy Plotinus proceeds to explain what it means for the soul to "ascend" to the One.

(x) But now, since a part of us is held by the body, as if someone had his feet in water, but the rest of his body was above it, we lift ourselves up by the part which is not submerged in the body and by this join ourselves at our own centers to something like the center of all things, just as the centers of the greatest circles join the center of the encompassing sphere, and we are at rest.

> νῦν δέ, ἐπεὶ μέρος ἡμῶν κατέχεται ὑπὸ τοῦ σώματος, οἷον εἴ τις τοὺς πόδας ἔχοι ἐν ὕδατι, τῷ δ᾽ ἄλλῳ σώματι ὑπερέχοι, τῷ δὴ μὴ βαπτισθέντι τῷ σώματι ὑπεράραντες, τούτῳ συνάπτομεν κατὰ τὸ ἑαυτῶν κέντρον τῷ οἷον πάντων κέντρῳ, ἀναπαυόμενοι.[87]

It is clear that, since henosis is not a physical exercise, man should lift himself up "by the part which is not submerged in the body". Exactly how this is done is explained in the following sentence "τούτῳ συνάπτομεν κατὰ τὸ ἑαυτῶν κέντρον τῷ οἷον πάντων κέντρῳ", which Armstrong translates into "by this [we] join ourselves *at our own centers* to something like the center of all things".[88] On this translation, κατὰ means *at* or *toward* and is a preposition denoting the *direction* of a movement, as in "Look *at* that!" And since τούτῳ refers to the part "not submerged in the body", the movement at issue should be the intellect's discursive activity. Therefore this translation suggests that henosis or the "joint" (τὸ συνάπτειν) consists of two stages: in the first stage we ascend toward our own centers, and in the second stage we proceed to ascend toward the center of all things. The entire process can be illustrated as follows, where the soul-circle

---

86   VI.9.8.13–16.
87   VI.9.8.16–22.
88   See also Richard Harder's German translation: "und damit berühren wir uns an der Stelle unseres eigenen Mittelpunktes mit der 'Mittelpunkt' aller Dinge", which, with the preposition *an* and *mit*, also suggests mediation.

moves toward the eccentric One-circle, touches it on the arc, and then finally coincides with it in the center (Fig. 1).[89]

Fig. 1

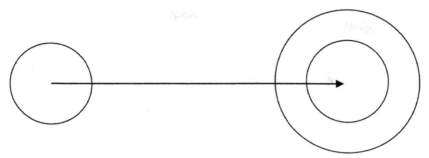

But this interpretation, based on the translation of κατά into *toward*, is in tension with two points brought up in the same chapter. First, according to (ix), "there is in her and around her the ancient nature..."; that is to say, the nature or "center" of the soul lies in the One. Figuratively speaking, the soul-circle and the One-circle must be *concentric* rather than eccentric, and the latter must be a greater one which encompasses the former, as is confirmed by the description "just as the centers of the greatest circles join the center of the encompassing sphere".[90] Second, to speak of the movement of the soul-circle, as is illustrated above, suggests that the soul has to *change* her nature so as to unite with the One. But according to (x), when the joint takes place, "we are at rest (ἀναπαυόμενοι)"; that is to say, it takes place without any change of the soul's nature. In light of (ix), this should mean that the soul remains in her natural state when the joint takes place, and that she does not change her nature so as to be united with the One.

89   See Hadot, 1994, 184–187 for a similar interpretation: "Cette coïncidence, Plotin l'imagine sur le modèle de la coïncidence entre les centres des grands cercles et le centre de la sphère, l'âme apparaisant ainsi comme un grand cercle de la sphère universelle, dont l'Un est le centre."

90   It is difficult to speculate on the difference between the two-dimensional circle and the three-dimensional sphere seems to me irrelevant in this passage. It might be that Plotinus calls the One a sphere rather than a circle in order to emphasize that the One, although present in the soul, is radically different from her intellect and sense organs, just as the sphere shares with the circle the same center but belongs to *another dimension*.

In view of this difficulty, I think it would make more sense to understand κατά as *in accordance with* or *by*, thereby relating κατὰ τὸ ἑαυτῶν κέντρον to several key phrases in the *Enneads*, such as κατὰ τὸ δυνατόν (as far as one can),[91] κατὰ φύσιν (by nature),[92] καθ' ἑαυτὸν (essentially, according to one's power)[93] and καθ' ὅσον (insofar as).[94] Thus construed, συνάπτομεν κατὰ τὸ ἑαυτῶν κέντρον τῷ οἷον πάντων κέντρῳ means: "we join something like the center of all things *in accordance with our own nature, or by ourselves*".[95] In other words, it is *by the soul's own nature* that she joins the One. To paraphrase with Plotinus' famous last words, we have to "try to bring back the *god in us* to the Divine in the All (πειρᾶσθε τὸν ἐν ἡμῖν θεὸν ἀνάγειν πρὸς τὸ ἐν τῷ παντὶ θεῖον)."[96] Aside from the textual supports found in the *Enneads*, this reading also avoids inconsistency with quotations (ix) and (x). First, what τὸ ἑαυτῶν κέντρον designates corresponds to the "primordial nature" from (ix), and the soul and the One are likened to two concentric circles, the former smaller than the latter, "just as the centers of the greatest circles join the center of the encompassing sphere". Second, since the soul joins the One by her own nature, she would remain in her natural condition when the joint takes place, which is why it is said in (x) that "we are at rest".

Figuratively speaking (see below), then, the process of unification starts from the center of the concentric circles, which represents the soul's divine nature, and proceeds via the elongation of the soul-circle's radius, until it ends in the *complete overlapping* of the two circles:

Fig. 2

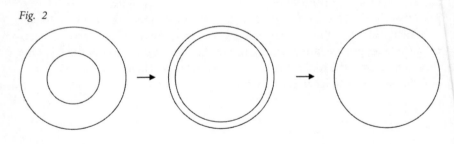

---

91   I.2.7.24, etc.
92   I.4.1.7, etc.
93   V.6.2.9, V.3.8.17, etc.
94   I.4.14.4, I.7.3.17, etc.
95   See Pierre Hadot, 1994, 101 for a similar translation: "nous coïcidons par elle *selon* le centre de nous-mêmes avec ce que l'on pourrait appeler le centre de toutes choses".
96   Porphyry, *The Life of Plotinus*, 2.25–26.

My contention in this section is that the complete overlapping between the soul-circle and the One-circle concentric with it represents Plotinus' illustration of henosis more appropriately than Fig. 1 does. Before turning to explain our guiding question with the help of this illustration in the next section, let us take note of some of its peculiar features. First, there is only one circle before our eyes, although it can be seen both as the soul-circle and the One-circle. We are not seeing different circles, but seeing the same overlapping circle *from different perspectives* which bring about *different appearances*, namely the One-circle and the soul-circle. This point accommodates the thesis in Section 3.1 that "vision" stands for the way an object is seen, rather than the object of direct observation.

The second point to note, however, is that this overlapping circle is not a reversible figure in the ordinary sense, such as the ambiguous duck-rabbit figure made famous by Wittgenstein:

Fig. 3

 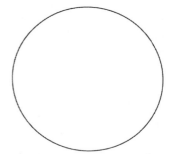

The duck-rabbit figure appears differently under different perspectives, first as a duck, then as a rabbit. The overlapping circle, on the other hand, appears first as the One-circle, then as the soul-circle. But these appearances differ only in *names*, and are exactly identical to each other in every *figurative* detail. Thus, as this illustration shows, although the same overlapping circle is observed from different perspectives, it appears exactly the same throughout perspective-change.

Last not least, while the duck-rabbit figure looks different from both the duck and the rabbit, the overlapping circle appears the same as the One-circle and the soul-circle as far as outward appearance is concerned. In the former case, it is possible *for the observer* to distinguish, in terms of observational language, the clear recognition of distinct images (duck and rabbit) from the vague perception of ambiguous image (duck-rabbit) which "lies behind them". For example, in observing the duck, the observer says that its head is turning toward the left, with its beak half-open. In observing the rabbit, he says that its head is turning toward the right, somewhat uplifted, with its mouth closed and ears standing straight up. While the rabbit looks somewhat nervous, the duck looks relaxed and is even smiling friendly. By contrast, the duck-rabbit appears to him just as a pencil-drawn irregular figure, with a black circle in the middle and three patches of white adjacent to it, and so on.

But things are different in the case of the overlapping circle, for there is no observational language *for the observer* to tell apart the overlapping circle, the One-circle and the soul-circle. Of course, he can resort to *conceptual* language and *conventional* practice to distinguish them. For example, the overlapping circle can be defined as that which is being observed directly, in distinction from the appearances arising through perspective-changes. The appearances themselves, in turn, can be dubbed whatever he likes, be it the One-circle, the soul-circle, the rabbit-circle, or whatever. In light of this, Plotinus' illustration also indicates the lack of real distinction, on the part of *the observer*, between what he takes to be *the underlying reality* and *the ways* he represents it.

3.3 An Interpretation of the Circle-Illustration

Now let us try to place the circle-illustration into the fabric of Plotinus' teaching. According to the illustration, the overlapping circle is the real object of direct observation, whereas the One-circle is an appearance thereof from a certain perspective. But since the One is certainly not a mere appearance in the fabric of Plotinus' metaphysics, it is clear that the One-circle cannot symbolize the One. It would be more accurate to say that the One-circle stands for the One seen from man' *perspective*, or man's limited knowledge of It. By the same token, the soul-circle does not designate man's nature, but man's nature seen from his *perspective*, or man's self-understanding.

Furthermore, since the One-circle is not the One Itself and the soul-circle not man's nature, the fact that they overlap each other does not mean that the One is *really identical* to man. Rather, it only means that man's limited knowledge of the One and his self-understanding differ in content but bear upon the same object, namely the ultimate reality. In terms of philosophy of language, the message of the circle-illustration can be put as follows: man has to realize that his limited knowledge of the One and his self-understanding are *intensionally different* but *extensionally equivalent*.[97]

Extension or reference-object, however, is itself a semantic concept. To see this point, we need only note that when we remain totally silent, we no longer refer to anything, but still remain in contact with the reality and are part of the reality. A reverse way to put this intuition is to see that we do not make contact with the reality just by conceptually distinguishing between the sense and the reference of an expression. Or we can rephrase it in terms of Plotinus' metaphysics: to say that the One is ineffable still ascribes something to the One, and it would be more appropriate for us to deny that we are even making such an ascription.[98] In view of this, we have to modify the above interpretation of the circle-illustration as follows: Man's *realization* that his limited knowledge of the One and his self-understanding are about the same reality does *not* make him ontologically identical to the One, but only changes his opinions about the One and himself. This realization is not the divinization of man's nature, but only the correction of his misconceptions about henosis.

My main thesis in Section 3 is that the above clarifications of the circle-illustration help to clarify our guiding question by *questioning its presuppositions*. The guiding question concerns how man should free himself from the illusive striving for henosis, and what henosis is when the illusion is dispelled. In raising these questions, we somehow presuppose that man's striving for henosis is successful only if it is *not* illusory. More pointedly, it is presumed that man's illusive striving and his true nature in which the One is present must be *incompatible*, that if man is naturally united with the One then he *cannot* fall under illusion, and that if man falls under illusion then the One must be *separate* from him.

In response, Plotinus' teaching of perspective-change, as illustrated by the overlapping circle, invites us to change our mind and to see our assumption about man's illusion as extensionally equivalent to our assumption about the One. To wit, since the One is unknowable and ineffable, we cannot say too much about Its presence in man's nature, either. That is to say, to the extent that the One is present in man's nature, a "negative anthropology" must go hand in hand with the negative theology of the One. In particular, to infer from the One's presence in man the assertion that man must be free from all kinds of illusion is to infer too much, for it presumes that the metaphysical ultimacy

---

97   I use the term *realize* to refer to the intellectual act involved here, in order to distinguish it from the intellect's proper function, namely the unification with the intelligible object.

98   Cf. V.5.6.26–34; see also Chapter 2 for the analysis of this passage.

proper to the One alone amounts to man's *infallible knowledge*. But this is problematic, because the anthropomorphic conception of the divine is incoherent with the ineffability and simplicity of the One. Furthermore, to the extent that the intellect dissolves itself in its *actuality*, the illusion thus generated must be necessary and cannot be unnatural or accidental. Seeing that man is so naturally inclined toward illusive striving, then, it is reasonable to infer that at least an important part of his true nature should already reside therein. Therefore, the *incompatibility* between man's true nature and his illusion about it is a man-made illusion. Now, while man's true nature and his illusion about it is not incompatible, they are certainly distinct. But in what sense should we understand the distinction in question? They are at least conceptually distinct as far as man's cognition is concerned: man's true nature obtains even when his cognition comes to rest, but man's illusion about his true nature presupposes the illegitimate functioning of his cognition. Now consider the real distinction between them. For the mind to tell that A is really distinct from B requires at least that the mind has access to the reality of both A and B. But since Plotinus insists that the One is present in man's nature without man being aware of Its presence, it is impossible for man to really distinguish It from anything. Of course, this does not mean that man is certain that there is *no* real distinction between his nature and his illusion. All it means is that even if there should be any real distinction between them, man still cannot say anything definite about it.

The upshot is that our guiding question rests on mistaken presuppositions and has to be dispelled. On this interpretation, the goal of Plotinus' mystical teaching, namely the "ascent" to the One, is neither to "attain" henosis by man's own doing nor to ontologically deify his finite nature. By contrast, all it aims at is to dispel man's mistaken beliefs about the One, his own nature, and henosis. Plotinus' teaching of henosis is therefore epistemologically critical and therapeutic in nature; its point, simply put, is to realize modestly that it is *natural for man to err* in our inquiry into henosis. In the eyes of theistic believers, such a teaching is bound to appear disappointing. Compare Aquinas with Plotinus: while Aquinas affirms on Christian faith that man can attain beatific vision in the afterlife, all that Plotinus says is that in this life all beliefs about henosis are illusory. However, these two lines of thought are not as incompatible as they seem, because Plotinus distinguishes sharply between henosis and his teaching thereof, and does not presume to say anything definite about henosis itself in his teaching. In this sense, theistic theologians might as well use Plotinus' teaching as an argument for the rationality of the theistic beliefs: if Plotinus' non-theistic teaching of henosis runs counter to our ordinary preconceptions of happiness, good-life and beatitude, and if the latter must underlie any theorization regarding the ultimate reality, then we have a reason to embrace theism and reject Plotinus' non-theistic thought.

By way of conclusion, let us note that the above interpretation of Plotinus' teaching of henosis can be understood as a variation of Proclus' Proposition 35 from *Elements of Theology*:

> Every effect remains in its cause, proceeds from it, and reverts upon it.

> Πᾶν τὸ αἰτιατὸν καὶ μένει ἐν τῇ αὐτοῦ αἰτίᾳ καὶ πρόεισιν ἀπ᾽ αὐτῆς καὶ ἐπιστρέφει πρὸς αὐτήν.[99]

The variation consists of two modifications: First, the verbs "remains (καὶ μένει)... proceeds (καὶ πρόεισιν)... and reverts (καὶ ἐπιστρέφει)" do not refer to three really distinct events, but three conceptual aspects ascribed to *one single state*. As such, to remain with the One, to proceed from the One, and to revert upon It amount to one and the same thing in reality. Second, the pronoun αὐτοῦ is specified as *of oneself* and interchangeable with the less common reflexive pronoun ἑαυτοῦ. Accordingly, that single state, that "one and the same thing in reality", is not the effect (τὸ αἰτιατὸν) considered apart from the cause, but the One's presence (παρουσία) in which It presents Itself (παρέχει). As E.R. Dodds points out, although a distinction in participation between the unparticipated (ἀμέθεκτον) One and the participant effect is discernible in certain passages of the *Enneads* (IV.2.1, IV.8.2.2–4, VI.2.20, VI.2.12, VI.4, VI.5), "Plotinus characteristically shrinks from calling the transcendent term ἀμέθεκτον (cf. esp. *Enn.* VI.v.3), though it is ἀμέριστον [i.e. indivisible] and ἀπαθές [i.e. impassible]—his mystical sense of the universe as the expression of a single divine force made the sharper distinction impossible for him."[100]

---

99 Cf. Dodds, 1963, 38–39.
100 Dodds, 1963, 211.

Concluding Remarks

My approach to Plotinus' mysticism rests on the semantic distinction between the reality of mysticism and the expressions referring to it: insofar as the mystics are also mystical writers, the former must be mediated by the latter remains irreducible to them. On the one hand, the same mystical experience *can* be referred to by different expressions in different ways; but on the other, expression-tokens of the same type *can* refer to different mystical experiences. Thus the task of the researcher is to figure out, on a case-by-case basis, how a specific expression refers to the reality of mysticism (cf. Introduction, Section 2.4). In Plotinus' case, since the only access available to me is his *Enneads* rather than his personal experience, I will only focus on the text itself and avoid essentialist and comparative issues. Instead, I agree with Armstrong that the *Enneads* can be understood as a book of spiritual guidance which offers instructions concerning henosis, and I take this didactic feature as foundational for my entire approach. Accordingly, the dissertation is orientated by two guiding questions: First, what are the methods taught in the *Enneads*? Second, in what specific way do these methods relate to their desired goal?

Plotinus' basic intuition is that the One is the ultimate reality of all beings, or rather that we use "the One" as a makeshift name for the ultimate reality of all beings for lack of a better term. This intuition underlies his metaphysics of the One, which serves as the framework for my interpretation of his mystical teaching. From this basic intuition Plotinus argues that the One must be *not only transcendent but also immanent*, and indeed so radically that man cannot and need not talk about It in any way. In Chapter 1, I appealed to this doctrine to contend that the attempt to prove the "existence" of the One via abductive argument is in vain, because the identification of the One with oneness runs counter to Its radical transcendence (cf. Chapter 1, Section 1). In addition, I also highlighted the implication of this doctrine for Plotinus' mystical teaching. Man's daily experience, at least *prima facie*, consists of two conflicting aspects: on the one hand, the One is already immanent in him; but on the other hand, he also desires to *know* the One, which desire in effect wrongly reduces the One to an intelligible being (cf. Chapter 1, Section 3). Thus understood, the aim of Plotinus' mystical teaching is neither to unite man with a certain deity nor to attain any extraordinary experience, but to resolve this apparent tension in man's daily experience.

The desire for knowledge sets the point of departure for Plotinus' mystical teaching. On the hierarchy interpretation, the desire for knowledge is nobler than all other desires, because its desired object, i.e. intelligible being, is the noblest. In Chapter 2, I rejected this interpretation on the ground that it does not take into account each desire's respective relation to the One. According to Plotinus, each desire's relation to the One is to be found in the desiring agent's relation to himself or herself; and all modes of desire have their common intrinsic structure in the desire for knowledge, because knowledge (or contemplation, to use Plotinus' technical term) leads to the contentment of the desiring agent (cf. Chapter 2, Section 1). I further showed that, for Plotinus, desire for knowledge is constitutive of the practice of philosophical inquiry (cf. Chapter 2, Section 2). Basing philosophical inquiry upon the desire for knowledge, consequently, renders the ascent to the One universally accessible to all rational human beings.

In Chapter 3, I drew from the comparison between Plotinus' and Dionysius' negative theology their respective distinctive features: while Dionysius' method of unknowing leads to the mystical knowledge of God, Plotinus' method of abandonment ends up in the dissolution of intellect (cf. Chapter 3, Sections 1 and 2). Regarding Plotinus' method of abandonment I argued for two theses: First, the dissolution of intellect results from its own doing and does not depend on any other factor. Second, the dissolved intellect is not an intuitive or "loving" intellect which is supposed, per impossibile, to unite with the One (cf. Chapter 3, Section 3).

The students fail to attain henosis by practicing the methods given in Plotinus' mystical teaching. So does it mean that his mystical teaching does not meet his goal? In Chapter 4 I suggested otherwise. Plotinus' intention is rather to let the students realize that it is natural for them to fail to attain henosis by their own doings, because the One is already immanent in them; and he teaches them a set of methods that inevitably fail, so as to remind them that, in practicing these methods, their motive (to attain henosis) and presupposition (henosis can be attained by personal endeavors) are wrong and have to be changed (cf. Chapter 4, Sections 2 and 3).

By way of conclusion, I shall highlight a central feature of Plotinus' mystical teaching which recurred throughout the preceding chapters, namely its *ambiguity*. To start with, the very way in which Plotinus discusses henosis in the *Enneads* is ambiguous. Since the One is simple and ineffable, henosis must also be simple and ineffable. This is one of the reasons why we do not find too many descriptions about what henosis is like in the *Enneads*; and where Plotinus does make such a description, it is not elaborate and conveys no serious salvific message concerning the One. Rather, as is emphasized twice in the *Enneads* that "whoever has seen, knows what I am saying", Plotinus is not outspoken in his teaching, but prefers to have the students follow his methods to "see" for themselves what he is talking about.

More important, Plotinus' conception of henosis is also ambiguous. In one sense, henosis is *man's natural condition*, because the One is the ultimate reality of all beings including man, such that he is always already united with It. But in another sense, it is also natural for man to fail to attain henosis. To wit, because man's natural condition already consists in henosis, he necessarily fails when he strives to attain it by his own doing. And to the extent that man's striving pertains to his natural condition as a rational, desiring agent, it is also natural for him to fail in such a striving. For Plotinus, then, man's natural condition in which he is united with the One is such that he fails to attain henosis by his own doing.

Because Plotinus' conception of henosis is ambiguous, it is difficult for us to contrast it sharply against Christian mysticism. To the extent that man is naturally united with the One, henosis is not attained in man's afterlife, nor does it consist in the transformation of his nature, much less does it presuppose man's belief about the One. Herein lies a great difference between Plotinus' non-theistic conception of henosis and the Christian conception of *unio mystica* (cf. Chapter 3, Sections 1 and 2, Chapter 4, Sections 1 and 3). However, Plotinus also maintains that man cannot attain henosis solely by his own doing. This point is not in essential conflict with Christian theology, according to which man alone, unaided by the grace of God, is unable to attain beatific vision. Besides, although in Plotinus' case man does not turn to the One as if It were a personal God or to any other deity, he does not do so out of pride or in order to take Its place, but simply because he is naively unaware of It. Thus, Plotinus' mystical teaching and Christian theology differ from each other in regard to their basic theological commitment, but their approach to salvation is not entirely incompatible.

Furthermore, the relevance of Plotinus' mystical teaching to the secular mentality is also ambiguous. *Formally* speaking, since Plotinus' teaching is addressed to lovers of sensible and intelligible beings who strive to fulfill their desires through the exertion of intellect, it is open even to non-religious people. Intellect and desire, however, are merely the basic pre-requisites for the target students of Plotinus' teaching of henosis, and by no means sufficient conditions for attaining henosis. *Substantially* speaking, because man's natural condition already consists in henosis, he necessarily fails when he strives to attain it by his own doing. While Plotinus' teaching appeals to non-believers because of its emphasis on their natural reason and natural desire, it also poses them a serious challenge for precisely the same reason: the challenge of meeting their ultimate concern solely by means of their imperfect powers.

The crux of Plotinus' mystical teaching is concerned with the practical problem of how man should cope with his failure to attain henosis, and even in this respect it remains thoroughly ambiguous. Since it is natural for man to fail to attain henosis by his own striving, it is absurd to encourage him to keep on trying in the hope that one day he would succeed. But since it is just as natural for man to strive to attain henosis, it is also unreasonable to ask him to give up his striving altogether. Plotinus' advice is simply that man should *change* his preconceptions concerning henosis and his failure to attain henosis. On the one hand, he should *dispel* the misunderstanding that if he is naturally united with the One, then his striving could never fail, or that if his striving fails, then he could never be naturally united with the One. On the other hand, man is advised to steer the *middle* way and realize that henosis and his failure to attain it are not really opposed to each other, even if they mean quite different things to him.

References

Primary Texts

Albert and Thomas: Selected Writings, ed. and tr. Simon Tugwell, Paulist Press, New York, 1988.

Anselm, Proslogium; Monologium; an Appendix in Behalf of the Fool by Gaunilon; and cur Deus Homo, tr. Sidney Norton Deane, Open Court, La Salle, 1903.

Aristotle, Aristotle's Metaphysics, tr. W. D. Ross, Clarendon Press, Oxford, 1953.

Augustine, The Confessions, tr. Maria Boulding, O.S.B., ed. David Vincent Meconi, S.J., Ignatius Press, San Francisco, 1997.

Diels, H. and Kranz, W., Die Fragmente der Vorsokratiker, 2nd edition, Weidmannsche Buchhandlung, Berlin, 1906.

Gregory of Nyssa, De Vita Moysis, in *Patrologia Graeca,* vol.44, ed. J. P. Migne, Imprimerie Catholique, Paris, 1863.

John of the Cross, The Collected Works of St. John of the Cross, tr. Kieran Kavanaugh, O.C.D. and Otilio Rodriguez, O.C.D., Institute of Carmelite Studies, Washington, 1991.

Plato, Plato: Complete Works, ed. John M. Cooper, Hackett, Indianapolis, 1997.

Plotinus, Plotins Schriften, tr. Richard Harder, Rudolf Beutler and Willy Theiler, Felix Meiner Verlag, Hamburg, 1956–1971.

—*Plotini Opera,* vol.1–3, ed. Paul Henry and Hans-Rudolf Schwyzer, Oxford University Press, Oxford, 1964–1982.

—*Plotinus,* vol.1–7, tr. A. H. Armstrong, Harvard University Press, Cambridge, 1966–1988.

—*The Enneads,* tr. Stephen MacKenna, Larson Publications, New York, 1992.

Porphyry, The Life of Plotinus, in *Plotinus,* tr. A. H. Armstrong, Harvard University Press, Cambridge, 1966–1988.

Proclus, The Elements of Theology, ed. and tr. E. R. Dodds, Clarendon Press, Oxford, 1963.

Pseudo-Dionysius, Dionysius: the Complete Works, tr. Colm Luibheid and Paul Rorem, Paulist Press, New York, 1987.

—*Corpus Dionysiacum*, ed. B. R. Suchla, G. Heil and A. M. Ritter, Walter De Gruyter, Berlin and New York, 1990–1991.

Seneca, Moral Letters to Lucilius 3 vols., tr. Richard Mott Gumerre, Harvard University Press, Cambridge, 1917–1925.

Thomas Aquinas, Summa Theologiae of St. Thomas Aquinas, tr. Fathers of the English Dominican Province, Benzinger, New York, 1947–1948.

Secondary Works

Adamson, Peter, *The Arabic Plotinus: a Philosophical Study of the "Theology of Aristotle"*, Duckworth, London, 2002.

—, "The Theology of Aristotle", *The Stanford Encyclopedia of Philosophy* (Summer 2013 Edition), Edward N. Zalta (ed.), URL = <http://plato.stanford.edu/archives/ sum2013/entries/theology-aristotle/>.

Aertsen, Jan, *Medieval Philosophy and the Transcendentals: The Case of Thomas Aquinas*, Brill, Leiden, 1996.

Almond, Philip C., *Mystical Experience and Religious Doctrine: An Investigation of the Study of Mysticism in World Religions*, Mouton, Berlin and New York, 1982.

Alston, William, 'Ineffability', *The Philosophical Review*, Vol.65, No.4, 1956, 506–522.

Armstrong, A. H., 'Plotinus', *The Cambridge History of Later and Early Medieval Philosophy*, ed. A. H. Armstrong, Cambridge University Press, Cambridge, 1967, 195–268.

—, 'Tradition, Reason and Experience in the Thought of Plotinus', *Plotino e il Neoplatonismo in Oriente e in Occidente*, 171–194, reprinted in Armstrong, A. H., *Plotinian and Christian Studies*, Variorum, London, 1979, XVII.

Arnou, René, *Le Désir de Dieu dans la Philosophie de Plotin* (3rd edition), Presses de L'Université Grégorienne, Rome, 1967.

Arp, Robert, 'Plotinus, Mysticism and Mediation', *Religious Studies* 40, 2004, 145–163.

Ashford, Bruce R., 'Wittgenstein's Theologians? A Survey of Ludwig Wittgenstein's Impact on Theology', *The Journal of Evangelical Theological Society* 50/2, 2007, 357–375.

Ayer, A. J., *Language, Truth and Logic*, Dover Publications, New York, 1946.

von Balthasar, Hans Urs, *The Glory of the Lord, vol.2: Studies in Theological Styles: Clerical Styles*, tr. Andrew Louth, Francis McDonagh and Brian McNeil C. R. V., ed. John Riches, Ignatius Press, San Francisco, 1984.

—, *Presence and Thought: Essay on the Religious Philosophy of Gregory of Nyssa*, tr. Mark Sebanc, Ignatius Press, San Francisco, 1995.

Beatrice, P. F., 'Quosdam Platonicorum libros. The Platonic Readings of Augustine in Milan', *Vigilae Christianae* 43, 1989, 248–281.

Beierwaltes, Werner, *Denken des Einen*, Vittorio Klostermann, Frankfurt am Main, 1985.

—, 'The Love of Beauty and the Love of God', *Classical Mediterranean Spirituality: Egyptian, Greek, Roman*, ed. A. H. Armstrong,: Routledge, London, 1986, 293–313.

—, *Selbsterkenntnis und Erfahrung der Einheit: Plotins Ennead V 3, Text, übersetzung, Interpretation, Erlaüterungen*, Vittorio Klostermann, Frankfurt am Main, 1991.

—, *Das wahre Selbst: Studien zu Plotins Begriff des Einen und des Geistes*, Vittorio Klostermann, Frankfurt am Main, 2001.

Benardete, Seth, 'On Wisdom and Philosophy: The First Two Chapters of Aristotle's Metaphysics A', *The Review of Metaphysics*, vol.32, 1978, 205–215.

Bréhier, Émile, *The Philosophy of Plotinus*, tr. Joseph Thomas, University of Chicago Press, Chicago, 1958.

Burrell, John, *Aquinas: God and Action*, University of Notre Dame Press, Notre Dame, 1979.

Bussanich, John, *The One and Its Relation to Intellect in Plotinus: A Commentary on Selected Texts*. Brill, Leiden, 1988.

—, 'Plotinus' Metaphysics of the One', *The Cambridge Companion to Plotinus*, ed. Lloyd Gerson, Cambridge University Press, Cambridge, 1996, 38–65.

—, 'Plotinian Mysticism in Theoretical and Comparative Perspective', *American Catholic Philosophical Quarterly* 71, 1997, 339–365.

de Certeau, Michel, 'Mystique', *Encyclopaedia universalis*, 11, Encyclopaedia universalis de France, Paris, 1968, 521–526.

Cooper, Stephen A., 'Marius Victorinus', *The Cambridge History of Philosophy in the Late Antiquity*, ed. Lloyd Gerson, Cambridge University Press, Cambridge, 2010, 538–551.

Corrigan, Kevin, *Reading Plotinus: A Practical Introduction to Neoplatonism*, Purdue University Press, West Lafayette, 2005.

Courcelle, Pierre, *Recherches sur les Confessions de saint Augustine*, de Boccard, Paris, 1950.

D'Ancona, C. 'Divine and Human Knowledge in the Plotiniana Arabica', *The Perennial Tradition of Neoplatonism*, ed. J.L. Cleary, Leuven University Press, Leuven, 1997, 419–442.

Deck, John, *Nature, Contemplation and the One: A Study in the Philosophy of Plotinus* (2nd edition), Larson Publications, Burdett, 1991.

Dodds, E. R., *Proclus: The Elements of Theology, A Revised Text with Translation, Introduction and Commentary*, Clarendon Press, Oxford, 1963.

Emilsson, Eyjólfur Kjalar, *Plotinus on Intellect*, Oxford University Press, Oxford, 2007.

Feingold, Lawrence, *The Natural Desire to See God According to St. Thomas and His Interpreters*, The Catholic University of America Press, Washington, 2004.

Findlay, J. N., 'The Logic of Mysticism', *Ascent to the Absolute: Metaphysical Papers and Letters*, Allen & Unwin, London, 1970, 162–183.

Fulmer, J. Burton, 'Anselm and the Apophatic: "Something Greater than Can Be Thought"', *New Black Friars*, Vol.89, Issue 1020, 2008, 177–193.

Gale, Richard M., 'Mysticism and Philosophy', *Journal of Philosophy* 57, 1960, 471–481.

Garside, Bruce, 'Language and the Interpretation of Mystical Experience', *International Journal for the Philosophy of Religion* 3, 1972, 93–102.

Gellman, Jerome, "Mysticism", *The Stanford Encyclopedia of Philosophy* (Summer 2011 Edition), Edward N. Zalta (ed.), URL = <http://plato.stanford.edu/archives/ sum2011/entries/mysticism/>.

Gerson, Lloyd, *Plotinus*, Routledge, London and New York, 1994.

—, "Plotinus", *The Stanford Encyclopedia of Philosophy* (Summer 2013 Edition), Edward N. Zalta (ed.), URL = <http://plato.stanford.edu/archives/sum2013/ entries/ plotinus/>.

Guenon, René, *The Crisis of Modern World* (4th, revised edition), tr. Marco Pallis, Arthur Osborne, Richard C. Nicholson, Sophia Perennis, Hillsdale, 2001.

Hadot, Pierre, 'Neoplatonist Spirituality: Plotinus and Porphyry', *Classical Mediterranean Spirituality*, ed. A.H. Armstrong, Routledge, London, 1986, 230–249.

—, *Plotin, Traité 38 (VI, 7)*, Les Editions du Cerf, Paris, 1987.

—, *Plotinus or the Simplicity of Vision*, tr. Michael Chase, The University of Chicago Press, Chicago and London, 1993.

—, *Plotin, Traité 9*, Les Edition du Cerf, Paris, 1994.

—, *Philosophy as a Way of Life: Spiritual Exercises from Socrates to Foucault*, tr. Michael Chase, Wiley, Malden, 1995.

Hankey, Wayne, 'French Neoplatonism in the 20th century', *Animus* 4, 1999, 135–167.

—'Neoplatonism and Contemporary Constructions and Deconstructions of Modern Subjectivity', *Philosophy and Freedom: The Legacy of James Doull*, ed. David G. Peddle and Neil G. Robertson, University of Toronto Press, Toronto, 2003, 250–278.

—'Neoplatonism and Contemporary French Philosophy', *Dionysius* 23, 2005, 161–190.

—'Jean-Luc Marion's Dionysian Neoplatonism', *Perspectives sur le neoplatonisme, International Socicety for Neoplatonic Studies, Actes du colloque de 2006*, ed. Martin Achard, Wayne Hankey, and Jean-Marc Nabonne, Les Presses de L'Universite Laval, Quebec, 2009, 267–280.

Hick, John, 'Mystical Experience as Cognition', *Mystics and Scholars: The Calgary Conference on Mysticism 1976*, ed. Harold Coward and Terence Penulhum, *Sciences Reilgieuses: Supplements 3*, 1977, 41–56.

Huxley, Aldous, *The Door of Perception*, Chatto and Windus, London, 1954.

Jacob, Pierre, "Intentionality", *The Stanford Encyclopedia of Philosophy* (Fall 2010 Edition), Edward N. Zalta (ed.), URL = http://plato.stanford.edu/archives/ fall2010/ entries/intentionality/>.

James, William, *The Varieties of Religious Experience*, Pennsylvania State University, 2002.

Jones, Tamsin, *A Genealogy of Marion's Philosophy of Religion*, Indiana University Press, Bloomington, 2011.

Katz, Steven, 'Language, Epistemology and Mysticism', *Mysticism and Philosophical Analysis*, ed. Steven Katz, Oxford University Press, New York, 1978, 22–74.

Knitter, Paul, *Introducing Theologies of Religions*, Orbis Books, Maryknoll, 2002.

Leftow, Brian, 'Divine Simplicity', *Faith and Philosophy*, Vol.23, Issue 4, 2006, 365–380.

Louth, Andrew, 'The Reception of Dionysius up to Maximus the Confessor', *Re-Thinking Dionysius the Areopagite*, ed. Sarah Coakley and Charles M. Stang, Blackwell Publishing, Malden, 2009, 43–53.

—'The Reception of Dionysius in the Byzantine World: Maximus to Palamas', *Re-Thinking Dionysius the Areopagite*, ed. Sarah Coakley and Charles M. Stang, Blackwell Publishing, Malden, 2009, 55–69.

Marion, Jean-Luc, 'Is the Ontological Argument Ontological? The Argument According to Anselm and Its Metaphysical Interpretation According to Kant', *Journal of the History of Philosophy*, Vol.30, No.2, 1992, 201–218.

—, *The Idol and Distance: Five Studies*, tr. Thomas A. Carlson, Fordham University Press, New York, 2001.

—, *In Excess: Studies of Saturated Phenomena*, tr. Robyn Horner and Vincent Berraud, Fordham University Press, New York, 2002.

McGinn, Bernard, *The Foundations of Mysticism: Vol. 1 of The Presence of God: A History of Western Christian Mysticism*, Crossroad, New York, 1991.

—, *The Flowering of Mysticism: Men and Women in the New Mysticism (1200–1350)*, Crossroads, New York, 1998.

Meijer, P. A., *Plotinus on the Good or the One (Enneads VI, 9): An Analytical Commentary*, J. C. Gieben, Amsterdam, 1992.

Miles, Margaret R., *Plotinus on Body and Beauty: Society, Philosophy and Religion in the Third-century Rome*, Blackwell Publishing, Oxford, 1999.

Mondello, Geoffrey K., *The Metaphysics of Mysticism: Commentary on the Mystical Philosophy of St. John of the Cross*, www.johnofthecross.com, 2010.

Niederbacher, Bruno, 'Ist Gott in allen Dingen?", *Gott suchen und finden nach Ignatius von Loyola* , ed. Josef Thorer, Echter Verlag, Würzburg, 2013, 54–58.

Nussbaum, Martha C., *The Therapy of Desire: Theory and Practice in Hellenistic Ethics* (2nd edition), Princeton University Press, Princeton, 2009.

O'Meara, Dominic, 'Plotinus', *The Cambridge History of Philosophy in the Late Antiquity*, ed. Lloyd Gerson, Cambridge University Press, Cambridge, 2010, 301–324.

O'Rourke, Fran, *Pseudo-Dionysius and the Metaphysics of Aquinas* (2nd edition), University of Notre Dame Press, Notre Dame, 2005.

Penulhum, Terence, 'Unity and Diversity in the Interpretation of Mysticism', *Mystics and Scholars: The Calgary Conference on Mysticism 1976*, ed. Harold

Coward and Terence Penulhum, *Sciences Reilgieuses: Supplements* 3, 1977, 71–81.

Perl, Eric D., *Theophany: the Neoplatonic Philosophy of Dionysius the Areopagite*, SUNY Press, New York, 2007.

Perrin, David B., 'Mysticism', *The Blackwell Companion to Christian Spirituality*, ed. Arthur Holder, Blackwell Publishing, Malden, 2005, 442–458.

Plantinga, Alvin, *Does God Have a Nature?*, Marquette University Press, Milwaukee, 1980.

Pletcher, Galen K., 'Mysticism, Contradiction, and Ineffability', *American Philosophical Quarterly* 10, 1973, 201–211.

Rist, John, *Plotinus: The Road to Reality*, Cambridge University Press, Cambridge, 1967.

Rocca, Gregory P., *Speaking the Incomprehensible God: Thomas Aquinas on the Interplay of Positive and Negative Theology*, Catholic University of America Press, Washington, 2004.

Rorem, Paul, *Pseudo-Dionysius: A Commentary on the Texts and an Introduction to Their Influence*, Oxford University Press, New York, 1993.

Schaeffer, Denise, 'Wisdom and Wonder in Aristotle's Metaphysics', *The Review of Metaphysics*, vol. 52, 1999, 641–656.

Schneiders, Sandra M., 'Approaches to the Study of Christian Spirituality', *The Blackwell Companion to Christian Spirituality*, ed. Arthur Holder, Blackwell Publishing, Malden, 2005, 15–33.

Shanley, Brian J., *Thomas Aquinas: The Treatise on the Divine Nature, Summa Theologiae I 1–13*, Hackett Publishing, Indianapolis, 2006.

Sleeman, J. H. and Pollet, Gilbert, *Lexicon Plotinianum*, Brill, Leiden, 1980.

Smart, Ninian, 'Mystical Experience', *Sophia* 1, 1962, 19–26.

—'Interpretation and Mystical Experence', *Religious Studies* 1, 1965, 75–87.

—'Understanding Religious Experience', *Mysticism and Philosophical Analysis*, ed. Steven Katz, Oxford University Press, New York, 1978, 10–21.

Stace, W. T., *Mysticism and Philosophy*, Macmillan, London, 1960.

Stump, Eleonore and Kretzmann, Norman, 'Absolute Simplicity', *Faith and Philosophy*, Vol.2, Issue 4, 1985, 338–353.

Swinburne, Richard, *The Existence of God* (2nd edition), Oxford University Press, Oxford, 2004.

Torrell, Jean-Pierre, *Saint Thomas Aquinas: Spiritual Master*, tr. Robert Royal, Catholic University of America Press, Washington, 2003.

Tyler, Peter, *The Return to the Mystical: Ludwig Wittgenstein, Teresa of Avila and the Christian Mystical Tradition*, Continuum, New York, 2011.

te Velde, Rudi, *Aquinas on God: the "Divine Science" of the Summa Theologiae*, Ashgate Publishing, Farnham, 2006.

Velecky, Lubor, *Aquinas' Five Arguments in the Summa Theologiae 1a 2, 3*, Kok Pharos Publishing House, Kampen, 1994.

Wainwright, William J., *Mysticism: A Study of Its Nature, Cognitive Value and Moral Implications*, University of Wisconsin Press, Madison, 1981.

van Winden, J. C. M., 'Das ἐκεῖ in Plotin Enneaden VI.9.7.4' in *Museum Helveticum* 37, 1980, 61–62.

Wittgenstein, Ludwig, *Tractatus Logico-Philosophicus* (revised edition), tr. D. F. Pears and B. F. McGuinness, Routledge, London, 1974.

—*Remarks on the Philosophy of Psychology, Vol. II*, ed. G.H. von Wright and H. Nyman, Blackwell, Oxford, 1980.

—*Last Writings on the Philosophy of Psychology, Vol. I*, ed. G.E.M. Anscombe and G.H. von Wright, Blackwell, Oxford, 1982.

— *Philosophical Investigations*, tr. G.E.M. Anscombe, Blackwell Publishing, Malden, 2001.

Yandell, Keith E., *The Epistemology of Religious Experience*, Cambridge University Press, Cambridge, 1993.

Zaehner, R. C., *Mysticism Sacred and Profane: An Inquiry into some Varieties of Praeternatural Experience*, Claredon University Press, Oxford, 1957.